Dancing with Dharma

Dancing with Dharma

*Essays on Movement and
Dance in Western Buddhism*

Edited by HARRISON BLUM

McFarland & Company, Inc., Publishers
Jefferson, North Carolina

ISBN (print) 978-0-7864-9809-3
ISBN (ebook) 978-1-4766-2350-4

LIBRARY OF CONGRESS CATALOGUING DATA ARE AVAILABLE

BRITISH LIBRARY CATALOGUING DATA ARE AVAILABLE

Front cover image *The Shape of Wind*, choreographed by
Wynn Fricke and danced by Zenon Dance Company members
(from left) Bryan Godbout, Amy Behm-Thompson, Greg Waletski
and Mary Ann Bradley (photograph by Bill Cameron).

Printed in the United States of America

*McFarland & Company, Inc., Publishers
Box 611, Jefferson, North Carolina 28640
www.mcfarlandpub.com*

With gratitude to my parents,
whose love is the foundation
upon which I dance.

Acknowledgments

This book would not exist without the generosity and effort of all the contributors whose work fills these pages. I'm indebted to them for their willingness to put into words what they bring to life with the body. I'd also like to thank my proofreading team—Ellen Grabiner, Andrew Merz, Christine Mitchell, Roman Palitsky, and Adam Groff—for their skillful help in fine-tuning this volume.

Zooming out a bit, I'd like to thank Mark Hilgendorf for recognizing and nurturing my spirituality as a high school student, my uncle Richard for helping to foster my curiosity and playfulness, my brother Morgan for being my confidant and dear friend, and my lovely fiancée Amorn O'Connor for her heartfelt support of this project, and everything else I do and am. Finally, a bow of thanks to everyone I've ever communed with through dance, for it's by sharing the wonder that it fully shines.

Table of Contents

Preface

In the summer of 2010, the Zen Peacemakers hosted the Symposium for Western Socially Engaged Buddhism. The first night featured entertainment by Krishna Das, a well-regarded kirtan singer. Personally, I was thrilled to hear and sing along with his Hindu devotional chanting. I was also a bit saddened that there was not a Buddhist arts performer to fill the bill. I wondered, would a progressive Catholic conference host a Jewish Klezmer band for its opening night entertainment? I hungered for Buddhist performance artists, especially movers and dancers, to be better known, celebrated, and connected to the broader landscape of Western Buddhism.

One aim of this collection is to do just that, to help kindred Dharma dancers out there feel part of an emerging Western Buddhist culture of movement and dance. As one author in this volume said to me, "I knew I couldn't be the only one, but I didn't know of anyone else doing work with Buddhism and dance." The field of Christian liturgical dance has been well documented in several descriptive and instructional books. This volume brings Buddhists and Buddhism into that conversation.

What you hold in your hands is the first of its kind—a comprehensive exploration of Buddhism merging with movement and dance in the West—and stands to become the foundational text on an emerging field. Amazon.com lists just ten titles in English with either "Buddhism" or "Buddhist" and "dance" in the title.[1] None of them focuses on dance in the West, and only one was published after 1990. The closest related works address the intersection of dance and religion more broadly, or the relationship between Buddhism or mindfulness and yoga.

In addition to recognizing and supporting a culture of Dharmic movement artists, this book invites wider participation in dance floor Dharma. I hope these essays will resonate with and inspire a variety of readers: meditation teachers and practitioners seeking to expand embodied practice; dancers and dance teachers interested in deepening the sacred elements of their work; body-based theater directors and actors; dance and religion scholars; dance/movement therapists; professionals in mindfulness-based modalities; and anyone embracing the spirituality of the body. This collection features created works, and also points toward what is possible and as of yet uncreated. It is offered as an ally for readers to discover and create their own visions, their own dances with Dharma.

The first five sections of this book are divided into the themes of Movement, Dance, Performance, Ritual, and Theory. While each is a robust and distinct genre, the borders between them are at times gray and overlapping. The boundaries between movement and dance, or practice and ritual, are subjectively held by movers and witnesses. Ultimately, it is an experience beyond language, beyond labels, that these artists pursue. One distinction I have chosen is to focus on movement and dance (as broad as these categories are) to the exclusion of bodywork, as bodywork modalities are many and beyond my familiarity.

In Movement, mediums include Authentic Movement, qigong, Continuum Movement, Gesture of Awareness, Dance/Movement Therapy, and Somatic Experiencing. Dance shares voices from Contemplative Dance Practice, 5Rhythms, Contact Improvisation, Tibetan Buddhist dance practice, and "Zenful Dance." The Performance section presents artists who take embodied Dharma to the stage. Their work ranges from embodied theater to professional dance to site-specific cultural pieces. We next hear of structures that bring the mover into a ritual space, from traditional Nepalese dance to Dances of Universal Peace to modern Buddhist dance liturgies. In the Theory essays, professional dancers, scholars of Buddhism and of dance, and senior Buddhist teachers reflect on the promise and practice of wedding Buddhism with embodiment, movement, and dance.

Finally, in section 6, Guided Practices, some authors from the previous sections present instruction for individual and group practices.

It was not possible to include all the voices of those working at the intersections of Buddhism, movement, and dance; there is a limit to how many essays can fit between two covers. Additionally, while I spent several years (and over 1,700 emails) working to identify, research, contact, and refine essays with as many relevant artists and experts as I could find, certainly there are more I have not yet heard of. As such, this volume serves more as a survey of an emerging field than as an exhaustive inventory. While most contributors have been developing their work for decades, some are in their first years. Several contributors have been colleagues in various capacities, and the inter-generational relationships among these writers also include Buddhist teacher–practitioner, dance teacher–student, and director-performer.

Across the range of work contained in these pages, the contributors all have a robust Buddhist practice. While not all these artists claim a Buddhist identity, neither did the Buddha. Beyond having a general sense that their movement work is spiritual or incorporates mindfulness, these authors have deeply explored the Buddha's teachings and their relation to the moving body. Many of these Dharma dancers articulate a non-separation between their movement or dance work and their Dharma practice or teaching. Across concepts and fields that might distinguish between dance and meditation, there is embodied consciousness in time and space. A practitioner can at once be both dancer and yogi, each aspect informing and becoming the other.

NOTE

1. Amazon.com advanced search for books with "Buddhism" or "Buddhist" and "dance" in the title. Accessed June 23, 2014.

Introduction

This book documents innovative work being done at the fertile intersection of Buddhist practice with movement and dance. Both Buddhism and dance invite the practitioner into present moment embodiment. The Buddha states in the *Anguttara Nikaya*, "There is one thing that when cultivated and regularly practiced leads to deep spiritual intention, to peace, to mindfulness and clear comprehension, to vision and knowledge, to a happy life here and now, and to the culmination of wisdom and awakening. And what is that one thing? Mindfulness centered on the body."[1] Within "this fathom-long body," he taught, "is the cosmos."[2]

Similarly, movement and dance training foster continuous mindfulness of the body. Artists in these fields spend decades fine-tuning their awareness and control of subtle sensations and movements. In the *Satipatthana Sutta*, the Buddha's pivotal teaching on the Four Foundations of Mindfulness, the First Foundation focuses on the body. Practitioners are guided to cultivate mindfulness of their breathing, postures, and movements. When "going forward and returning … looking ahead and looking away … when flexing and extending … when eating, drinking … when walking, standing, sitting, falling asleep, waking up, talking, and keeping silent" the practitioner is to maintain continuous mindfulness.[3] This list encourages embodied awareness in everything we do, in all our moments. Movement and dance artists practice, create, and perform in this realm. They are masters of the First Foundation.

Amidst this inherent synergy between Buddhist and dance practice, the climates of Buddhism and dance in the West are aligning in new ways that offer unprecedented opportunities for cross-pollination. Most Western Buddhists are lay people. As such, there are now multiple generations of Western Buddhists who have deep Buddhist practices alongside other life pursuits. There are practitioners sitting intensive Buddhist retreats and meditating daily as they work as choreographers, dance teachers, theater directors, and bodyworkers. There are also Buddhist lamas, nuns, teachers, chaplains, and professors integrating movement forms into their Dharma teaching. While Buddhism has always focused on the body, embodied practice modalities are now increasing and spreading in novel ways. Walking meditation is no longer the only moving alternative to seated meditation.

Amidst current innovations, there is a rich history of movement and dance as Buddhist practice, a connection shared by most religions across time and culture.[4] Tibetan Buddhist Cham dance, performed by monks, dates back over a thousand years.[5] Writing in the 15th century, Japanese Nō theater master and devout Buddhist Zeami Motokiyo claimed, "The fundamental properties of dance and song have always arisen from the

Buddha-nature that is stored in all sentient beings."[6] A century later, Japanese samurai and Rinzai Zen master Takuan Sōhō wrote of a state of pure perception that "'applies to all activities we may perform, such as dancing.'"[7]

In the 20th century, Buddhists writing as, or for, Westerners embraced the connection between Buddhism and the arts. Anagarika Govinda wrote on "Art and Meditation" in the 1930s.[8] A few decades later D. T. Suzuki, whose work greatly popularized Zen in the West, wrote that with a spontaneity born of presence, "'all arts merge into Zen.'"[9] Jump forward another few decades to the 1970s and Sangharakshita, founder of the Friends of the Western Buddhist Order in the UK, was writing of a "religion of art" grounded in "'the expansion of consciousness beyond the boundaries of selfhood.'"[10] Naropa University and Shambhala lineage founder Chögyam Trungpa Rinpoche spoke of Dharma art as "'art that springs from … the meditative state.'"[11] Also in the latter half of the 20th century, Buddhist teacher Ruth Denison loosened the structures of meditation retreats and incorporated movement and dance. Reflecting in the 1980s on her approach to teaching, Denison shared, "'When there is strong awareness, one can be creative. A new approach is no problem.'"[12]

Sacred and therapeutic dance in the West, meanwhile, has blossomed. The turn of the 20th century saw individual dance performers, such as Isadora Duncan and Ruth St. Denis, focusing on the sacred element of their work. As modern dance gave way to postmodern dance in the 1960s, some dance artists began to embrace a process-over-product orientation. This shift was perhaps best exemplified by the Judson Dance Theater, which grew out of classes taught by Robert Dunn, a student of Buddhist *Abhidharma*.[13]

Buddhist concepts have recently been tied to contemporary dance in a novel way by theoretical chemist and religion scholar Dr. David Glowacki. He writes, "It seems increasingly common to hear chemists and bio-chemists invoke choreographic and dance analogies to describe the dynamics of molecular systems—referring to molecular dancefloors or chemical choreographies."[14] Such languaging points to modern understandings of matter as comprised of dynamic movement instead of static objects. The Buddha expressed kindred notions 2,500 years ago, teaching that upon careful investigation "whatever kind of form there is, whether past, future, or present … would appear … void, hollow, insubstantial. For what substance could there be in form?"[15]

With the help of professional dancers, computer programmers, and electronic musicians, Glowacki brought this molecular world into tangible experience in 2011 through *danceroom Spectroscopy* (*dS*). *dS* creates a "feedback cycle" wherein projected images and sound are created based on movers' "real time [energy] field perturbations … within a dynamic atomic system."[16] Simply put, dancers are now able to see and dance with their energy fields, while simultaneously affecting and being affected by sound created from their movements. Those who have taken part in *dS* "often hinted at how it left them with a sense of interconnectedness to nature and others, beyond the limits of their material body."[17]

Experiences of transcendence and interconnection in dance are hardly limited to high-tech museum installations. Movement and dance has become widely available as a spiritual practice for untrained dancers, with programs offered from large retreat centers to the yoga studio around the corner. Some of this momentum arises out of yoga's growing popularity. The Kripalu Center for Yoga and Health, for example, offers multiple yoga-dance fusions, from "Let Your Yoga Dance" to "Salsa and Yoga" to "Shake Your Soul: The Yoga of Dance."[18] Artists in contemporary dance are also contributing. JourneyDance,

5Rhythms, Soul Motion, and Spiritweaves are examples of visionary movers formalizing and sharing their practices of sacred dance. Some of these even offer teacher trainings in their respective forms.

In 2007, Mark Metz founded Conscious Dancer, an online and print magazine, to document and serve this expanding culture. Metz states that since that time he has observed huge growth in the number and style of conscious dance events. "Ten years ago there would be one or two weekly events in major cities. Now there's something every night of the week, sometimes more than one."[19] Their Fall 2010 issue listed ten conscious movement and dance modalities that have gained an international critical mass, and one hundred that are well established though less widespread.

The field of Dance/Movement Therapy (DMT) has emerged as another arena of conscious movement and dance, harnessing the therapeutic potential of the moving body. Originating in the 1940s, DMT arose "out of the merger of the modern dance movement with existing theories

Contemporary dancer Miyako Asano performing "Hidden Fields" using *danceroom Spectroscopy* at the Barbican Arts Centre, London, March 2015. Photograph by Paul Blakemore.

of group and individual psychology and psychotherapy."[20] Distinct from talk therapy or technical dance training, DMT honors and examines expressive embodiment as a source of insight and healing. In a move toward professionalization, the American Dance Therapy Association was established in 1966, and began with 73 members.[21] Their online directory currently lists close to 900 members, most of them formally trained in the field.[22]

Perhaps most noteworthy in the current landscape of dancing with Dharma is the ever-growing popularization of mindfulness meditation. Amazon.com lists two thousand books for sale with the word "mindfulness" in the title. More than half of these have been published in the past five years.[23] Mindfulness was a cover story of *Time* magazine in 2014 and was featured on popular TV show *The Colbert Report* in early 2014. By one National Institute of Health study, there could be as many as "one million new meditators every year" in the United States.[24]

In many settings, mindfulness meditation is not being taught or practiced in a Buddhist context. In his recent book *Evolving Dharma*, scholar and contemplative Jay Michaelson states that "in the last quarter century the dharma has evolved by disappearing: it's been taken out of its religious context, abstracted, and now appears in any number of secular (and multi-religious) forms instead."[25]

While high profile figures, from the Dalai Lama to Buddhism scholar Robert Thurman, have supported the rise of meditation outside of Buddhism, mindfulness has largely been popularized by clinical application and research drawing directly from Buddhist practices and teachings.[26] Mindfulness-Based Stress Reduction founder Dr. Jon Kabat-Zinn and Mindfulness-Based Cognitive Therapy co-founder Dr. John Teasdale both credit Buddhism, specifically the Insight Meditation tradition, with influencing the establishment of these therapeutic models.[27] Buddhism stands to continue gaining attention in the West as mindfulness continues to grow in popularity.

The rise of Western Buddhism, sacred dance, and Dance/Movement Therapy, along with the mindfulness meditation boom, offer a climate of unprecedented opportunity in the West for Buddhism to inform movement and dance practices, and for Buddhist practice to be shaped by movement and dance artists. As this volume demonstrates, this interweaving is already well underway. Buddhists are now dancing the Dharma in many shapes and forms.

* * *

While this book focuses on intersections of Buddhism, movement, and dance in the West, it would be simplistic and inaccurate to credit the West with innovation and the East with tradition. As Professor David L. McMahan writes in his book on Buddhist Modernism, Western Buddhism "is a facet of a ... global network of movements that are not the exclusive product of one geographic or cultural setting."[28] Furthermore, the dichotomy of traditional and new Buddhist practice may need nuancing, as "traditions inevitably become hybrids of what were already hybrid traditions."[29]

Beyond my introductory comments and the thoughts expressed within these chapters, I imagine senior scholars of Buddhism and dance will have much to contribute in terms of further contextualizing and making meaning of the practices presented in this volume. While I have studied and practiced Buddhism for the past eighteen years, including at the graduate level academically, I entrust specialists more versed than I to further analyze the implications of the work presented herein. Thoughtful consideration will include attention to how Buddhism and Buddhists might be both aided and also perhaps disserved by these emergent practices.

Similarly, while I have been an avid improv dancer for a similar length of time and have danced in almost a dozen performances, I am not a dance scholar. This volume, written by creators and/or students of emergent forms and practices in Buddhism and dance, is necessarily somewhat apologetic in tone. As such, it serves as firsthand testimony that can be both studied and adopted. Some readers will analyze this collection toward academic ends while others will embrace it as an instructive manual on new forms of Buddhist and movement practice. I hope and trust it will serve well for both purposes.

Beyond supporting the study or practice of Buddhism and dance, this book claims that Buddhist practice has the opportunity to grow in new directions in the West, and seeks to expand that opportunity. Beyond sitting silently in meditation or listening to Dharma talks, Buddhists in the West are wedding practice to other modalities, from visual arts to ecological advocacy to hip-hop music. Broadening the vehicles of Buddhist practice holds the promise of expanding access to the teachings. Some who might never cross the doorway of a meditation center could thrive in a mindfulness-based dance class at a YMCA.

As the Buddha taught with the main purpose of alleviating suffering, I believe Dharmic artists have a responsibility not only to integrate the Dharma, but to also examine whose suffering their work remedies, and how. The immediacy of the body offers a universal gateway to the present moment and the possibility of peace in that moment, a gateway that needs widening to accommodate more identities, more colors, classes, ages, and abilities. It is my hope that Dancing with Dharma will be one vehicle for expanding access to the Dharma in the West.

May the work and intentions shared in this book ripple outward, bringing greater ease and joy.

Notes

1. Gil Fronsdal, *The Issue at Hand: Essays on Buddhist Mindfulness Practice* (Redwood City: Insight Meditation Center, 2001), 47–48.

2. Thanissaro Bhikkhu, trans., *Handful of Leaves—Volume Three: An Anthology from the Aṅguttara Nikāya* (Valley Center: Sati Center for Buddhist Studies & Metta Forest Monastery, 2003), 82.

3. Analayo, *Satipatthana: The Direct Path to Realization* (Cambridge: Windhorse Publications, 2010), 5.

4. Margaret Taylor, *Dance as Religious Studies* (New York: Crossroads Publishing Company, 1993), 15.

5. "Cham," Core of Culture. Accessed May 31, 2015. http://www.coreofculture.org/cham.html.

6. Zeami Motokiyo, "A Mirror Held to the Flower," in *On the Art of the Nō Drama: The Major Treatises of Zeami*, trans. Thomas Rimer and Yamazaki Masakazu (Princeton: Princeton University Press, 1984), 77.

7. Takuan Sōho in a letter to a student, in D.T. Suzuki's *Zen and Japanese Culture* (Princeton: Princeton University Press, 1959) as quoted in David McMahan, *The Making of Buddhist Modernism* (Oxford: Oxford University Press, 2008), 129.

8. McMahan, 135.

9. McMahan, 128.

10. McMahan, 136.

11. McMahan, 143.

12. Ruth Denison as quoted in Lenore Friedman, *Meetings with Remarkable Women: Buddhist Teachers in America* (Boston: Shambhala Publications, 2000) 154.

13. Ellen Pearlman, *Nothing and Everything—The Influence of Buddhism on the American Avant Garde: 1942–1962* (Berkeley: Evolver Editions, 2012), xiv.

14. David R. Glowacki, "Using Human Energy Fields to Sculpt Real Time Molecular Dynamics," in *Molecular Aesthetics*, ed. Peter Weibel and Ljiljana Fruk (Cambridge: MIT Press, 2013) 249.

15. Samyutta Nikāya 22:95, *In the Buddha's Words: An Anthology of Discourses from the Pāli Canon*, trans. Bhikkhu Bodhi (Somerville: Wisdom Publications, 2005), 343.

16. Glowacki, 250.

17. Glowacki, 255.

18. Kripalu Center for Yoga and Dance, "Calendar of Programs." Accessed June 20, 2015. https://www.kripalu.org/program/theme/CADAN.

19. Phone communication, July 17, 2013.

20. Fran J. Levy, *Dance Movement Therapy: A Healing Art* (Reston: American Alliance for Health, Physical Education, Recreation and Dance, 1992), 6.

21. Levy, 15.

22. "Find a Dance/Movement Therapist," American Dance Therapy Association. Accessed July 10, 2013. http://www.adta.org/Find_a_DMT.

23. Amazon.com advanced search for books with "mindfulness" in the title. Accessed February 20, 2014.

24. "Meditation: An Introduction," National Institute of Health 2006, in Jay Michaelson, *Evolving Dharma: Meditation, Buddhism, and the Next Generation of Enlightenment* (Berkeley: Evolver Editions, 2013), x.

25. Michaelson, 7.

26. Michaelson, 16, 19.

27. Richard Gilpin, "The Use of Theravada Buddhist Practices and Perspectives in Mindfulness-Based Cognitive Therapy," *Contemporary Buddhism* 9.2 (2008): 227–251.

28. McMahan, 6.

29. McMahan, 19.

SECTION 1

Movement

Gesture of Awareness[1]

CHARLES GENOUD

Say what one will, something has begun.

Almost twenty-five years ago I discovered a practice called Sensory Awareness at a workshop led by Michael Tophoff, a Dutch psychotherapist. Participants were asked to walk, sit, or lie down. Sometimes we were asked to work in groups of two or three, placing our hands on the shoulders or feet or some other part of the body of another person. We were asked to take the arm of another and to move it slowly.

It was a simple, powerful practice, and such interactions found immediate reflection in the quality of my attention. Straight away I was fascinated by the work, by its power to bring forth life in present experience, by its power to allow present experience to shine. By that time, I had practiced meditation in the Tibetan and Theravada traditions for over ten years. The impact of Sensory Awareness in my meditation practice was profound. It helped me to be grounded, more balanced. And I loved the playfulness of it.

After the first workshop, I decided to learn more about Sensory Awareness, and to use it as a stepping-stone for the practice of meditation. I attended more workshops with Tophoff in Spain, France, and Switzerland, and I attended workshops in Mexico with Charlotte Selver, the pioneer in the field of Sensory Awareness. All the while I continued with my studies and practice of Tibetan and Theravada Buddhism. When I started to lead Gesture of Awareness classes, I didn't know whether it would only help introduce people to meditation or if it would also lead to insight and wisdom.

Gesture of Awareness is simply a name, one I have given to a meditation of inquiry and mindfulness. It is based mainly on awareness through sensations of the body, and yet it does not imply observation of movement or position. Gesture of Awareness is rather an invitation to experience oneness of body and mind. It is an invitation to experience the body as a body of presence. Experience is not through concentration, but through awareness manifesting as a gesture. Awareness manifesting as hearing, seeing, thinking, tasting, and touching and smelling. But awareness can be veiled by thoughts.

I might guide the practice something like this:

can I be
can I stand
as a way
of being
a simple way
of being

you may walk
and stop
and see
where has your walking gone
you may walk
where has your standing gone

11

you may move
and stop
and know
where has your moving
gone

can we be moving and
standing still
at the same time
you may try

Through the years, through every retreat I led, I would discover new ways of disclosing the many preconceptions that shape and restrain our lives; the preconceptions that lead us to be taken in by the fiction of time and space, here and now; the preconceptions that lead us, for example, to perceive the world through the notion of efficiency.

The practice we engage in during Gesture of Awareness retreats is an inquiry into the nature of such fictions. It questions the chains of time in all their myriad forms: the chains of transformation, improvement, usefulness, and of movement—questioning, and yet not looking for conclusion, for knowledge, as that would reduce one's experience to the concept of experience.

can you move your arm
from left
to right
in front of you

just feel
the movement
feel the weight
of your arm moving

can you move your arm
from right
to left

now in the past
move your arm
in the past

you may try
move your arm
from left
to right
in the past

now in the future
can you do it
in the future

move your arm
from left
to right
in the future

can we
make a movement
in the past
make a movement in the future

then explore
the movement in the present
from left
to right
from right
to left

experience the presence
of a movement

In the practice of Gesture of Awareness, we don't explore how the world of form merges with space or how words blend ineluctably with silence. We explore how physical sensations never depart from the nature of awareness. The body is the main place of inquiry in Gesture of Awareness. The body knows itself not as this sensation, or as that sensation, but as pure presence. As Meister Eckhart said, the soul is the place where god knows himself.

Early on, the body played a major role in the practice of Buddhist meditation. In the *Satipatthana Sutta,* it is said:

> Furthermore, when walking, the monk discerns that he is walking. When standing, he discerns that he is standing. When sitting, he discerns that he is sitting. When lying down, he discerns that he is lying down. Or however his body is disposed, that is how he discerns it.

Later Buddhist traditions, however, fascinated by other aspects of spiritual life such as rituals, visualizations, and investigations into the nature of consciousness, put the body aside. The body was no longer viewed as a powerful locus for awakening, but seems to have been viewed with contempt; yet all sensory fields are commonly used in Buddhism to discover not the nature of the object but the nature of the perceiving subject.

If the sensory experience of hearing can be a skillful means of awakening, so can other fields of sensory experience. Why wouldn't we realize our true nature by inquiring into the nature of bodily sensations?

how much of the movement can we experience at a time	how much of the movement can we experience at the same time
can we experience the beginning and the middle at the same time	can our hand be at two places at the same time
can we experience the middle and the end at the same time	if not if our hand is at one place at a time how is movement different from stillness

A meditation that finds expression in mindfulness of the body is not concerned with an objective knowledge, but rather, as in all Buddhist traditions, with a way to know oneself deeply and be free.

So much importance in our present-day culture is given to the body, but to the body as object, not as subject; the body as seen by others, and not as it is, a body experienced in intimacy. We are concerned with the body we own and not with the body we are. Seeing the body in this way, we may find that it is rather like a cage in which our mind, or our soul, to use Christian terminology, is kept captive. But when deep intimacy with the body is developed, the cage-like body dissolves in the space-like mind.

Many mystical traditions teach that the body does not limit the mind but rather is simply an amalgam of phenomena experienced by the mind. For the Indian Guru Ramana Maharshi, the body is just a thought. Some Buddhist traditions would say that it is just the play of awareness. Such a statement, though, is not to be understood as a negation of external phenomena, as notions of what may constitute inner and outer are the mere play of awareness.

According to Meister Eckhart, the body is more in the soul than the soul is in the body. Clear perception of the experience of the soul through the body isn't something one necessarily expects from Christian philosophers, many of whom tend to consider the body as a source of evil. Some masters teach that the soul is essentially in the heart but this isn't so, Meister Eckhart said, and they are mistaken in such respect. The soul is completely and totally undivided in the foot, in the eye, in any member of the body.

For a meditator who devotes attention to the body, whether in sitting or walking meditation, it may be of benefit to learn what other people in other contexts have to say about awareness of the body. Observing people walking across a meditation hall, I noticed how the walker's quality of presence can captivate the attention of the observer. It was not long before I turned to the world of actors and dancers to learn how they approach this aspect of their art. I found inspiration.

There was a performance by Bill T. Jones in Paris. Walking slowly to the middle of the stage—there was no music, only the man walking, naked. The intensity of the situation was vivid. Nothing else was needed. I imagine that he wasn't thinking, but simply and completely walking. If he'd been lost in his thoughts, there wouldn't have been a dance performance. It all seemed easy, natural. Later I learned in an interview that this wasn't so. He explained how risk itself was essential to him.

Jerzy Grotowski, the Polish theater director, worked with actors for months, even years, without being preoccupied by any need to present a show to an audience. He compelled the actors to undertake rigorous training, and they were transformed by it into spiritual seekers of a kind. The skill of the actors arose from their quality of mindfulness, one that is similar to the practice of meditation. Grotowski's notion of a total act was also deeply interesting to me. "I mean the very crux of the actor's art: that what the actor achieves should be a total act that he does whatever he does with his entire being."[2] I'm well aware of the difference in perspective between performer and meditator. But as presence is not all there is to meditation, I likewise assume it's only one of many qualities needed by an actor, and yet it is an essential one.

Dancers spend thousands of hours in the practice of walking, standing, leaping, moving. They have developed a deep knowledge of the experience of the body and a vocabulary to express it. They may also certainly face the problems that can arise when any dichotomy between body and mind is made. "When we say that the actor/dancer uses her body, we may wonder," Eugenio Barba said in his essay "The Credible Body."[3] That is, we may wonder who is using what.

The body of the accomplished dancer, the master, becomes "a body of presence and attention," as the French dancer and choreographer Dominque Dupuy said. When we develop true intimacy with our body, we become intimate with ourselves. We learn to be present as a whole. We open to discovery of our essence when the dichotomy of body-mind is dropped.

That is precisely the purpose of the practice of Gesture of Awareness. In this practice we explore movement to discover the nature of awareness. We inquire even of the sensation of tension in the neck—becoming aware not of the sensation but of the consciousness of it; becoming aware not of the consciousness of it, but of the essence of the consciousness. If the body is just a thought, the play of awareness, then ultimately an intimate knowledge of the body is an intimate knowledge of awareness.

It is skillful to use the body as a means of inquiry into one's true essence. Buddhism has a long tradition of employing meditation on sound, but sounds flicker. They're unstable; they're dependent on external conditions. This is much less the case with the body. But in order to explore one's true essence one needs to stop elaborating on what is happening; one needs to let go of the habitual tendencies of judging, evaluating, of labeling every experience.

just be
standing

experiencing
nothing to change
nothing to improve

can we feel the floor
beneath our feet
feel its
temperature
feel its
texture

is it hard or
soft
cold
warm

can we just be
standing

without interfering
without changing anything
without keeping anything

It is hard to lead classes without any suggestions of what a given experience should be—to lead classes in an ever-open way. We're so used to modifying our experiences that the bare attention of one kind of experience may draw us on to try to transform or improve what is happening—thereby drawing us out from the experience. If asked, for example, "Can you be aware of your breath?" some participants may notice that their breath feels contrived, and immediately try to improve it. If asked, "Can you let the breath be contrived or free?" participants may interfere much less with their experience.

I've noticed when teaching meditation how often I, too, perpetuate a sense of time and duration. We're often too casual, too loose, in our way of speaking. First, second, or third day has no meaning with respect to present experience. What does it mean to sit or walk for fifteen minutes, or for an hour, from the point of view of being present? Language is conceived from the point of view of the experience and the experiencer, from the point of view of duality. When exploring modes of being, language can mislead us.

Sometimes I've noticed when participants work together in groups of three that each takes for granted that he or she will be in the middle during the next turn. They take this for reality. I bring this reality into question by stopping the exercise after two participants have had their turn in the middle, leaving one with their expectations unfulfilled. In *Lama Yangthig*, by 14th-century Tibetan master Longchengpa, I found a similar instance. Here, the teacher asks the student to walk to a place some distance away. When the student has reached the midway point, the teacher asks the student to stop, and to return. This surprises the student and leaves him thoughtless, free of conceptualization.

The practice of Gesture of Awareness is, at times, akin to a koan: a koan not based on words but on situation. Not asking, "What is the sound of one hand clapping?" but rather, for example, asking when walking, "Can we be at two places at the same time, and if we have time, why not?" Many aspects of this practice find their source in Buddhist sutras like the *Satipatthana Sutta* and the *Bahia Sutta*. References can also be found in the texts of the great Indian commentators. As Nagarjuna, the illustrious teacher and commentator on the Buddha's teachings, says:

> Walking does not start
> In the steps taken or to come
> Or in the act itself.
> Where does it begin?
> Before I raise a foot,
> Is there motion,
> A step taken or to come
> Whence walking could begin?[4]

When asked what the writing of James Joyce was all about, Beckett said that it wasn't about something, but rather was the thing itself. I imagine that could be said about Gesture of Awareness.

At the beginning of each session, I question some aspect of what we take to be the reality of our experiences so that all participants, including me, may be drawn into a state of perplexity, into a mood of investigation. Some hunting tribes used to perform a dance before going off on their expeditions as a way of tuning in to the spirit of the hunt. I see the questioning at the beginning as a dance of inquiry. And after, we explore through movement, gesture, and contact the truth of each moment.

NOTES

1. This essay was created, with permission, from excerpts of Charles Genoud's *Gesture of Awareness: A Radical Approach to Time, Space, and Movement* (Somerville: Wisdom Publications, 2006).

2. Jerzy Grotowski, *Toward a Poor Theater* (London: Methuen Drama, 1968), 91.

3. Eugenio Barba, *Le Corps en Jeu* (Paris: CNRS Edition, 1994), 251–252.

4. Nagarjuna, trans. and arr. Stephen Batchelor, *Nagarjuna: Verses from the Center* (New York: Riverhead Books, 2001), 84.

Body
The Foundation of Insight

BHIKKHUNI THANASANTI

Integral Awakening through the Body

Many people come to meditation with the idea that if they just focus and concentrate hard enough, they'll be happy and peaceful. In fact the opposite is true. When we're relaxed and happy, then our minds focus and we become still, naturally. Stillness doesn't come from a concerted, restricted effort clamping down on the object; it comes from relaxation and allowing the object of our attention to fill awareness. As our bodies relax, our minds focus. Without dispersion and distraction, insight can emerge. Our sense of well being is critical to developing deep meditation.

One of the things I do when teaching is to begin sitting meditation with standing. This always evokes laughter because you're not supposed to sit standing. You're supposed to sit sitting! I do this because people feel more grounded and settled. They feel more relaxed. And when they then sit it takes much less time to focus on what's going on.

I was recently teaching a retreat and noticed that the community I was in had a very high level of determination, diligence, and commitment, and very little joy, spontaneity, and body awareness. Eventually, I encouraged them to stop doing formal walking meditation and to do aimless wandering, where they weren't using any particular technique, but just using their body as an access to being open, alive, and responsive to the nature around them. They loved it because it helped bring balance and allowed them to feel a joy, ease, and spontaneity that they had been lacking. As a result, many reported insights that were new for them.

One of the most significant *suttas* in the Pali scriptures is the *Satipatthana Sutta*. This *sutta*, or discourse, describes a path to freedom using meditation. It clearly emphasizes attention to the body as the First Foundation of Mindfulness. In this teaching, the Buddha speaks on body awareness by asking that we pay attention to our posture, breath, daily activities for getting dressed, moving, eating, and using the toilet, internal components of the body, the elemental qualities within the body, and the body's nature to decompose. The Buddha establishes the foundation of insight with the body as a precursor to other insights. The body is an important anchor for meditation practice. It stabilizes the process of opening up to the other three foundations—feelings, thoughts, and the contents of one's mind.

17

Mindfulness of the body is the place from which we can understand and have insight into the feelings we have, the things that we think, and the way we are reacting to stuff that is going on. This works because each of these other foundations has a somatic counterpart. Every thought and feeling has a sensation that we can feel in our body. Anger may have heat in our abdomen. Fear might feel like a constriction in our throat. Desire to be free may feel like a tingling in our back. Every thought, every feeling can be traced to a corresponding sensation. Every reaction to a thought or feeling we can notice in our body. When thoughts are complicated, or we're going through something that is difficult to understand, we can shift our frame of reference. Instead of focusing on the thought, we can bring our attention to the impact of the thought in our body. As we focus on the physical sensation connected to the thought, it brings perspective. This perspective often can help us find a wise response to what's happening.

In a traditional approach, the assumption is that our transcendent insights are key and everything else that is important will follow. If our transcendent insights into the nature of reality don't translate into other parts of our life, then it's not important. In my experience, and in my observations of people around me, it's very possible to have transcendent insight and for it *not* to eradicate the issues that we experience in our personality, core beliefs, and relationships—domains that are part of the external world. An integral perspective of awakening does not presume that an interior insight is going to automatically translate into these other domains. As I have worked directly with my body and become a little more skilled at relaxation and how to direct energy through my body, it has supported seeing my core beliefs, some of the characteristics of my personality, and the way these things have played out in my relationships. The shifts happened from understanding the importance of bringing care and attention into these domains and from utilizing my body as an anchor for these insights.

In an integral approach to awakening there's an interest to see that the body is opening and relaxing. There's an interest to see that we're actually doing the work we need to on our psychological structures and personal relationships. There's an interest to see that the power dynamics that we are involved in are useful for the context that we're in. We are not only interested in the interior domain of reflective awareness, but in how this expresses itself in the forms, structures, and relationships in our world. Integral awakening is interested in development in all parts of our personal lives, and seeing our interconnection with the culture and the environment of which we are part.

The Power of the Subtle Energy Body

As a Buddhist nun, my life is based on meditation and renunciation. Yet, even though this is the focus of my life, I found that my capacity to make use of Buddha's teachings increased when I started learning about qigong and subtle energy through alternative sources. After having been meditating for fifteen years, five of which I had been a nun, I started qigong practices.

I was first introduced to qigong by reading a book. As I read and started doing the practices, I noticed it had an enormous impact on my ability to stay present and attentive to my own body sensations. Like many people I know, bringing attention to my body was not an easy task. My attention would get entangled in thoughts and I wouldn't feel what was going on in my body. I was often thinking or planning and not attentive to what I was feeling physically. Doing qigong exercises helped me to focus, helping me to pay attention what was happening in my body.

I noticed that by doing the qigong practices from a book, without a teacher or community of support, it still had a significant impact on my ability to relax, focus, and concentrate. As a result of my own beneficial experience, I felt compelled to share qigong with those who attended my meditation retreats. Most people coming on retreat can't relax. They don't really know what it feels like to have attention immersed in the body. They don't know what it means to look for or feel subtle energy and to attune to the nuances of what is going on in the body. For modern people coming on retreat, beginning with instructions to sit and focus on your body isn't helpful. They are too tense to feel much of anything that is going on.

The Pali scriptures of the Theravada tradition don't talk directly about qi or energy of the body. Yet the tradition that I was first ordained into, the Thai Forest mediation masters, teaches it. Some of them understand this subtle energy and how to activate it. If you look at the teachings of Ajahn Lee Dhammadharo, his breath meditations activate the subtle energy of the body. He's a Forest meditation master in the Theravada tradition. The Tibetan, or Vajrayana, tradition has many practices and teachings around the subtle energy body. Within the Vajrayana tradition, though, many of the teachings and practices that activate the subtle energy of the body require preliminary practices to have access to them.

Qi, the Subtle Energy Body and Emptiness

Practicing qigong can open up the life force, the qi energy. This happens whether or not you have any conceptual understanding of qi. When qi flows, your muscles warm up and soften and your body becomes more open. These physical attributes of relaxation make it possible for attention to settle much more easily.

Practices that open that up and direct the subtle energy can be powerful tools. They help us shift our understanding that our body is solid, stable, and unchanging. This insight lets us see that all of nature is the same way. When there isn't something that is stable, solid, or unchanging that we can find in any thing, we have an insight into the empty nature of existence. Being empty of inherent existence is not the same as being without of any kind of existence. What this means is that things do exist, but they don't have a substantial unchanging component that is the basis for their existence. One of the most beneficial aspects of working with the subtle energies of our bodies is their capacity for stabilizing the mind in emptiness. Understanding how qi can stabilize the mind in emptiness is profound work. It is for this reason that the subtle energy body is so important.

Qi and subtle energy are not separate from meditation, but are directly connected to what's happening in our mind. With the view that qi, body, and mind are connected, the path opens up that values body awareness practices, more understanding of the subtle energy body and how to work with it, and the way that our body and the kind of qi we are experiencing affect our moods and mind states.

In our North American post-modern society there's an overemphasis on individuality and will as being the energy source that makes everything happen. When we start working with qi and get a feeling for our life force, we can begin to understand how to

Bhikkhuni Thanasanti leading Sherin Shaaban and Dan Arias in qigong at Northeastern University, April 2015. Photograph by Harrison Blum.

do things from this different source of energy. We can be fueled by qi, breath, and awareness. As we feel and connect with this in our own body, we can open up a window to see how that might also apply in other areas of our life. Because we can't consolidate a sense of a permanent individuated sense of self around qi, it also can be a support for insight into what we actually are made of—a co-dependent arising phenomena based on many different circumstances. There isn't one entity that we can know, name, and label as "myself" that doesn't change. This, too, is part of stabilizing our attention in emptiness, to see the connection between the way that who we are is dependent on all these various things coming together.

Different Containers, Different Practices

A monastic life is based upon renunciation. We refrain from dancing, singing, going to shows, and beautifying ourselves. Renunciation does not place a judgment on these activities as being immoral, bad, or wrong. Renunciation streamlines our focus and priorities. The premise of renunciation is based in the power of harnessing our attention and utilizing our energy for awakening. While certain forms of spiritual dance can be very reflective, a lot of dancing is not about waking up. It's about following impulses and desires.

There are many ways dance can be both expressive and meditative, but this doesn't mean dance should be introduced as part of monastic lifestyles. A monastic tradition is designed to focus attention on contemplation. Just because monastics live with this level of renunciation doesn't mean that this is the ideal everyone should live up to, that we should try to get dancers to do this, too. Dancers are not going to want to give up dancing, as dancing is what they do! Likewise, monastics don't need to include dance in order for certain contemplative dance practices to be legitimate for dancers. Everyone doesn't need to be living with the same standards in order for each of us to feel confident in our path.

Yet, no matter what our path and precept commitment in life, we all have bodies, we all experience stress, and we all want to be happy. When we see that our bodies support where we place attention and how we work with what is arising, we gain more understanding, confidence, and independence. As we become more independent and confident we have more capacity to work with what is arising. This is the ground from which a way of being fully alive and loving can emerge, one rooted in insight, and in which one is free to choose how to live and be of service in this world.

Movement as Skillful
Means to Stillness

Lori Wong

"When going forward & returning, he makes himself fully alert; when looking toward & looking away ... when bending & extending his limbs ... when carrying his outer cloak, his upper robe & his bowl ... when walking, standing, sitting, falling asleep, waking up ... he makes himself fully alert. And as he remains thus heedful, ardent, & resolute ... his mind gathers & settles inwardly, grows unified & centered."

—*Kāyagatāsati Sutta*[1]

Recently, I met in private with a woman who was very interested in learning meditation, but she said she couldn't sit still—she'd never been able to sit still her entire life. She was now retired, but was completely uncomfortable with not being busy in mind and body. We talked a bit about the practice of mindfulness as not forcing the mind to stop thinking, but actually just paying attention to our experience and seeing our relationship with that experience. I could see that she was fidgeting as I spoke to her and sensed that she was anxious—little twitches and nervous movements in her face were noticeable. I suggested that we didn't have to sit still to practice mindfulness. We could start practicing mindfulness by just paying attention to the body in a very specific way. I asked if she would be willing to stand up and try a brief experiment with me.

We were standing on top of some mats on the floor, so I asked her to feel the surface she was standing on (in bare feet) and to pay particular attention to how the weight was distributed on the bottoms of her feet. I asked her to shift her weight and to pay attention to how that felt on the soles of her feet, and then to come to a slow stop. When she seemed comfortable with that, I asked her to close her eyes and to notice how that might change the perception of her feet to not have the distraction of visual input. She noticed that her feet needed to grip the floor and that there were little adjustments that her body had to make to stay balanced. While she had her eyes closed, I then directed her attention into one hand—to specifically sense each finger from the inside, one by one, starting with the little finger, progressing to the thumb, and then to sense the palm and back of the hand and finally, the whole hand. Then, I asked her to widen her attention to take both hands into her awareness and notice if the hand she had been paying attention to felt different than the one we had ignored. She opened her eyes and indicated that yes, it did. The hand she had paid attention to felt warmer, bigger, more alive. She was very surprised! We spent only a few minutes with that exercise, but she had a very concrete experience of directing her attention intentionally. I asked her if she noticed anything else while her attention was on the hand. No. It was as if everything else faded out.

I mentioned to her work that Catherine Kerr has done at Brown University showing that directed attention placed in specific parts of the body may attenuate or modulate the perception of pain and regulate emotional response.[2,3] So, by placing attention purposefully in her hand, this woman's directed attention dimmed any other sensory input coming into her brain.

While we did the standing exercise, I could tell she was much calmer, less nervous. I thought it might be a good time to try some meditation in a seated posture. She was still anxious, but much less so than when we started. I suggested that we try a seated movement as a gateway to becoming more still. I led her in a series of movements that start with hands flat on the thighs and gradually progress to both hands on the chest over the heart.

This sequence is a variation of a technique from a Southeast Asian Theravada Buddhist practice called Mahasati Meditation developed by Luangpor Teean Jittasubho (1911–1988). I was first introduced to this movement meditation by one of my Buddhist teachers, Larry Yang, while I was in the Community Dharma Leader Program through Spirit Rock Meditation Center. This sequence of movements starts with hands on the thighs, then one hand is moved in a sequential pattern: from palm down, to placing the hand on its edge on the thigh, raising it, then placing the hand on the chest, then repeating the sequence with the other hand. Once both hands are placed on the chest, the pattern sequence is reversed, returning the hands back to the thighs. This sequence can be repeated over and over again as a complete practice and can be used not only to settle the mind but as an effective tool to see the nature of the mind—seeing our identification with thoughts, sensations, and emotions which are actually transitory and ephemeral.[4]

As she followed the sequence and got to the point when she had both hands on her chest, I could see that this was really soothing for her, so I suggested she could stay there as long as she felt it was helpful. I could see her relax visibly and she was much calmer. After a few minutes, she resumed and completed the first sequence. At that point, I suggested that if she felt calm enough to stay there and focus on her breath, she could do so. She did not repeat the sequence. We sat there for five minutes as she followed the movement of her breath. She did not fidget, was not restless, and was completely tranquil.

* * *

In my experience teaching mindfulness to various populations, including children, adults, and incarcerated people, I have found that using movement can often be a skillful entry point not only to stillness, but to truly connecting to our lived experience in the moment. This was just one example of how powerful that can be for someone who may be anxious and might find sitting still to be too challenging without some other way to begin. I have used this and other kinds of movement to help practitioners be in touch with their physical body and the felt sense of their experience. This investigation of felt sense through movement in the body provides a gradual and natural way for the mind to prepare to enter into the stillness of meditation.

Once, I had an opportunity to teach this modified Mahasati practice to a small group of children between the ages of six and eleven years old. In this group, there was one child whom I was told was autistic. He seemed to have trouble keeping his attention focused and was mostly disengaged during the other mindfulness practices that required being still, so I decided to switch to mindful movement to see if that might help entice him. When I introduced the Mahasati meditation initially, this child seemed just as distracted and inattentive as with the other mindfulness practices. However, when I asked the children to engage in a "slow" race—to see how slowly they could do this sequence of movements, this child actually participated and it was quite evident that he had paid attention while I was teaching the sequence, even though he did not appear to be following along. When I deliberately slowed the sequence down, this appeared to capture his attention fully and he seemed to be much calmer during the "race."

If I have a group of children that seems energetic or restless, I will often use some qigong, or other mindful movements, to direct their attention into the body and then gradually slow the movements down so we can move to a still, seated posture. One such movement mimics walking in place as if through tall grass—lifting the legs and arms in a synchronous movement. I ask the children to see if they could do this without making any sound—which requires them to focus attention on how lightly or heavily they place their feet on the floor. This activity also begins to quiet them down as we go slower and try to make less and less noise. The children become more still and settled as they naturally slow the movement down to be quiet. As illustrated by this activity, children seem to respond more readily to movement, and using a moving awareness practice as a means to bring focus into the body while gradually slowing down seems to help them move into a still posture without as much fidgeting or restlessness. This serves two purposes: it simultaneously engages the mind and diverts attention away from being caught in thoughts, and gently moves the child into stillness through the encouragement to slow down and move quietly.

* * *

This kind of strategy also works well with adults, although I might introduce it differently. As a volunteer teaching mindfulness in prison, the incarcerated men we visit may not be used to sitting quietly and still for any length of time, so we often start out using some kind of movement to engage them and move them towards a seated, still posture. Men, in my opinion, may be less aware of their body—less used to paying attention to bodily sensations—so using movement as a mindfulness practice also trains their awareness of sensations in different parts of the body. This is very useful when we use mindfulness to experience emotions in the body, rather than allowing emotions to spin off into ruminative thinking.

In a prison visit, we might use yoga, qigong, or tai chi as the mindful movement prior to a period of sitting meditation. Using mindful movement, we direct their attention to the somatic experience rather than externally oriented thinking. We remind the men to come back to the physical sensations when they find themselves thinking about something else. In this way, we begin to introduce emotion regulation through choosing not to follow a particular train of thought and instead to intentionally focus on the physical sensation of the movement we're engaged in. Sometimes, I have asked the men to practice a single leg balance (it could be yoga or qigong). This pose requires a lot of attention to keep from losing one's balance. It usually gets pretty quiet as the men try to keep their balance. At the end of the balancing, I will ask the men if they were thinking about anything else while holding the pose. Many of the men say they couldn't think of anything because they were too busy trying to stay upright! And, most of the men who were thinking of something else lose their balance because they weren't paying attention to balancing. This is a very quick and easy way to demonstrate the power of intentional attention and how it can foster a quieter, more focused mind.

One study suggests that tai chi can increase tactile acuity through training specific attention on the body's extremities (hands and feet).[5] This kind of attention training might also be a beneficial element to enhancing emotional and cognitive processing, as well as reducing chronic pain and negative, ruminative thinking.[6] I know from my own direct experience with practicing tai chi or qigong that the mind can become quite concentrated and free of distraction and thinking as one develops the attention and sensitivity to the sensations in the body as it moves. This body awareness is an important element in mindfulness meditation. Enhancing body awareness is considered a key element of mindfulness based therapies as well as Buddhist insight meditation.[7] The *Satipatthana Sutta* (*Majjhima Nikaya* 10), in particular, points to mindfulness of the body in various postures (sitting, standing, walking, lying down) as an essential training. The Insight Meditation tradition, one of the main forms of Western Buddhism, relies heavily on the *Satipatthana Sutta* as a foundational practice.

* * *

At times, when someone is caught in ruminative or obsessive thinking, introducing sequenced movement may help by giving the mind something to do, while breaking the ruminative or obsessive pattern. One woman was struggling with PTSD and could not meditate focusing on the breath for any length of time, as that would exacerbate her distress or produce more anxiety. I asked her to try the modified Mahasati sequence and this was helpful for her to calm the mind enough to gain some normalcy in her life. In one specific situation after some practice with this sequence, she realized that her PTSD was being triggered. She was able to excuse herself to go to another room and close the door. Once she felt secure behind the door, she used the movement sequence to be able to regain enough calm and clarity to be able to go back out and re-engage successfully. Adopting these movement techniques allowed her some self-regulation of emotions that would have otherwise derailed her for days. This was only one instance, but it points to the power of using mindful movement to disrupt particular strong patterns in the mind.

Developing internal awareness also helps to introduce the idea of experiencing sensations without having to "fix them." We can learn to just attend to the sensations as they arise without needing them to be different. One standing exercise develops this awareness by asking participants to shift their weight to one foot. I ask them to notice if that is painful or unpleasant. Then, as time passes and they keep the weight on the one foot, I ask if they notice if it is now painful or unpleasant. Given enough time, the posture becomes unpleasant. I let them shift and ask them to notice how it is now pleasant to shift the weight and ask them to notice how long the pleasantness lasts. Using this simple movement exercise can also be done in a seated posture, asking someone to shift from one side to another. This not only brings the focus into physical awareness in the body, but begins to point to the changing nature of what we feel and experience—that even if we move to change from unpleasant to pleasant, it's not a lasting change. So, carrying this experience to a still posture, we can start to see that squirming and shifting in our seat does not guarantee any lasting relief. This can be a helpful understanding about reactivity that might come up in sitting still—we feel unpleasant and try to make it pleasant, only to be thwarted over and over again. This helps us to develop some tolerance and capacity for learning to still the body and mind.

Buddhism historically has adapted into the culture and society in which it spread. The popularization of *vipassana*, or insight, meditation (and mindfulness as we know it today) is accredited to Ledi Sayadaw in late 19th-century Burma.[8] Much of insight meditation taught in the West was highly influenced by Burmese and Thai meditation masters—and the model adopted in the West predominantly focuses on retreat practice in which stillness is strongly emphasized. As mindfulness has become more widely accepted and practiced in both Buddhist and non-Buddhist settings, mindfulness in movement has been gaining popularity as a useful technique and skill that not only has its roots in the Buddha's teachings, but allows a wider population to participate that might not easily sit still for long periods of time. In retreat centers over the last ten years, it's become more common to find offerings of yoga, tai chi, or qigong as an adjunct to sitting and walking practices. Upon leaving retreat, one of the difficulties that many people face is bringing aspects of their sitting practice into daily life. This can also pose a challenge for people who practice formally outside of retreat and relate to their practice as something separate from the rest of their life. The many variations of mindful movement could be an essential element facilitating the integration of mindfulness into the activities of our everyday lives. Beyond supporting general well being, mindful movement can also be a powerful and skillful means toward developing the stability of mind leading to awakening.

NOTES

1. Kāyagatāsati Sutta, Majjhima Nikāya 119. Trans. Thanissaro Bhikkhu. Accessed May 6, 2015. http://www.accesstoinsight.org/tipitaka/mn/mn.119.than.html.

2. Catherine E. Kerr, Matthey D. Sacchet, Sara W. Lazar, Cristopher I. Moore, and Stephanie R. Jones, "Mindfulness Starts with the Body: Somatosensory Attention and Top-down Modulation of Cortical Alpha Rhythms in Mindfulness Meditation," *Frontiers in Human Neuroscience* 7.12. doi: 10.3389/fnhum.2013.00012.

3. Alex Knapp, "Catherine Kerr on the Science of Meditation," *Forbes Magazine*, Sept. 9, 2011. Accessed May 6, 2015. http://www.forbes.com/sites/alexknapp/2011/09/09/catherine-kerr-on-the-science-of-meditation/.

4. Mahasati Insight Meditation Association, "What Is Mahasati." Accessed May 6, 2015. http://mahasati.inspiredlens.com/mahasati/.

5. Catherine E. Kerr et al., "Tactile Acuity in Experienced Tai Chi Practitioners: Evidence for Use Dependent Plasticity as an Effect of Sensory-Attentional Training," *Experimental Brain Research* 188.2 (2008): 317–322. Accessed November 21, 2014. http://link.springer.com/article/10.1007%2Fs00221–008–1409–6.

6. Catherine Kerr, "Mindfulness Starts with the Body: A View from the Brain," talk given at TEDxCollege Hill, May 12, 2012.

7. Wolf E. Mehling et al., "Body Awareness: A Phenomenological Inquiry into the Common Ground of Mind-Body Therapies," *Philosophies, Ethics, and Humanities in Medicine* 6.6 (2011). doi: 10.1186/1747–5341–6–6.

8. Erik Braun, *The Birth of Insight: Meditation, Modern Buddhism, and the Burmese Monk Ledi Sayadaw* (Chicago: University of Chicago Press, 2013), 257.

Finding Our Flow
Continuum Movement and Buddha Dharma

ADRIANNE E. VINCENT

Luminous pearlescent light interpenetrated by radiant royal blue orbs swirls close by and through me as an infant lying on my back in my crib, wide open, one with all, in ecstatic bliss. My preverbal memories are filled with this state. This complex of rapturously joyful sensate memories, combined with luminescent visual impressions of my gently swaying and bobbing beloved bluebird mobile, endure. They can saturate my present spiritual practices of Continuum and Buddhism today and serve as access points to moments of total absorption, no matter what may be arising in my inner or outer world.

I have come full circle over the course of my life. I found my calling to healing modalities during the earliest years of my life, and during the subsequent years I sought to nurture it through my studies and work as a movement therapist, counselor, and hands-on healer. During the first few years of my life I experienced what Freud calls the "oceanic feeling," that is, a profound feeling of being one with everyone and everything else. I felt that the boundaries between the world and me were fluid, and that they were constantly shifting, often vanishing such that I blended into the world and the world blended into me. During such moments, I experienced the entirety of nature and the universe as a unity and myself as an intrinsic part of it. My early childhood experiences had all the hallmarks of mystical experiences, as they were defined by immense feelings of peace, harmony, and joy.

The memory of these profound and powerful early spiritual episodes stayed with me as I grew older. I gradually realized that everything I did spiritually, professionally, and personally during the subsequent years of my life could be traced back to my initial experiences of unity with the world and inspired me to seek supportive spiritual and personal communities and scholarship that understand and have helped foster the insights of those awakenings.

Origins

I was born and grew up Catholic in San Francisco in the sixties. When I was four years old, I began attending mass with my family, as well as studying and practicing three

27

types of dance: ballet, modern, and tap. The Catholic Church and the dance studio were two key sites where I continued to encounter my early experience of being one with the world. Studying these several types of dance supported the evolving and opening of my body, but soon the dance studio became too rule-filled to sufficiently support me in finding the sense of peace and unity with the world I was seeking. In my teens, I realized that while dance indeed enabled me to actively utilize my body, it did not enable me to cultivate the kind of deep bodily awareness that I desired. My dance teachers prioritized the attainment of certain bodily forms over the attainment of a deep awareness of the body. I understood I needed the body as a territory within which I could recognize essential experiences in order to ground my developing consciousness, but the forms I had chosen were not leading to that path.

In the Catholic Church I learned the stories of the saints who transcended themselves, achieving egoless states allowing them to fully devote themselves to the service of others. Listening to these stories I understood that my early experiences of being one with the world were profoundly similar to the egoless states that these saints strived to cultivate. Furthermore I realized that, like these Catholic saints, I, too, wanted to transcend my ego self again, recreating my early experiences of being one with the world, but now as a path to wholeheartedly dedicating myself to the service of others. Contrary to the Catholic saints who actively renounced and negated their bodies in their devotional practices, I understood instinctively how deeply I must live in my body, experiencing its sensations to affectively become sensitive to others. I felt that it was only by becoming fully attentive to my own bodily experience that I could transcend myself, and become deeply attuned to the bodily experiences and suffering of others.

Therefore, when I turned fifteen years old I started doing yoga to cultivate a deeper awareness of the body while embarking on my path of spiritual development. Yoga helped me to cultivate an awareness of myself as an embodied human being, to experience a sense of kinship with all human beings and all other beings, and ultimately all of nature and the universe.

As I immersed myself into yoga practice, I also began listening to Alan Watts, who did a weekly radio program, *Psychotherapy: East and West*, in which he discussed insights from Vedanta, New Physics, Cybernetics, Semantics, Process Philosophy, Natural History, and Anthropology. While listening to Watts' discussion of modern sociology and psychology, particularly the sociological theories of Emile Durkheim and the psychological theories of Carl Jung, I realized that my own early experience of being one with world was not unique, but rather it is a universal human experience, and one with antecedents and parallels across time, space, and culture. Furthermore, listening to Watts' program enabled me to learn about a host of Eastern spiritual traditions, including Buddhism, Hinduism, Vedanta, and Jainism. In particular, Watts drew my attention to the possibilities that meditation, particularly Buddhist meditation, offered to transcend the ego and to cultivate a mystical experience of oneness with others, the world, and nature.

As a result, in 1980, when I was in my early twenties, I began to pursue Buddhist meditation under the supervision of Jack Kornfield and Robert Hall, who belonged to the tradition of Theravada Buddhism, practiced *vipassana* (insight) meditation, and, in Hall's case, taught emergent body therapies and embodied psychotherapy. Kornfield and Hall taught ten-day meditation and movement retreats in the Yucca Valley desert of Southern California. These *vipassana* meditation retreats primarily focused on sitting and walking meditation, with Lomi movement sessions (described below) led by Hall each afternoon and Dharma talks twice a day. My concepts about what kind of spiritual growth was possible for the "lay-person," or the non-monastic, were blasted wide open at my retreat. It was such a revelation for me that I stayed on another two weeks, sitting part time and working part time on staff, so I could continue to practice and deepen the insights I discovered during the first ten days.

Deepening the Dharma Movement

Subsequent retreats revealed to me the aim of Buddhist practice, the alleviation of suffering by achieving "awakening," or enlightenment, through bringing wise attention to the experience of the present moment. It was at these retreats in Yucca Valley that much deeper layers of suffering began to reveal themselves to me and drop away. By virtue of cultivating an awareness of each passing moment, I became more skilled and prepared to pay attention to my own body, becoming more deeply aware of myself as an embodied and sentient being than I had ever been before. My awareness of my own bodily and sensory experiences, in turn, allowed me to conceive of myself as a being in the context of nature and the universe. The more I immersed myself into my bodily and sensory experience, the more states of non-identification with them became predominant, as I couldn't grasp an experience or mind-state. I deeply understood they were not "mine" to have. And if they weren't mine to have, then they were no one else's either, and the suffering, I was beginning to understand, was therefore inherently universal.

Spontaneously, upon grasping these realizations, endless waves of compassion arose within me, for not only my own misery but also for the misery of the entire human race. Not one of us will come to the end of our lives unscathed by anguish of one sort or another. As I grasped the impermanence of all thought forms and felt the impact of that realization after just one retreat, I became certain that the insights I sought in order to do the healing work I was called to do were to be found within the deep contemplative practices of Buddhism.

I also realized, rather ironically, that it was only by cultivating a profound awareness of my bodily existence that I could transcend myself and attain an egoless state. By virtue of this egoless state I could become fully aware of my deeper connections with the whole of creation, bearing witness first to my pain and then that of others, enabling me to serve them unconditionally. Through the exquisitely nuanced focus which Buddhism brings to bear upon our incarnated existence, and my interest in the embodiment aspects of the Buddhist teachings, I was unwittingly cultivating the fertile ground for the concepts of Continuum, which I wouldn't actually learn about until several years later.

In the meantime, I deepened in my study and practice of Lomi Bodywork. Lomi Bodywork incorporates deep-tissue massage, classic Rolfing techniques, Polarity and Gestalt therapies, and *vipassana* meditation in order to help people release deeply held emotions and open the flow of energy in the body. In a typical session, clients may work seated, on the table, or in movement exploration as the practitioner guides them to attend to their breath and bodily sensation. It was while training to become a Lomi Bodywork practitioner that I learnt about Emilie Conrad, the founder of Continuum.

Continuum Movement

Continuum Movement was founded in 1967 by Emilie Conrad on the basis of her life-long exploration of dance, nature, and a variety of cross-cultural spiritual practices. As I explored Emilie's work, I discovered that she combined my interests in dance, meditation, philosophy, self-transcendence, and science more effectively than the other movement forms I had explored until that point. Thus, in 1982, when I was in my mid-twenties, I reached out to Emilie and Susan Harper, her collaborator in the development of Continuum, and received their direct guidance and supervision.

Continuum is based on the premise that we are the products of an on-going biomorphic evolution occurring for billions of years—a universal, continual, and all-encompassing process. Being products of this cosmic process, we are profoundly tied to everything else that is a part of this universe, including all kinds of animate and inanimate objects, such as plants, animals, and stars. The atoms in our bodies were once part of stars, and for a long period of our evolutionary history we lived in the ocean, and only gradually moved to the land. Despite moving from the ocean to land, we continue to carry our oceanic origins within us and thus we are fundamentally fluid beings. In other words, we are "moving water brought to land," and by virtue of being fluid beings we can potentially spill, expand, pour, and unfold in an omni-directional way, building a wide range of connections with other beings, nature, and the universe.

However, the repressive constraints of modern life impair our vitality, spontaneity, creative intelligence, and our ability to expand and to connect with others. As a result, we become confined to our inner shells and suffer from a variety of maladies, including immobility, depression, isolation, and fatigue. The goal of Continuum is to enable us to become aware of ourselves as fluid and embodied beings as a means to enable us to experience our profound interconnections with the entire cosmos, and to unlock and expand our spiritual energy and creative intelligence. These women taught what I experienced as the exquisite interface of Buddhism with dance. My body and mind had found a true spiritual home.

Emilie worked in conjunction with Susan to translate the ideas of Continuum into a series of exercises. In one Continuum exercise in which I participated, we were instructed to lie on our backs on the soft carpeting in a light filled room in a Catholic University atop a hill with 360-degree views of San Francisco—the city, bay, hills, and all. While the fresh ocean breezes blew through the eucalyptus trees

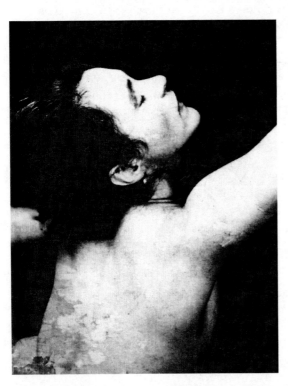

Adrienne E. Vincent practicing Continuum, San Francisco, 1997. Photograph by Christine Alicino.

outside our room, we were instructed to guide the gentle breezes of our breath through our bodies, focusing our attention inside. Susan demonstrated, seated in a chair, knees wide apart, undulating her spine, that when we shaped with our mouths the inhalation and exhalation, we could "drop" these winds of our breath into different areas of our bodies. Caressing the exhalation by shaping our lips into an "O" circle, dropping the sound of the exhale into our lowest sound register, and gently touching our bellies we might discover something about ourselves. Then she asked us to work with the undulation of our spines in conjunction with the opening offered by our breath.

As I lay staring at the ceiling, Susan put beautiful deep Tibetan chants on the sound system, and I began cautiously touching my lower abdomen with the finger-tips of my right hand while over and over again dropping the sound through my open throat, down through my chest and into my belly. I allowed the vibrations of sound to soften my glottis, epiglottis, and all the tissues of my throat, neck, spine, and chest. At times I actually felt what I thought she had spoken of in her instructions, the rippling out of sensations from this core of deep resonant sound. At other times I simply allowed the monks' chanting to move through me, opening me to sound, light, and a certain kind of transcendence. At points I gave myself over to the fact that I had hardened, dense, thickened areas which wouldn't relent to my repeated attempts to soften and open.

In the midst of the endeavor, I felt that the exercise was qualitatively different from the Buddhist meditation that I had practiced earlier in the desert. Unlike those Buddhist practices which were extremely focused and structured in terms of their rules and requirements, this Continuum exercise simply invited me to live, to awaken not only to the now, but to the organismic moment of unfolding, the birthing of undulations I had never before known or valued. The tiniest reverberations intensified as we were left to explore for hours without specific guidance. It was the first time within memory that I felt safe and invited to simply be with sensations, sounds, and movements, without sexual overtones, without medical analysis, without dance instructions, without any agenda but simply to witness the majesty of the "universalness" of life unfolding before my very eyes, within my very body.

I was one of sixty undulating bodies that afternoon, awakening with awe and fear and reverence. Hour upon hour I was in turns fascinated and bored, reborn and dying, the entire panoply of existence revealing itself to all of us, equally, simply, and without differentiation. I felt that I was deeply aware of myself as a fluid organism and at the same time I was aware of my kinship with all other organisms and with the universe, which was itself an organism.

The Dharma of Continuum

Continuum Movement shares with Buddhism a number of similar insights into the human condition. Buddhism and Continuum Movement teach us that we are profoundly connected with each other. In Buddhism, the notion of *pratityasamutpada,* or dependent origination, underscores that nothing independently arises or comes into being. Rather, all things are mutually dependent, and they come into being by virtue of their dependence on other things. Continuum shares this Buddhist insight as it also teaches that we are profoundly connected with everything, as we are products of billions of years of cosmic evolution. Continuum teaches that we are fluid and embodied aggregates of vibration, sound, and movement, and are imbedded in the organismic movement and unfolding of the universe.

From this view of interdependence, both Buddhism and Continuum emphasize self-lessness and emptiness. The self is not discrete and autonomous, but rather is deeply connected with everything else. The origins, the persistence, and the very nature of the self are shaped by its intimate and myriad connections with the rest of the universe. Things are thus inherently empty, and they acquire their being, subsistence, and meaning by virtue of other phenomena. All bodies in the universe are what they are by virtue of their connections and mutually dependent bonds with all other bodies.

Additionally, both Buddhism and Continuum prescribe various spiritual exercises to enable us to cultivate a deep awareness of our embodied existence and our connections with the universe. Buddhism prescribes meditation in order to help us to hone our attention to the present moment so that we can become deeply aware of ourselves and our suffering. We learn to focus on our breath, and to register the multifarious and minute movements inside our bodies, and learn to treat ourselves with compassion. Our awareness of our own fragile and bodily existence allows us to appreciate the fragile experience of other sentient beings and the rest of creation.

Like Buddhism, Continuum also prescribes various spiritual exercises to enable us to become more fully aware of ourselves and of our ties with the rest of the world. However, unlike Buddhist meditation, which is based on general methods, structures, and forms for all practitioners, Continuum encourages individual practitioners to try, dissolve, and recreate different forms in light of each body's unique biomorphic call for healing. Therefore, whereas Buddhist meditation may be experienced as a set of practices imposed from without, Continuum enables practitioners to organically tailor their practices in light of their specific, individual needs. Amidst some such differences, Buddhism and Continuum can be construed as broadly similar, even complimentary, approaches that aim to enable us to become deeply aware of ourselves and of our ties with others.

A Drop of Healing into an Ocean of Being

Buddhism and Continuum mutually enrich my practice as a teacher, therapist, and healer. In my own work, I draw on the analogous insights shared by Buddhism and Continuum, and I try to demonstrate how these insights can be translated into various exercises and techniques that cultivate bodily awareness, self-transcendence, and connection with and care for others.

In the mid–1990s, I taught a MBSR (Mindfulness-Based Stress Reduction) class at a hospital in Santa Rosa, California. While not exactly a class on Buddhism per se, MBSR is based on Buddhist concepts and practices of mindfulness meditation. One of the students in my class had been in an accident that damaged her spinal cord, leaving her completely paralyzed from her first cervical vertebrae down through her body. She was unable to move or speak. Her caregiver wheeled her into the classroom on a gurney with an IV tube for fluids in her arm.

My class had twenty-four able-bodied students in addition to this woman, and although her suffering seemed most apparent, we all shared the same enormous desire to be free from suffering, whatever form it was taking. We were in it together, facing down our demons using millennia-old techniques from Buddhism combined with the innovations of Continuum.

I encouraged this patient to make a repetitive circular motion with her eyes, first one direction then the other. Her face was virtually frozen in place, restricting any movements other than her eyes and mouth. She was unable to communicate any emotion non-verbally, and her speech was barely a mumble. As she became more comfortable with moving her eyes in circles as well as moving them up and down, I encouraged her to extend her capacity to communicate by rhythmically humming, causing vibrations through her head and creating dimensionality and depth in her capacity to feel sensation. I then instructed her to blow air through her closed lips as means to create a larger oscillation of movement in the frozen facial area, essentially flapping her lips. While quite contained, such movements and sounding vibrations are consistent with the spiritual practices espoused by Continuum.

Within forty-five fine minutes of practicing these micro eye movement exercises and the micro/macro sound-movement exercises, her face began to soften and her skin developed a flush from the influx of blood to the newly awakened areas. As well, supported by the resonant field of a classroom of students, she began sensing her own vibrations, vibrations which she could modulate and control at will; two things which had been absent from her somatic life since her accident. She had liberated herself from the prison of sensations being "done to her" by the medical system and transformed into the co-creator of her experience, as limited and circumscribed as it was.

She continued to attend the eight-week course on MBSR and gradually became adept at making a variety of micro-movements, which in turn enabled her to break out of her physical, psychological, and emotional isolation, and to cultivate a deeper awareness of herself, her body, and her spiritual bonds with others. In this, and countless other classes and sessions, I have seen a gentle interweaving of Buddhism and Continuum create fruitful inquiries into the fluid resonance of the human body, mind, and spirit with this universe in which we live.

Permissive Movement as a Dharma Door

BRIAN KIMMEL

From Yoga to Buddhism: Finding a Path

Twenty years ago, at age sixteen, I began a quest to find meaning in movement and meditation as an integrated path. I had passed my first quarter of six in hatha yoga at Everett Community College in Washington State. I was receiving college credit there as a high school student in place of Physical Education (PE). I mark my insistence on taking yoga instead of PE as the beginning of my spiritual path. I knew deep down that the health of the body depended upon more than physical exercises, but on all aspects of a person's life. I learned, through the mentoring of my first yoga teacher, Marsha Valentine, about the "Five Principles" including: proper diet, relaxation, breathing, concentration practices, and physical exercises.[1] The aspect that I loved most in yoga and was easily drawn toward was meditation. Marsha noticed this inclination and introduced me to the teachings of Thich Nhat Hanh. It was then that my interest in Buddhism grew.

Thay, which means teacher, and is how Thich Nhat Hanh is known by his students, epitomized mindfulness in everyday life. His life, a model of engagement and integrated practice, includes but is not limited to sitting meditation. Thay's teaching centers around the "oneness of body and mind" and the use of the breath as a "harmonizer" of body and mind.[2]

In 2009, in my early thirties, I began studying dance and psychology at Naropa University. I brought with me to Naropa a wellspring of practice in Thay's integrative mindfulness framework. At Naropa, I was introduced to Contemplative Dance Practice (CDP), a form derived from many streams of somatics including Authentic Movement, avant-garde performance including influences from Judson Theater, Merce Cunningham, and John Cage, and meditation from Chögyam Trungpa Rimpoche. These various streams were woven together by CDP founder, Barbara Dilley.[3]

CDP is a very intricate form of Dharma Practice and Deep Play. It combines sitting, and sometimes walking meditation, with two improvisatory sessions: "Personal Awareness Practice," undertaken solo, and "Open Space," where virtually anything goes. Each session of CDP ends with a short sit and an informal discussion.

After three years of studying and practicing this form with Dilley and esteemed teachers who learned CDP from her, I began to modify and adapt the practice for my

Brian Kimmel in Stina Hoberecht's Awake in the Dark, Naropa University, January 2014. Photograph by Dave Andrews.

own use as a meditation teacher and movement educator and facilitator. CDP in its prime form is practiced in about two-in-a-half hours. What I was really looking for was the elements of CDP, but in a condensed format that could be added on to other formal or informal practices.

When I first came to CDP I was obsessed with being "good." My body learned through the ages that being good meant being quiet and still. What that looked like in my body was an extremely rigid spine while in a seated meditation posture and in every-day life. This rigid spine routinely immobilized me, and caused lower back pain and tension in my neck and shoulders to the point of injury, which in my current view was a form of self-harm. In its pursuit of being "good" my body forgot how to breathe. That's when I gradually learned, through the form of CDP, how to live in my body again, how to move as my body moved, and in other movement forms, how to be with myself more fully, more authentically, and to be gentle, loving, and kind to myself. All of this is what led me to design a form more applicable to everyday life and formal meditation settings. I call this adapted form, Permissive Movement.

Permissive Movement: Solo and Group Forms

Permissive Movement, I propose, is an easy way to incorporate movement and dance into any kind of Dharma practice. Permissive Movement is done both solo and in groups. It can be incorporated within regular sitting and walking periods or periods of chanting. The format I follow most often is sitting, walking, short sitting, Permissive Movement, and chanting, in that order. The time frame is up to you or whoever is facilitating. It depends mostly upon how much time there is allotted for movement if done as a part of a meditation group or other formal practice group. I find twenty minutes to be a good enough amount of time in more formal meditation settings. I also use a shortened version alternating sessions of Permissive Movement and sitting practice as a solo practice. Permissive Movement with the addition of sitting practice of any length could be an entire practice period. This is to say that Permissive Movement is a Dharma practice itself that can include a sitting period or just sitting as a form of Permissive Movement.

The following is an example of what might happen in a solo Permissive Movement session:

After sitting and walking meditation, I clear a space before my cushion for me to move. I bow to the space to acknowledge the sacredness of this moment, and to honor the practice I am about to begin. I see myself in the space standing. I see a particular posture of standing in a particular spot before me. Gently, I move to that place. I find the posture. I stand in just the right angle that feels right in my body. I saw myself with closed eyes, and so I close my eyes. I am not sure what happens from this place or this posture. I only saw myself standing still. And so I stand still. I stand just to stand. I stand and notice what it is like to stand. I encourage the breath in my body. I witness the breathing. I feel and I notice what it is like to stand and breathe.

After a few moments, my body begins to twist slightly to the right and left. I have twisted right and left in a similar way before. At first, I enjoy doing something familiar, but then I take a risk. I let go and allow my body to be moved—familiar or unfamiliar does not matter now. I want to be present for what happens now. I want to be present now. And so I follow the impulse, a sense in my body to continue. I experience the delight directly, as my body twists slightly. Then my right arm raises. I feel it raise. I notice what it is like for my arm to raise. I breathe with my arm raising. I follow the impulse, the sense in my body to continue. I raise my arm as far as it wants to raise and then lower my arm to the side of my body.

That's Permissive Movement. Just notice. Just allow being moved and being still. Nothing fancy or out-of-the-ordinary. You may want to notice when things seem like they stay the same. Notice when things seem to change.

In solo Permissive Movement practice you can do whatever you want. There is no one else in the room with you to dictate how long or short, how loud or quiet you are. You can just be. What is beneficial in groups, however, is the possibility of being witnessed, of seeing and being seen. I agree with Authentic Movement expert, Zoe Avstreih, who said, "To see and be seen is the intimacy of true presence which invites healing." In this way, both being witnessed and witnessing is an act of mindfulness.[4]

Witnessing as an act of mindfulness encourages a nonjudgmental attitude. This happens as nonjudgment of others and oneself. Seeing things as they are without judgment or pretext is a form of insight consistent with the aims of Buddhist practice, a form of waking up from the dream of delusion that radically shifts one into a new way of moving and being in the world. Witnessing and being witnessed can, in this way, influence the practice of Permissive Movement and affect impulses to move, thoughts, and perceptions of oneself and others.

Permissive Movement in groups adds to the transformative potential of movement in contemplative contexts. We are born as social creatures with social and cultural ways of moving, thinking, speaking, acting—and all the dos and don'ts. When we begin to move in mindfulness with others, we may begin to see and to feel how we have been moved as social and cultural beings. If parts of these social and cultural movements are not authentic, in Permissive Movement we can change, we can begin to move in a new way as individuals and as part of a group. That, to me, is liberation.

The following is an example of what a group Permissive Movement session might be like as recalled by a mover in the space:

> I am mover in the space. The facilitator guides a few movements we do as a group, like rais-ing the arms while breathing in and lowering the arms while breathing out. Raising the shoul-ders toward the ears on an inhalation, lowering the shoulders to neutral on an exhalation. Right after the facilitator mentions bringing the shoulders to neutral, the facilitator invites us to move as we wish to move. Maybe to begin with the shoulders, or not. I am drawn to close my eyes, so I close my eyes. The facilitator invites us to give ourselves permission to listen to our bodies, offering ourselves our undivided attention. I feel drawn to tears. I think to myself: "No one has ever allowed me to be myself. I am always told what to do. I depend upon it. Sometimes I feel like crying, but others tell me not to. That's okay, but right now with my eyes closed, I feel a sense of sadness in my chest." My attention is brought to the center of my chest. I move my left hand to my chest based upon an impulse inside of me. I feel the warmth of my hand and the coolness of my chest. I feel my sternum press outward against my palm on the inhalation and recede on the exhalation. My chest begins to warm. I feel my spine breathing and moving upon each exhalation and inhalation. I extenuate the movements of my spine. The sense of sadness in me turns to appreciation. The facilitator asks if there are any movements or gestures or postures we have yet to explore but would like to explore.
>
> "Now is the moment," the facilitator says. "This is it." I open my eyes and look around the room. I want to see the other people in the space move. The facilitator then says, "Perhaps you see a movement you want to try on for yourself, and you begin to try on that movement. Pick up influence from others and put influence down."

That's what Permissive Movement might look like in groups. What might follow is the facilitator guiding towards playing, moving responsibly with others if called or continuing in personal practice. The only restriction in Permissive Movement is: Do No Harm. This means to not harm ourselves, others, or the space.

Differences and Similarities of Permissive Movement to Other Movement Forms

In the description of solo Permissive Movement, the mover found delight in movement. This comes from CDP, to discover and follow "kinesthetic delight," or joy in the body. Following impulse, however, comes more from Authentic Movement. In Permissive Movement, impulse can come from anywhere in the body, but stems from a feeling, a sensation, or an intuition in the mover. As in the Four Foundations of Mindfulness taught by the Buddha, mindfulness of the body, even the body while moving, helps to bring and keep the practitioner close to themselves and intimate with their direct experience.

CDP and Authentic Movement bring the mover to very different points than Permissive Movement. CDP depends more on a form. In Permissive Movement, the form is not so crucial, but the development of the mover's sense of themselves and their relationship to others is. Authentic Movement comes from Depth Psychology and is usually practiced with one person as a witness, which helps develop a therapeutically relevant attachment bond to help the mover explore and integrate subconscious material through improvisatory exploration and active imagination.

The body in movement and stillness is very ordinary. What is perhaps unusual about movement and stillness as it is practiced in Permissive Movement is that it is done within a contemplative context, and in this is an explicit intention to follow impulse, to move or to be still as called from within. What begins to move is not a preconceived or vetted movement, but an authentic sense of moving as the body moves, a sense of being real, a sense of wholeness and "oneness of body and mind."[5] Following impulse in this way with mindfulness, concentration, and insight is a Dharma door, a Dharma practice. It leads to fuller awareness of one's experience, and a direct experience unencumbered by habitual thoughts, speech, and action. Whenever the body breaks out of its habitual patterns of doing, thinking, and acting, a new neural circuitry, or pathway of change, is created. That is the basis of Dharma, promoting a discovery of the elements of liberation in oneself, and going on that journey to benefit oneself and in the service of others.

Finding Permissive Movement as a Dharma Door

I am compelled to find new disciplines, as in practices and forms like Permissive Movement, as Dharma doors that help elicit authenticity. This motivation is aligned with feminist Dharma theories. Boucher wrote: "At a woman-led retreat you may find yourself dancing in a circle, reaching to the sky, touching the ground … many Buddhist institutions have become more sensitive to women's particular needs."[6] I argue that this is true not just with the needs of women but people of all genders and sexual orientations, including a newer gender-ation of gender non-conformists, lesbians, gays, bisexuals, and transgender people, and people of numerous ethnic, social, and cultural makeups.

American Buddhism and 21st-century Dharma are adapting to our current world and its current social climates. Maybe one day Buddhist monastic orders will openly and unapologetically ordain transgender and gender-queer monastics, not to mention fully ordaining female monastics, as is the effort now in some sects. Our current world demands new kinds of Dharma, new Dharma doors. I believe movement to be one of those doors.

Ways That Movement Is a Dharma Door

In Somatic, or body-oriented psychology, I am particularly invested in the understanding that "movement is life."[7] In fact, the body is always moving when it is alive. For some scholars and clinicians: "movement is the *modus operandi* of all life."[8] One might see the very breath as a form of movement with the expansion and deflation of the lungs. No matter how subtle the breath becomes in meditation the autonomic function of the breathing mechanism propels movement, the pumping of the lungs as an organ, the contraction and expansion of the abdominal diaphragm and the ribs, and all the tiny muscles that move or engage for us to breathe. Another necessary movement is our beating heart. The surge of blood through the veins, and the various valves that open and close throughout the body providing life—sustaining oxygen and blood throughout the body and allowing the exiting of wastes and dead cellular material. All of this happens without the conscious effort of the meditation practitioner as you sit. Without even being aware of this, the body is taking care of itself. The body is moving to sustain itself and you. Awareness of this process engages the mind in the physical body, essentially bringing mind back to the body. That's the meditation the Buddha proposed in his Sutra on the Full Awareness of Breathing (*Anapanasati*), and the Four Foundations of Mindfulness (*Satipatthana*). The awareness of the body in its organic movement internally and externally helps to establish intimacy with oneself. Concentration and insight develop through this natural inquiry into the process, the organic, life-sustaining movements of the body. That's the effect and indication of mindfulness in the body, and is one practical use of Permissive Movement.

Additionally, awareness of movement and following impulses to move, like rolling the neck and shoulders in sitting meditation every once and a while or between sits, can help move stagnant energy. Because the mind is one with the body, when the body moves so does the mind. So if the mind is stuck, move the body. If emotions are stuck and one cannot experience the joy indicated by the Buddha in the Sutra on the Full Awareness of Breathing, move the body.

Thay has often taught not to discriminate between body and mind. One should smile just to smile, and if one does not feel joy, not to wait for joy to smile. Smile first, and joy will come. The smiling is the joy. Similarly, Thay describes joy or peace in the body while meditating as a form of liberation. When the body is not at peace, move in a way that brings peace. Sit in a way that brings peace.

Finally, in stark contrast to the body's perpetual movement, practitioners often believe that sitting practice is the only practice Buddha recommended. However, the Buddha, in the Four Foundations of Mindfulness, mentioned four postures (sitting, standing, walking, and lying down) and many variations.[9] He also mentioned the practice of joy and breathing into the body. All of these indicate modern-day Dharma practices that allow for the discovery of mindfulness within all variations of sitting, walking, standing, and lying down. Permissive Movement and other movement forms within Dharma lineages offer methods to bring mindfulness to the body in all its various postures and movements. Dance and creative movement through space can become Dharma doors, practiced for the purpose of peace, enjoyment, and liberation. This is the work I learned in CDP, and what I have brought to Permissive Movement.

Conclusion

What I discovered in my own personal journey with Permissive Movement, as a facilitator and in solo and group practice, is a profound shift in my ability to confront myself without judgment. Permissive Movement has made my journey in the Dharma more intimate. Bearing Permissive Movement in mind, I now enter sitting meditation with more gentleness. I listen inside of myself for a posture that will support my well being. As I begin to sit on my meditation cushion, I breathe deeply. I listen for the posture to come organically from within. I am not looking at a photograph in my head, trying to make myself look like the Buddha in the picture. I am looking deeply into myself as a Buddha, listening for what the Buddha in me has to say. That Buddha is my internal witness, my internal guide, my mindfulness showing me the way.

I have taken pride in the many people who have come up to me after I have led group Permissive Movement during meditation retreats. They have talked to me about the transformation they felt and experienced in "moving as they felt called to move," and how different and refreshing it is to be prompted in giving themselves permission to move just as they move. Then, when they returned to the cushion, they brought that permission with them—the permission to listen deeply to oneself, the permission to be oneself, that's Permissive Movement.

I didn't anticipate when I started my journey many years ago with yoga and Buddhism that I would create a form of practice, and that it would be oriented around movement. It gives me strength and courage to know I can make a difference in people's lives through offering opportunities to move. Everyone moves. I hope to bring Permissive Movement to people who have forgotten that they can and do move, and that movement itself, if done with awareness and precision, can bring happiness and peace. I hope you will join me.

NOTES

1. Sivanda Yoga Center and Vishnu Devananda, *The Sivananda Companion to Yoga: A Complete Guide to the Physical Postures, Breathing Exercises, Diet, Relaxation and Meditation Techniques of Yoga* (New York: Simon & Schuster, 1984), 20–21.

2. Thich Nhat Hahn, *Transformation & Healing: Sutra on the Four Establishments of Mindfulness* (Berkeley: Parallax Press, 1990), 42–43.

3. Melinda Buckwalter, *Composing While Dancing: An Improviser's Companion* (Madison: University of Wisconsin Press, 2010), 55–56.

4. Zoe Avstreih, "Achieving Body Permanence: Authentic Movement and the Paradox of Healing," in *Authentic Movement: Moving the Body, Moving the Self, Being Moved*, ed. Patrizia Pallaro (London: Jessica Kingsley Publishers, 2007), 270–273.

5. Nhat Hahn, *Transformation & Healing*, 42–43.

6. Sandy Boucher, *Opening the Lotus: A Woman's Guide to Buddhism* (Boston: Beacon Press, 1997), 50.

7. Patricia Pallaro, *Authentic Movement: Essays by Mary Starks Whitehouse, Janet Adler and Joan Chodorow* (London: Jessica Kingsley Publishers, 1999), 11.

8. Christine Caldwell, *Getting in Touch: The Guide to New Body-Centered Therapies* (Wheaton: Theosophical Publishing House, 1997), 101–110.

9. Bhikkhu Bodhi, trans., *The Middle Length Discourses of the Buddha: A New Translation of the Majjhima Nikaya* (Boston: Wisdom Publications, 1995), 146, 1191.

Fostering Equanimity and Mindfulness through Dance/Movement Therapy and Authentic Movement

Joan Wittig

Dancing is not getting up painlessly like a speck of dust blown around in the wind. Dancing is when you rise above both worlds, tearing your heart to pieces, and giving up your soul.—Rumi[1]

What then did these people do in order to achieve the progress that freed them? As far as I could see they did nothing but let things happen.—Carl Jung[2]

I spent hours of my childhood dancing in the living room with my sisters. I was a child of the 60s, so our dance was not so much made up of steps, but rather, we improvised. Self-expression was everything. I don't know why, but dancing is perhaps the only area of my life where I have never experienced any self-consciousness. I have never cared how I look. I only care about the joy that is mine when I dance.

When I went off to college, I majored in biology, thinking to be a researcher. It didn't take long to see that this wasn't a good plan for me. My one shining moment every week was my dance improvisation class. I woke up happy every Wednesday morning, anticipating this class. I stayed happy all day, and sometimes all the next day. As a result, I changed my major to dance, with an emphasis on dance therapy. I didn't really know much about dance therapy then, but I figured that if one improvisation class could have such an impact on my emotional life, there must be something to this profession of dance therapy.

I am a board certified dance/movement therapist. I use movement and body-focused work as my primary way of practicing therapy. I don't privilege words; rather, I invite my clients to rely on the wisdom and memory stored in their bodies, and to let this guide their access to emotions. My work has been informed by my increasing understanding of the need for mindfulness as a constant in the work. Some approaches to therapy work by delving deeply into the past. Though this is valuable work, the work that I do requires attending to what is happening now, in this moment. Mindfulness in Dance/Movement

Therapy means noticing what is happening right now, in one's thoughts, feelings, and bodily sensations. Only by attending to what is happening now can we make sense of what has gone before, and how this is meaningful in our lives today.

I am drawn to Buddhayana Buddhist practice, an inclusive approach to Buddhism that draws on wisdom from all Buddhist traditions. Buddhist practice, most specifically *vipassana* meditation, has taught me about compassion. Jack Kornfield, co-founder of the Insight Meditation tradition, tells us that in meditation we face our own greed, unworthiness, rage, paranoia, and grandiosity, and the opening of wisdom and fearlessness beyond these forces.[3] I remember so well my early days of meditation, what a relief it was when I didn't have to do anything except sit, and breathe. This experience has filled me with a sense of compassion for myself, and I see how ridiculously hard I work most of the time. I am so busy in my thoughts that I miss out on opportunities to be kind to myself, and to others. Realizing this allows me to extend my compassion out into the world, toward all sentient beings. This allows me to feel love for each of my clients as fellow humans, even when it is challenging to love them.

Interweaving Fields: Movement, Therapy and Dharma

Dance/Movement Therapy is a form of psychotherapy, different from traditional psychotherapy in that its focus is on nonverbal, primarily physical, forms of expression, rather than on the use of words. The American Dance Therapy Association defines dance therapy as "the psychotherapeutic use of movement as a process which furthers the emotional, physical, and cognitive integration of the individual."[4] In each session, dance/movement therapists look for a balance of talking and moving that allows our clients to "experience, clarify, and eventually integrate feeling, thinking, and moving."[5]

Authentic Movement, sometimes used in Dance/Movement Therapy, is a simple practice in which a mover waits in stillness for an impulse to emerge from the unconscious, and follows the impulse into movement. A mover participates by being willing to make space for whatever emerges, and to enter deeply into the movement, the experience and expression, without judgment. The mover moves in the presence of a witness, and when Authentic Movement is used in Dance/Movement Therapy, the witness is the therapist.

Dance/Movement Therapy and Authentic Movement often incorporate the Buddhist concept of equanimity, wherein desire and aversion are tempered, and the pleasant and unpleasant are neither pulled toward nor pushed away. Understanding comes through just being with, and leads the mover toward a non-judging awareness, without attachment to outcome, that allows patience, compassion, and acceptance. In Buddhist practice, equanimity is neither a thought nor an emotion. It is the steady conscious realization of reality's transience. *Vipassana* meditation is a practice of mindful meditation, a way of self-transformation through self-observation, a way to cultivate equanimity. As we sit, we pay attention to all our sensations rising and passing away. We allow whatever arises to be received in a spirit of friendliness and kind affection; and we allow it to pass away. We develop a quality of loving kindness, which facilitates an integrated life. Kornfield speaks of the opening of the body and mind as "the beginning of what the Elders described as the Insight Meditation path of dissolution."[6] Tibetan Buddhist teacher Chögyam Trungpa, in teaching the necessity of taming the neurotic mind, reminds us that in sitting practice, we experience the mind, the body, and the breath working together.[7]

Improvisation as Therapy

What really drew me to dance therapy was the improvisational aspect of it. Though not all improvisation is therapy, all good therapy is improvisational in nature. Dance/Movement Therapy sessions vary in form from therapist to therapist, but all dance therapy sessions use improvisation to find expression in movement. The act of improvising requires a presence that brings with it a sense of being alive, with no particular expectations, no regrets, no sense of loss. There is only this moment. This presence brings a sense of peace, a sense that all is as it should be. This presence invites patience, compassion, and acceptance—those same qualities that one learns through meditation. With even a small amount of meditation experience, most practitioners are humbled by their inability to fully control their minds. As such, flexibility and allowance toward experience are essential allies on the cushion, allies also crucial to cultivating the open presence of improvisation.

Musician Stephen Nachmanovitch believes it is possible to become what you are doing. Buddhists call this state of selfless, absolute concentration *samadhi*. Both meditation and dance are ways to achieve this selfless state. Nachmanovitch posits that in improvisation "memory and intention (which postulate past and future) and intuition (which indicates the eternal present) are fused.... The work of the improviser is to stretch out momentary flashes (of creative inspiration) until they merge into the activity of daily life. We then begin to experience creativity and the free play of improvisation as one with our ordinary mind and our ordinary activity."[8] This is the goal of therapy—to be free.

Meditation assists us in becoming free. Sakyong Mipham, Trungpa's son and current head of the Shambhala Buddhist lineage, reminds us that gathering the mind is a gradual process. We begin, following our breath, acknowledging thoughts as they arise, and then releasing the thoughts. In so doing, we realize that the mind's movement isn't "me." Releasing the thought and returning to the breath gives a sense of space and relief.[9] This helps develop the ability to hold the place of a non-judging witness, supporting compassion for oneself and for others.

In dance therapy, we begin with the body, with movement—the mover bends at the waist, and her head drops toward the floor. Next there is sensation—the mover notices that her head feels heavy, as though she cannot support its weight. Then there is emotion—as her head drops toward the floor, the mover notices she is filled with a deep sadness. She longs for someone to be here with her, to help her support her heavy head. She has an experience in her body, and it leads her to expression of her feelings. She remembers when no one was there to help her. Her memory, long stored in her body, emerges through this movement. The memory frees the emotion, also long stored in her body. As she moves, the memory and the emotion are dislodged, set free into the world; and now there is space in her for something new, where before there was no space. This memory and this experience are neither good nor bad, they just are. It is the stuck-ness of both that causes suffering, the unwillingness or inability to set these old happenings free, the clinging, either consciously or unconsciously.

Just as all good therapy is improvisational in nature, all good therapy relieves suffering. The relief comes through allowing the memory and emotion to come into the present moment, to be felt, and to be released; and through realizing that this experience was in the past, and is not happening now. This is similar to meditation, where we notice a thought, and set it free, focusing once again on the breath, and on what is happening right in this moment as we breathe in, and breathe out. That said, we work with attention to finding a middle way—that is, not always seeking the fastest possible way to relieve suffering, but rather coming to understand one's suffering as a natural and useful part of life.

The process of therapy is not always joyful, but being present in the moment ultimately brings a sense of joy and possibility. Sharon Salzberg, another co-founder of Insight Meditation, writes that the state of love-filled delight in possibilities and eager joy at the prospect of actualizing them is known in Buddhism as bright faith. She explains, "With bright faith we act on our potential to transform our suffering and live in a different way."[10] I have seen this come to life when giving my second year graduate students the task of improvising around what inhibits them at their internships, where they are practicing to be dance therapists. To assist in knowing this, I invite them to improvise around a memory of a time when either they were inhibited, or they were free from inhibition, any time in their past. N., who has suffered much loss in the past two years, chooses to remember a time when she felt uninhibited, and she explores this in movement. When she is finished, she tells of feeling joyful, and of wondering what allows her to be joyful. She thinks for a moment, and tells us it is being present in the moment that allows her to feel her joy—in her memory of being uninhibited, and right now.

The Conscious Collective

One of the most powerful aspects of dance therapy is the experience of being a member of a group. In Buddhism, we would think of this as the Sangha, one of the "Three Jewels."[11] The Three Jewels refer to the Buddha, the Dharma (the teachings of Buddha), and the Sangha. In the traditional sense, Sangha refers to the community of ordained monks and nuns, or to the community of "noble ones" who have attained at least the first stage of awakening. In the west, sangha is used as a collective term for all Buddhists, for the community of Buddhist practitioners.[12]

Many of the people I have worked with over the years have not had any good experiences as members of a community or group, including their primary groups—their families. In dance therapy groups, members mirror each other, joining each other in movement, and reflecting back to each other. This allows each member of the group to know that they are seen, and accepted, as the other members join their movement. This can be a profound experience, to know that there is a place for one in the group, and that one belongs here.

Some years ago, I was working in an inpatient psychiatric hospital with a group of three patients, two of whom were suffering from severe depression, and one who had been diagnosed as schizophrenic. We were moving with the image of stepping over obstacles. We jumped over a puddle of water; then one mover pretended to take off his coat and spread it over the puddle so the rest of us could safely cross over. We encountered another obstacle, a big hole. To solve this problem, we decided to fill the hole with sand

Advanced Dance/Movement Therapy course given by author for Inspirees Institute for Creative Arts Therapy, Beijing, China, May 2014. Uliana Dzyuba and Xijing Chen mirror each other in movement. Photograph courtesy Inspirees Institute.

and rocks. Once more an obstacle presented itself, a huge boulder. Together we lifted the boulder and moved it out of the way. As each obstacle came up, the group worked together to transcend it. For each of these patients in a psychiatric ward, this was a deep and unfamiliar experience, one of being helped and supported while also offering help and support.

Another profound aspect of dance therapy, and in particular Authentic Movement, is the experience of being seen by a non-judging witness. Janet Adler, dance/movement therapist and teacher of Authentic Movement, teaches, "The witness's relationship to suffering, her capacity to bring a compassionate enough presence … marks the boundaries of the mover's work in a mysterious way…. A compassionate witness accepts what is, remains nonattached, and expects nothing."[13]

I remember being in the studio with a young woman, engaging in Authentic Movement. Her plane was flying over New York just as the World Trade Center was attacked. She was relocating to New York that day. I see her bend over, mouth open. As her witness, I have an image of letters and words falling from her mouth. When we speak, she tells me this is exactly her image. She feels seen by me, as she struggles to find her words, her voice in the world. On another occasion, I am teaching dance therapy in China, in Beijing. The group is lying on the floor, close together. Each person begins to chant her name, very softly. I invite them to increase the volume little by little, until each person is chanting her name loudly and energetically. Along the way I invite each person to add movement as she is so inspired. The group members relate feeling touched by this exercise, as they describe what it was like to hear their names in relation to the others. They have felt a sense of belonging to the group, in a way they have not experienced before. On still another occasion, I am working individually with a woman who suffers from anxiety. I join her in movement. She leads, and I follow. I lead, and she follows. We move together, and she tells me that this has brought up old memories of nobody wanting to play with her. She feels the sadness; but she also has a new experience, one of finding someone who wants to play with her.

Dance Therapy and Buddhism—An End to Suffering?

What is the origin of suffering? The Second Noble Truth tells us that suffering comes from ignorance, which leads to craving and clinging. Psychoanalytic and psychodynamic theories have much to say about the origins of suffering, mostly agreeing it comes from early childhood events or losses. Suffering is a great motivator, for entering therapy and for learning to meditate. What is it that finally allows a surrendering, a willingness to seek relief? Humanistic psychologist Marilyn Ferguson suggests that maybe it is anything that shakes up one's old understanding of the world.[14] The urge toward greater freedom, toward a fuller life, is natural.

It is true that every life will hold many present "here and now" moments of suffering. But how many more moments do we spend, remembering and reliving the suffering; or fearing we will suffer again and trying to figure out how to prevent it, thereby missing the present moments in which we are not actually suffering? Both Dance/Movement Therapy and meditation can lead to a decrease of suffering. They can teach us to let go of the past, to let go of the suffering that is already over, and move into the present moment, which is so often free from suffering.

Dancing, living in our bodies, moving, all can be sources of joy. Think of walking down the street with a child, who runs up the street and back, runs circles around you, zig-zagging from curb to stoop to curb, all for the pure pleasure of moving; and all this while you just walk. Likewise, meditation can be a source of "peaceful abiding,"[15] of stability, clarity, and strength. It can lead us to know our natural peace.

Dance/Movement Therapy and Authentic Movement invite an integration of feeling, thinking, and moving. They invite the mover to make space for whatever emerges, without judgment. In a similar fashion, meditation invites the meditator to observe the arising and passing away of thoughts and sensations, and to do so without judgment and with compassion. Therapy involves an improvisational process, a process that requires a presence that brings with it a sense of being alive, with no particular expectations. Both Dance/Movement Therapy and Buddhist practice offer a sense of belonging to a larger community, a way out of the isolation that so often contributes to suffering. Both invite a process not of fleeing suffering, but of recognizing it and coming to accept it through an embodied experience. This acceptance leads to freedom. May all sentient beings be free.

NOTES

1. Jallaludin Rumi, *The Matbnavi*, in Stephen Nachmanovitch, *Free Play: Improvisation in Life and Art* (New York: Jeremy P. Tarcher/Putnam, 1990), 53.
2. C.G. Jung, in Nachmanovitch, 158.

3. Jack Kornfield, *A Path with Heart: A Guide Through the Perils and Promises of Spiritual Life* (New York: Bantam Books, 1993), 7.

4. American Dance Therapy Association, "Fact Sheet" (Baltimore: ADTA National Office, 1966).

5. Joan Naess-Lewin, *Dance Therapy Notebook.* (Washington, D.C.: American Dance Therapy Association, 1998), 9.

6. Kornfield, 19–20.

7. Chogyam Trungpa, *The Path of Individual Liberation* (Boston: Shambhala Publications, 2013), 133.

8. Nachmanovich, 17 – 19.

9. Sakyong Mipham, *Turning the Mind into an Ally* (New York: Riverhead Books, 2003), 59–63.

10. Sharon Salzberg, "Suffering and Its Partial Cure," in *Adventures with the Buddha: A Buddhism Reader,* ed. Jeffery Paine (New York: W.W. Norton, 2005), 355.

11. Jan Willis, "An African-American Woman's Journey into Buddhism," in *Adventures with the Buddha,* 280.

12. Richard H. Robinson, Willard L. Johnson, and Thanissaro Bhikkhu, *Buddhist Religions: A Historical Introduction* (Belmont: Wadsworth/Thompson, 2005), 327.

13. Janet Adler, *Offering from the Conscious Body* (Rochester: Inner Traditions, 2002), 79.

14. Marilyn Ferguson, as quoted in Rick Fields, Peggy Taylor, Rex Weyler, and Rick Ingrasci's *Chop Wood Carry Water: A Guide to Finding Spiritual Fulfillment in Everyday Life* (Los Angeles: Jeremy P. Tarcher, 1984), 1.

15. Mipham, 5.

"Hell Is the Land of Tranquil Light"[1]

Dance/Movement Therapy in a Single Moment of Life

CRISTINA LIVINGSTONE

Prologue

I am standing alone in the group room of an acute inpatient psychiatric unit in an impoverished city hospital, moments before gathering patients for my Dance/Movement Therapy (DMT) group, reflecting on how I came to find myself in this particular position. My thoughts veer towards the way in which dance and Buddhism have been entwined for most of my life. While in the dressing room after taking a ballet class when I was 15 years old, I overheard a dancer I admired talking to someone else about Nichiren Buddhism and the Soka Gakkai International (SGI), which means Value Creating Society in Japanese. Nichiren Daishonin (1222–1282) was a Japanese Buddhist reformer who, after studying the Buddhist Sutras for decades and being ordained as a monk, established his teaching based on the Lotus Sutra. The SGI is the lay Buddhist organization of practitioners of Nichiren Buddhism, currently under the leadership of Daisaku Ikeda. Since 1960, when Daisaku Ikeda became president of the organization, its members spread Nichiren Buddhism from Japan to 192 countries and territories worldwide.[2] As a matter of fact, I was living in Argentina when I was introduced to the practice.

Her explanation paralleled one written more recently by Clark Strand:

Soka Gakkai members chant the mantra-like title of the Lotus Sutra, Nam-myoho-renge-kyo, as a way of harnessing the universal life force inherent in their own bodies and minds. According to the teachings of Nichiren Buddhism, that mantra activates the basic, positive creative energy of the universe—a force that animates all sentient beings, driving them to grow and express their true nature eternally, from one lifetime to the next. By chanting Nam-myoho-renge-kyo and working for the happiness of others, Nichiren Buddhists seek to improve their current life condition and demonstrate "actual proof" of the Buddhist principle that all things are interconnected—that an inner change in the life of one individual can trigger outer changes in their community, their environment, and ultimately the world at large.[3]

Deeply impressed by Nichiren's philosophy and the simple accessibility of the daily practice, I took faith on August 4, 1985, when I was 16 years old. As an SGI member, I was immediately encouraged to write down my goals and use my desires as fuel to pray so I could fulfill my *bodhisattva* vow to benefit all beings and contribute to world peace using my own specific talents. My first goal was to become a professional dancer. My second goal, which emerged spontaneously, was to become a psychotherapist. During the intervening decades, my Buddhist practice served as a sturdy ship from where I navigated the many ups and downs of my life, not the least of which included a 26-year professional dance career. And it was through a chance encounter with a former dancer and fellow SGI member that I was introduced to the field of Dance/Movement Therapy (DMT). This psychotherapeutic modality allowed me to utilize the knowledge I gained as a professional dancer within a psychodynamic context, thereby giving me the opportunity to fulfill the second goal I had set for myself when I joined the SGI so many years before. So in a way, I'm standing here now because of my Buddhist practice.

DMT is based on the premise of the interconnectedness of mind, body, and spirit; and is defined by the American Dance Therapy Association as "the therapeutic use of movement to further the emotional, cognitive, physical, and social integration of the individual."[4] Since entering the field, I have become aware of the ongoing discussion in the DMT community regarding what exactly constitutes "movement" or "dance" within the modality. Modern dance choreographer Erick Hawkins (1909–1994), my dance mentor, believed that "the kinesthetic sense, the sensing of movement, is the heart of dance."[5] He also asserted, "What we all have in common as human beings is the human body.… If we feel what goes on in our bodies, we also feel what goes on in the body of another human being we are close to."[6]

Cristina Livingstone with Erick Hawkins at his summer intensive workshop, circa the time she was accepted into his dance company, Hunter College, July 1993. Photograph by Joy McEwen.

Personally, I'm not interested in trying to differentiate between these terms while I'm running a DMT session because trying to do this ironically interferes with my ability to be fully embodied and present with my patients. Too much analysis pulls me into cognition and out of feeling, which is at the heart of dance and the human experience. I remember Hawkins telling me during a rehearsal to "deeply search for the miles of depth of feeling contained in each step." For me, the essence of what makes DMT a special therapeutic modality is contained in this statement. When a simple, everyday movement becomes imbued with feeling, it reveals its symbolic meaning and is transformed into a true dance of relationship and communication with self and others. It becomes the dance of our shared humanity, which cuts across the isolation that is the hallmark of so much mental illness and disease.

These are depressing times for all of us working in mental health. The economic collapse of our system has turned units like mine into pioneers of what I facetiously call "the five day cure for psychosis." Like countless others, I came into this milieu armed with beautiful psychodynamic theories designed to provide care and facilitate deep, meaningful change over a protracted period of time—months, if not years. But since 2012, I have been faced with the stark reality that I will rarely work with a patient more than once during their inpatient stay, and I have become accustomed to entering the unit daily and not knowing half the patients as we turnover up to three quarters of our census every week. I feel that I am navigating through uncharted territory, and I fear that none of us on the frontlines of acute psychiatry know what real treatment is anymore.

The exhaustion generated by trying to cope with the dizzying speed of intakes and discharges on my unit made me lose confidence in my ability to engage with patients in a value-creating way. Bitterness, jealousy, and despair flowed through my heart and out of my pores during many peer supervision sessions, as I listened to the other dance/movement therapists (dmts) speak about the relationships and interventions they developed for patients they were able to work with in other settings over a period of weeks. In contrast to them I felt like a joke, an expert at writing intake and discharge notes all day long, but not a clinician by a long shot. I was burnt out despite my regular therapy, supervision sessions, and self-care activities, so I sought guidance from one of my SGI leaders, who was also a psychologist and well acquainted with the pressures of modern day institutional work. First, my leader reminded me of the principle of *Essho Funi*, or the "oneness of life and its environment," which explains that "life and its environment, though seemingly two distinct phenomena, are essentially non-dual; they are two integral phases of a single reality" because "'life constitutes a subjective self that experiences the effects of its past actions, and 'its environment' is an objective realm in which individuals' karmic rewards find expression."[7] Based on this principle, he then challenged me to use my prayer to manifest the concept of "changing poison into medicine"[8] in order to transform my work environment.

After receiving this guidance, I began to chant Nam-myoho-renge-kyo concretely to find the best way to adapt the theories and methods I'd learned in graduate school to the manic pace of my unit. Through continuous personal prayer, coupled with ongoing engagement in SGI group activities, I realized that basing myself on the theory of the "mutual possession of the Ten Worlds," which is part of the principle of *Ichinen Sanzen*, or "3,000 realms in a single moment of life," was the key to restoring my confidence in my ability to provide a meaningful experience for my patients using the tools of DMT.

"The Ten Worlds are the ten states of life: hell, hunger, animality, anger, humanity, heaven, learning, realization, bodhisattva, and Buddhahood," that all sentient beings experience, and "the mutual possession of the Ten Worlds means that each of the Ten Worlds has all of the Ten Worlds inherent within it."[9] The Ten Worlds are not linear and hierarchical. They are constantly in flux and when one is salient, the other nine remain latent within the overt "world," or life condition. Nichiren explained to his followers that through chanting Nam-myoho renge-kyo and recognizing the true relationship between the Ten Worlds, one could find that "neither the pure land nor hell exists outside oneself; both lie only within one's own heart…. Awakened to this, one is called a Buddha; deluded about it, one is called an ordinary person…. Hell is itself the Land of Tranquil Light."[10]

Most of my patients are in hell due to their profound suffering, and many staff members, myself included, get plunged right along into that same world due to the constant exposure to vicarious trauma. Animality, hunger, and anger are the other predominant life conditions I notice among patients and staff. The theory of *Ichinen Sanzen* and the mutual possession of the Ten Worlds helps me fight against the sense of powerlessness induced by my institutional environment, because it reminds me that I am like a miner, using DMT to dig deep enough to discover the gem of Buddhahood that is hidden inside the world of hell.

The Session

I am now standing in a circle in the group room, surrounded by five male patients. I have no way of knowing what will happen, what feelings will be expressed in patients' bodies nor which interventions I'll make in order to create the most therapeutic holding environment possible, but this is what I see in the initial "single moment" of this group's life:

Pedro is a 22-year-old, monolingual Spanish-speaking Mexican man.[11] His arms look like withered branches, his hands clenched in fists. He can punch but he cannot reach out safely into the world. His eyes are dull and his face is contorted into a scary grimace. I feel his hostility directed at me, but I sense that it serves to hide his deep fear. Powerful loneliness enters my being. Pedro has spent most of his life in and out of mental institutions, and he was just released from prison after attempting to rape and murder his mother while in the throes of untreated paranoid schizophrenia. Pedro's body feels to me like it's fossilized inside the realm of hell.

Andres is a 30-year-old, monolingual Spanish-speaking Dominican man, and this is his first psychiatric hospitalization. Yesterday he emerged from a drug induced state of psychosis, which lasted for two weeks and landed him in prison, prior to being brought to our facility for psychiatric evaluation. He is smiling and looking at me with dreamy, childlike eyes, which seem to be saying, "I love you, mommy, and I'm going to marry you when I grow up." Ah, yes—the Oedipal complex is alive and well over here in acute psychiatry. Every male patient I have worked with has unresolved mother issues. Andres feels to me like he's in the world of heaven, elated just because he's "close to mommy."

Sam is a 40-year-old, English-speaking Caucasian man who appears closer to 60 years of age. He is unkempt and disheveled, with long dirty fingernails, and a mass of tangled hair that extends around his head like an electrified barbed wire fence. He has spent most of his life in psychiatric institutions and suffers from disorganized schizophrenia. First he tries to hide in a corner, but eventually he accepts my invitation to join our circle. Sam's feet feel disconnected from the floor, and I get this image of him as a helium balloon. Just as I think, "I'm losing him, he's floating away in a psychotic haze," Sam asks me, "Am I on planet Earth?" He isn't joking and I reassure him that, yes, he is on planet Earth with the rest of us. He gazes at me with wide-open, opaque eyes, and I can tell that visual hallucinations are clouding his field of vision. Sam closes his eyes, smiles enigmatically, and declares, "I have to shield myself from the power of the energy." He's paranoid, but nonetheless retains a light, gentle kindness which makes me feel like he's in the world of humanity (despite his not being fully convinced that he himself is human and living on Earth).

Vidal is not psychotic but suffers from depression. He is a 35-year-old, monolingual Spanish-speaking Puerto Rican man who moved to the city a few months ago, and he's the only patient I know "well" because he was recently re-admitted. He seems genuinely happy because he's being discharged today, and I can only hope that his second five-day-long hospitalization is more successful than his first. It's his first time in a DMT session and he is surprised that we aren't going to be dancing bachata. He appears curious, and I feel he's flowing between the realms of heaven and learning.

Ralph is a 55-year-old, English-speaking Caucasian man with a long history of violence, sexual predation, incarceration, drug abuse, and psychiatric hospitalizations. The treatment team and I suspect that he's mostly antisocial (formerly referred to as psychopathic/sociopathic) and not psychotic at all. He was admitted after assaulting staff at his shelter while high on K2. He licks his lips with a predatory tongue as he stares at me. I feel my back broaden and my stance widen as I reinforce the boundaries of my kinesphere in response to his sexual acting out. Ralph is embodying the most maladaptive aspects of the world of hunger, and he wants me to know that he sees me as an object at his disposal.

Ichinen Sanzen ceases to be a theoretical concept and becomes a live, full-bodied experience as the powerful waves of each patient's unmet needs crash into me. I feel a torrent of emotions, expectations, and desires projected onto me in this single moment of life: mother, lover, teacher, authority figure, a privileged and unattainable object/being that induces desire, fear, confusion. I feel my feet reach firmly into the ground and my spine lengthen. My embodied experience tells me that the dominant life condition of this group is shifting between hell and hunger. I take a deep breath, and then it's show-time.

I explain that I will be conducting the session in Spanish and English in order to bridge the language difference. Then I set a very structured agenda because we are all new to each other and there is already much sexual preoccupation/competition, which requires both safe expression and containment. I begin by delineating personal physical boundaries as a warm-up and, since I am still having trouble remembering everybody's names, I start with the "name game." In this sequence, patients take turns saying their name and doing a gesture, which is then repeated by the group and eventually becomes a choreography combining everybody's movements. The name game falls apart because the patients remember only my name and movement but forget each other's. They keep their distance from each other but try to get closer to me as they engage in an increasingly primal, competitive dance, with me as "the prize." Sam is the only exception. He has been unable thus far to engage with me or anyone else, and appears to have landed on another planet as he steps out of the circle and tries again to hide in a corner. I wonder if "the power of the energy" that he needed to "shield himself" from is the unbound testosterone that is flying around the room. This session is taking on the life condition of animality, and the questions for me become: "What can lead us to embody the more positive aspects of competition? Is it possible to facilitate some sort of group cohesion? Can this group even go there?"

I grab a Kush ball (a toy that fits in the palm of my hand and resembles a sea urchin made out of soft, short rubbery strands) and I toss it over to Pedro, who then passes it to Andres. The ball introduces an element of lightness, speed, and directness into the patients' movement repertoires, as well as surprise and laughter. Soon sports images emerge and the patients organically divide into two teams: the Latin American, Spanish speaking patients relate to fútbol, while the American patients engage in baseball images. The patients are continuing to explore competition, but now it isn't strictly over me. They are engaged in teamwork and are using sports metaphors to explore cultural differences. The patients then create a "fútbol/baseball game," complete with its own set of rules, and they allow me to take turns playing on each team (I try my best to spend an equal amount of time with each). I notice that Sam has been able to engage in the game, and that the sports metaphor has allowed Ralph to sublimate his sexual preoccupation. The group's life condition is now shifting from animalistic competition towards the world of humanity.

Once this game plays itself out, I toss a Spaghetti ball into the mix (this is a collection of six-inch long silicone strands that are bound in the middle). Due to its weight and elliptical trajectory when thrown into the air, this toy elongates, slows down, and grounds the patients' movement repertoire. Raucous laughter erupts from the room as images of food swirl while we continue to toss the "spaghetti." Every patient takes turns sharing his favorite food and creating movements that represent it. We are symbolically exploring nourishment, and I wonder what I am capable of feeding them. What can they digest and take in? I receive my answer when the patients spontaneously begin to create a "group recipe" combining all of their movements into a choreographed dance: they don't need me to "feed them" anything because right now they are capable of "feeding each other." The same patients who half an hour earlier were so entrenched in competition that they couldn't even remember each other's names, are now using dance as a metaphor for nourishment and caring for each other's needs.

The group has now moved and danced its way out of the realms of hell, hunger, and animality into the compassionate world of *bodhisattva*, which is the foundation of Buddhahood. In this moment, I feel privileged to be a dmt because I am able to witness my patients as they embody the beauty and hope of the mutual possession of the Ten Worlds. There is no need to physically go anywhere special or far away. This place of suffering has been transformed into a Buddhaland through the patients' dance. In this very moment they are embodying Nichiren's assertion that "hell is itself the Land of Tranquil Light."[12]

We are fully absorbed in this sublime experience when a psychiatric technician abruptly enters the room. He dumps Mario inside and quickly scurries away. Mario is a 45-year-old, monolingual Spanish-speaking Puerto Rican male, with a body and mind fully ravaged by AIDS. He is standing alone in the middle of the room, lost in a stultifying stupor. Mario's AIDS dementia renders him unable to care for his basic needs to the point of being unable to feed, bathe, or clothe himself. He's mute most of the time, and when he does manage to say some words, they are incoherent utterances. I can see the outline of his soiled diapers under his pajamas and I catch a whiff of the smell. Mario looks afraid. The other patients look stunned and all movement has ceased in response to this interruption.

I am suddenly in the world of anger because I had specifically informed staff that Mario required individual care at this stage of his treatment, and that his impaired cognition and frail physical state made him unsuitable for this particular group. I am aware of the complex staff dynamics that create conditions where a group that reaches a higher stage of development is then sabotaged, but this knowledge is not going to help resolve my current dilemma—how to integrate Mario and rebuild the group. I once again feel my feet reach into the ground and my spine lengthen. I think of "changing poison into medicine" as I deepen my breath and become determined to find a way to create value out of this disruption.

I go back to the basics, asking the group to re-form a circle in order to integrate Mario. He remains still, practically catatonic, so we arrange ourselves around him. I decide that a concrete task will be the most expedient way to facilitate group cohesion, so I grab the Kush ball again and we begin to play a simple game of catch. I notice a glimmer of curiosity in Mario's eyes as he follows the trajectory of the ball, but the other patients appear bored. I add the Spaghetti ball as well, and the original group members become more engaged as we try to manage tossing and catching the Kush and Spaghetti balls simultaneously. We are finally developing a new group rhythm when Mario ends up holding both toys. We look at him expectantly, but he remains still. I repeatedly ask him, as clearly and simply as possible, to throw even one of the balls to any patient so we can continue playing, but Mario is unresponsive. I am at a loss and I feel exhausted. I feel as if my feet are covered in deep, heavy mud, and I am mute and paralyzed, just like Mario. I feel like I'm stuck in hell as I experience Mario's induced kinesthetic countertransference.

After a seeming eternity, I notice out of the corner of my eye that Pedro is walking towards Mario. The very same Pedro who began the session with his hands clenched in fists is now gently reaching out to Mario's right hand and softly says in Spanish, "Hey, you can let go." Sam, who began the session by hiding from everyone else is now following Pedro's example. He walks up to Mario and encouragingly says, "It's OK, man." It doesn't matter that he is speaking English—in that moment, Mario wakes up from his stupor in response to his peers' compassion. He smiles and gives the Kush ball to Pedro and the Spaghetti ball to Sam, and the rest of the patients cheer, welcoming Mario into the group.

Sam and Pedro come towards me and return the toys. I feel inspired and humbled by all that transpired since the group began. What initially started as a manifestation of the hellish isolation of mental illness gradually moved from hunger and animality to the world of *bodhisattva* and Buddhahood as the patients were able to engage their creativity and feel, at least for a moment, that they are more than their disease and suffering, and that they have something of value to offer each other. The disruption that I first perceived as an obstacle to the flow and development of the group process proved to be another opportunity for group members to reveal the life condition of *bodhisattva*, because without Mario's appearance Pedro and Sam would not have had the opportunity to manifest their compassion so fully.

I gaze at the patients and see that they are smiling in a very relaxed manner. Just as I am about to proceed with a cool down that will facilitate processing and integration of all that happened, we hear lunch being announced over the loudspeaker. Never mind that it arrived half an hour early, the psychiatric technicians are already banging on the door of the group room, ordering the patients to go to the dining room. I have to laugh as I think back to the theme of food and nourishment that had emerged earlier in the session. The group quickly falls apart as the patients scramble out of the room. This wasn't the ending that I'd had in mind, but such is life in a psychiatric unit.

Epilogue

I am once again standing alone in the group room. Soon I will be locked up in my office writing notes during my lunch hour. I will then go to my peer supervision group, where I will receive clinical feedback about today's session. I'll answer questions about my interventions and choices, such as not using music but using the toys, and I'll delve into what I could have done better or differently while also processing the myriad factors that contributed to the specific flavor of my group. Though I still long to work in an environment where I could have a longer period of time with which to work with patients, I notice that I don't feel like a "faux" clinician. A session like today's helped reinforce my belief in the importance of DMT as a necessary therapeutic modality, given that a group of patients such as these—separated by age, language, culture, and different clinical diagnoses—would have had a much harder time becoming actively engaged, manifesting empathy, and experiencing group cohesion had they been sitting in a more traditional verbal psychotherapy group. Most importantly, I understand that I can provide a safe, healing, and embodied space for patients, even if it's just for "a single moment of life."

As I leave the group room and start walking to my office, I think of one of my favorite quotes from one of Nichiren's letters:

> Great events never have minor omens. When great evil occurs, great good will follow.... Even if you are not the Venerable Mahakashyapa, you should all perform a dance. Even if you are not Shariputra, you should leap up and dance. When Bodhisattva Superior Practices emerged from the earth, did he not emerge dancing?[13]

Though Nichiren Daishonin did not prescribe a specific movement ritual as part of his Buddhist practice, I feel in my heart that he understood DMT.

Notes

1. Nichiren Daishonin, *The Writings of Nichiren Daishonin* (Tokyo: Soka Gakkai, 1999), 456.
2. Soka Gakkai International, "Nichiren Buddhism and the SGI." http://www.sgi-usa.org.
3. Clark Strand, *Waking the Buddha: How the Most Dynamic and Empowering Buddhist Movement in History Is Changing Our Concept of Religion* (Santa Monica: Middleway Press, 2014), 5.
4. American Dance Therapy Association, http://www.adta.org.
5. Erick Hawkins, *The Body Is a Clear Place: And Other Statements on Dance* (Princeton: Dance Horizons Book Co., 1992), 14.
6. Hawkins, 126.
7. Soka Gakkai. *The Soka Gakkai Dictionary of Buddhism* (Tokyo: Soka Gakkai, 2002), 477.
8. Daisaku Ikeda, "The Practice for Transforming our State of Life," *Living Buddhism*, November 2014.
9. Daisaku Ikeda, "Three Thousand Realms in a Single Moment of Life," *Living Buddhism*, August 2014.
10. Daishonin, 1274.
11. All names have been changed to protect patients' identities.
12. Daishonin, 456.
13. Daishonin, 1119.

Dance

Doing Being
Tibetan Buddhism and Postmodern Dance Improvisation

KAREN NELSON

Don't quote me. Isn't that what the Buddha meant with his final advice, to rather speak for ourselves as we discover our innate potential for freedom?

I am sensing my feet in contact with the earth. I am standing. My awareness opens to include fingers fluttering slightly as if to catch a branch or leaf of a tall tree. Warm, gentle exhales through both nostrils sound like a small ocean wave caressing the rocky and sandy shore. Toes branch out, roots of this nervous system are gaining purchase on the moving planet. Blood circulates, describing pulsating messages of life. It is a heart-pounded lettering, a gentle flowing script, subtle and intimate.

Buddha Dharma and Post-Modern Dance arrive in my life at the same time and place—1977 at Naropa Institute in Boulder, Colorado. I go to discover formal dance and find myself joining the sitting and walking practices too. I am attracted to meditation, drawn to the shrine room by the red cushions and all the people silently being in stillness. It's like this: A gong rings and the whole room changes. There is a rising in the space and a movement of through and around. The humans are a flock, walking on a path marked by bright cushions and silk bannered walls. We calibrate our steps, measuring to the person in front and return to our seats when called by the gong.

Later, in a Berkeley workshop, Judson era postmodern choreographer Steve Paxton introduced me to "the stand" through his dance work called Contact Improvisation. In class, Steve utters an image and our perceptions shift in that moment. He says, "easy breathing" or "let gravity have you" or "the three centers of weight are counterbalancing along your spine." The room starts dancing although we appear to be still. We are practicing a reflexive standing, witnessing the tiniest reflexes of our nervous system as it holds us upright. The movement is barely visible.

The Four Thoughts That Turn the Mind, common to all lineages of Tibetan Buddhism, are Dharma contemplations that help us freshly connect with the path. The first thought is that our human body is precious and that inhabiting it fully is a doorway to presence. Whenever I practice standing, this first thought lives in me. I am flooded with sensations of gratitude, purpose, and meaning.

It is late 1977 in Salt Lake City, and I am encountering my first workshop in Contact Improvisation, a dance form where communication between partners occurs through touch. I am at an evening jam, a casual atmosphere of self-guided practice that contrasts the teacher-led mood of a class. I begin moving in the space, noticing that a particular young man I avoided partnering with during class is possibly my only option for duet practice. Moving while considering this potential encounter, I taste my aversion.

The second mind-turning thought is that of death and impermanence: how everything disappears, changes. As I'm dancing, I am aware of an unreasonable prejudice I have based on the appearance of the young man. I judge his oddly-shaped, humpy spine, bumpy skin, and tangled hair. I imagine stale sweat and yellow teeth. I also sense a glimmer for change in my outlook towards him.

Soloing, I'm playing with the sensation of weight sloshing from my upper back to the side of my hip to leg to arm, sensing, too, the peripheral and impending choice of partnering in duet. I am discovering disorientation and spherical space as I dance, falling softly into the floor and relaxing tensions. The third thought that turns the mind could be described as taking responsibility for our actions and relationships with others. A bit frightened, I consider how this man and I are moving in each other's sphere of influence. Any action I do reveals my consciousness. What will I choose?

We come into close range. Either one or both of us could make a move to partner by extending a touch. The fourth mind-turning thought is to consider our ability to choose a bigger view for our lives. The sensation of my body opening and relaxing is more compelling than the tension or closing sensation that comes from evaluating and fearing. A powerful curiosity leads the edge of my skin and cells. This dancing body does not believe the mental story my aversion is telling.

My partner and I connect through touch at our backs. The smell of him is musty, his t-shirt a little stiff from dried sweat. We are both new at this. Our bodies' learning curve cracks jokes that our dancing naturally knows how to humor. There is a third thing created between us that we share and listen to. Aversion melts like glacial rivers aligning with the fall of the mountain. Our reflexes begin to entrain. My whole body is opening, surrendering further. We are discovering together new territories in the movement as we dance in the sea of equanimity.

Witnessing the life and death of a patterned habitual story line is an enlightening experience. Emerging whole and equal through discovering the release of a tight self towards a feared other removes a veil of ignorance. Buddhist teacher, writer, and translator Ken McLeod speaks of the power of attention. Attention notices the reactivity in the first place and then witnesses the pattern's entire life-death cycle. We are left with naturally arising qualities of mind which inspire true caring for countless other beings. These qualities are known in Tibetan Buddhism as the Four Immeasurables: love, compassion, joy, and equanimity. Discovering such remarkable qualities arising naturally in the course of a dance is both profound and very ordinary.

Tuning in Transcendence

The Six *Paramitas*, or Transcendent Perfections, of generosity, patience, discipline, effort, meditation, and wisdom are also palpable experiences in the course of a collaborative dance-making process. Of the Six *Paramitas*, generosity is said to have been the first taught by the Buddha. Tuning Scores, invented by visionary dancer, choreographer, and performing artist Lisa Nelson, are compositional in nature. Like Paxton, one of her

A Contact Improvisation performance at Naropa Institute [University], Boulder, Colorado, 1986. Shown here from foreground to background: Karen Nelson, Steve Paxton, Nancy Stark Smith and Tomaj Trenda. Photograph by Bill Arnold.

long-time collaborators, Lisa freely extends her experiments to the collective community—no permissions or certifications are required for me to carry my learned version of Tuning Scores into my own work. The openness of generosity is a spirit that uplifts every piece of the action—the giver, receiver, and the gift itself. Generosity is a nice place to begin.

Tuning is based on constructing dances in space and exposes communication between the dancers. The practice includes using verbal calls like "pause," "play," "reverse," and actions like physically entering or exiting the space. These calls and actions reveal the dance-making desires of the collaborators, something that usually remains mysterious and vague during dance improvisations.

I am imagining a Tuning "run," while also tracking my inner life of practicing Dharma. In this fantasy, I am sensing the room and my fellow collaborators gathered on the edge of the composing space for the dance. The room is bare. I see a dancer enter the space. I empathize with how her weight shifts into the balls of her feet. I'm in a state of "open presence," a meditation state described by Tibetan masters such as Yongey Mingyur Rinpoche as simply opening attention, relaxed and unedited. In open awareness, the dancers are tracking personal compositional desire and processing this information as it becomes expressed in space.

I track the motion, vision, sound, and story of this lone dancer entering the space. As she enters, I hear the musical chirp of floor boards creaking, the percussive swish of her feet on the wood. I see and feel the spirals in her body as she simply walks. I register surprise as she suddenly stills herself mid-stride. I see her inner balancing systems reaching for organization. My imagination jumps to life. What has led her to compose stillness then and there?

Another dancer suddenly crashes into the space, shocking my reflection on the first dancer's statue-like stillness. The *paramita* of patience in Sanskrit means "absence of anger." Implicit in that definition is the presence of anger, craving, and the frustration of suffering. At the sound of the entering dancer's crashing form, an electric feeling of fear verging on anger moves through my chest and arms. My right ear is leading the turn of my head towards the source of the sound. My heart is beating more quickly. My mouth is dry and a tension overtakes my whole form, now slightly paralyzed. Patience is the deep listening to the fear and anger as it arises and subsides while I watch the dance composition change. I note that the previous world I had been acquainting myself with is gone forever.

The *paramita* of discipline is tied to cleanliness of action. When does an action have a residue, a left over sense of remorse or guilt? "Pause" is called in a gently singing voice from a dancer to my right. The ensuing stillness in the room reveals the sounds of a dragonfly battering its wings against the window and a tractor mowing the field beyond. By attending to our sensations and feelings, we can discover our own ethical discipline. We can bow to our mistakes and begin again.

The two dancers in the composing space simultaneously begin a lyrical stepping duet as if they had suddenly been placed into a completely new scene. The previous image of extreme contrast, stillness and a loud crashing movement, is transformed. The dancers' unison movements travel through space and seem to be accompanied by sounds of life around us.

Watching the duet I notice my body is sinking into a dull, numb state. The *paramita* of effort is about remembering to practice waking up. I register this sinking and discover a curious seeker in me that begins to chart sensations: heavy, tired, a remote sadness in my face and heart, short breaths. Transcendent effort is remembering that forgetting is not something we can control. Beating oneself up for forgetting is violent and off the point. The moment of remembering is a cause for celebration, no matter what. Cued by my body's symptoms, a visual memory of the Tuning run's first image appears in my mind: the woman alone walking into stillness. I realize I am mourning its loss.

The recognition of the mourning brings a warmth and tenderness, followed by a new spirit of vitality. The *paramita* of meditation is the ongoing flow of awareness in every aspect of our lives, including the celebration and joy of having a practice. I open my eyes and ears to discover a pocket of space in the room that invites me to enter the dance composition. Inspired by the original image that disappeared, I want to offer a memorial to it. I walk into the space and stop mid-stride.

I am joined by a dancer entering from the edge who touches my arm with her elbow. We begin to move together. While the other duet continues its unison step dancing, my partner and I explode into a vigorous counter-point dance in physical contact. The *paramita* of wisdom is the surrender of letting go, allowing natural mind to effortlessly reveal itself. We are taking each other's weight, flowing into and out of the floor. I am lifted to a balance high on her shoulder as we turn spinning like a pinwheel and just as suddenly we fall.

Ken McLeod once asked a crowd during a public talk something like "What exactly are you trusting when you let go and fall backwards in a trust-fall exercise, where a couple of people are behind you prepared to catch your blind fall?" Ken provided his own answer after some comments from the group. I heard him utter, "What are you trusting? Nothing whatsoever."

As a dancer I know this "nothing" so well. Recall the falling moment of the duet mentioned above, a third thing is happening there that is beyond either my or my partner's conscious choices. I am falling and sliding down my partner's landscape of flesh, muscle, and bone. It is as if our fluid states of weight and balance have combined. I have no conscious sense what will happen next. It is a gap, experiential knowledge of "nothing whatsoever." Our bodies' tissues are open to this falling moment where unconscious reflexes are firing and we survive the fall, with glee.

Between the Earth and Me

By taking the earth as witness to his enlightenment, the Buddha offers me the suggestion that presence in the body is the pure witness of our lived experience. Embodiment and the earth are interconnected. The human experience of touching the earth is constant as we continuously relate to the call of gravity. Although constant, like breathing, our sense of gravity can be completely ignored or taken for granted and not experienced.

In dancing, I sometimes conflate the *idea* of moving with the actual *sense* of moving. The idea of moving is disembodied and has a quality of ambition. Sensed moving is embodied with awareness flowing throughout the body and is related to curiosity.

Recently, in a solo performance, I was trying so hard to feel the movement that I missed the sensing of my body, even as I appeared to move. Afterwards I discerned that my ambition was connected with an effort to please others, a life-long pattern related to a wobbly sense of self-worth. In a second performance there was a shift; everything that came to awareness while dancing was welcome. Curiosity guided and included everything, even the sensation of ambition with its metallic hardness and the easy stretch of yawning with its supreme neglect of the audience.

In Dharma practice, ambition appears as my wish to be fixed. When examined closely, this "fix me" fantasy has physical sensations that include tense jaws, arms, and hands, tight and searching vision, thoughts like "must do," and a sense of hovering or about to explode. In moments of pausing and simply looking closely into the sensations, there is a returning to presence and a natural, easy curiosity begins.

Physical contact is earthy. In contact there is a transmission of blessing between humans, environments, and objects. Taking a pilgrimage walk around Tibet's sacred Mount Kailash, spreading our bodies completely on the ground in a gesture of surrender, touching holy objects, dancing with endless varieties of people, seeing live performance, video and photos, reading writings—in these ways and more, transmission occurs. Our practice of dance or Dharma is energized as embodied knowledge passes along, one body to the next.

It is profound to discover, over decades of living, my place in a lineage of dance or Dharma. Even more, it is vivid and meaningful beyond words to sense how my participation contributes to the evolution of these forms. Gratitude towards my teachers, collaborators, and companions on the path arises naturally. Coming to presence and letting sensation radiate is a choiceless act of freedom. Alive, I touch the earth constantly and receive unconditional support for this life.

5Rhythms

A Moving Meditation Practice

LUCIA HORAN

"It takes discipline to be free."—Gabrielle Roth

Throughout time, spiritual practices have offered the promise of salvation and freedom. But what does it mean to be free? Each spiritual lineage has its own answer to this question. In the lineage of the 5Rhythms®, freedom is attained through the gateway of the body. In order to find freedom, one must turn their attention inward. Free the body, and the heart and mind will follow.

From the perspective of Theravada Buddhism, "enlightenment will come if you work for it. The path is a gradual one that leads against the stream. One breath at a time we make progress towards freedom."[1]

Through meditation, it becomes possible to transform the chattering mind into a mind of awareness. Through disciplining the mind to pay attention to the body, one builds concentration and can expand the capacity to be with what is. This might sound simple, but it is a mighty and sacred task. I found this to be most true in my own life when surviving just one breath at a time felt like an accomplishment.

The Buddha said that meditation should be practiced standing, walking, sitting, laying down, and in all bodily functions. So then, it is not enough to just sit in a formal practice or to just practice in movement. Meditative stillness and movement inform each other, and are cathartic in combination. Becoming skillful in both of these realms helps us step away from *dukkha* (suffering) and into *nibbana* (peace).

The 13th-century poet Rumi often speaks of the relationship between stillness and movement. He suggested that in order to fully understand stillness, one must dance. And in order to truly understand the dance, one must be still. It is through stillness that I have come to understand the truth of the dance, and it is through the dance that I have come to understand the Dharma (the way, truth) of stillness. If practiced in conjunction, insight occurs. I have found this to be true as both a practitioner and a teacher.

As I dance, I am always aware of the still-point inside me. As I meditate, I am always aware of the movement inside me. It is of great value to hold these two perspectives while in practice. It allows for the freedom of a larger view to be perceived in any given circumstance.

In my journey toward healing, I have primarily used the 5Rhythms in combination with the Dharma. This pairing, sprinkled with a good dose of therapy and Somatic Experiencing trauma work, has been life changing and transformational. It is my intention to share with you how these two practices complement and support each other in the path to finding a peaceful heart.

Breaking Free from Identifications

How do you define yourself? I am a dancer. But who would I be if I had no legs? I am a mother. But who would I be if my child has passed on? I am a wife. But who would I be if I divorce? How we define ourselves says a lot about how flexible we are to change. You see, we are spirit and energy moving. We are not fixed by any of these titles. Titles only tie us to the false reality of self. They are a way to understand this world, but they also support the ego's illusory foundation of safety because, as we know, all "I am"s are impermanent. If we go further in our investigation, we can then find the true source of who we are and where our happiness comes from. If our happiness is based on conditions, as soon as the conditions change, so then does our happiness. If one learns how to find happiness beyond causes and conditions, then one can find lasting peace.

One must become intimate with each state of being that life requires from us. There are times where one may need to open to inspiration, or put it into action. There's a time to surrender to what that action may become, to allow it to transform, or simply to sit quietly in the stillness as a witness. If we limit ourselves to one way of being, such as "The Giver" or "The Doer," then we may miss out on receiving the good life has for us. It is very limiting to say, "I don't do stillness." But we can imagine plenty of New Yorkers making that statement. Now imagine dancers making the statement. "I don't do stillness." Now imagine sitting meditation practitioners saying, "I don't dance." Sure, it has been said! What I have found, though, is that by stepping out of the comfort zone, one can greatly expand the possibility of insight.

By breaking the patterns of identification that imprison, one is then able to be free from their limitations. For example, while working at an Against the Stream Insight Meditation Retreat,[2] I found myself giving a discourse and demonstration. The room was mostly filled with "tough guys," their knuckles and necks tattooed, arms crossed, staring down at me with a look of "You have to be kidding me. She wants us to dance?" They were immediately confronted by the limitations of this attitude. They had to shatter their image of the "tough guy" in order to participate. Those who did not left the room. They either broke through right there, or the next day they returned with the insight of how limiting this attitude actually is.

They had been avoiding feeling what was buried below the surface. For many, addiction is used to mask the pain for a time, but ultimately does not free us. Once people become sober, they can then attend to the source of the wound and begin to heal it. As soon as they began to move, they began to feel. Once the feeling is activated, whatever needs to be free has the opportunity to do so.

There was one man who returned, deciding to participate after seeing this. He was a war veteran who had fought in Bosnia. He told me that he had not cried for many years since his tour. It was the meditation and the dance that allowed him to melt the armor of tears guarding his heart. Once the tears had washed his heart, it was possible for him to find joy again. He wrote me a letter some time afterward:

Hi Lucia,

I'm not sure if you remember me or not but I was at the ATS retreat last summer. That experience was life and heart changing for me and I wanted to thank you for being part of that. 5Rhythms was a real stretch of my comfort zone to say the least. I use to love music but after a mission with the military to Bosnia in the early 90s everything changed. I lost some really good friends and saw the worst humans have to offer. I had lost my ability to have a genuine laugh, I wasn't ticklish anymore and I lost any sort of enjoyment for music. Today that changed! I listened to a Bob Marley song and the tears poured! My heart has healed another step. I am writing to tell you because, well, for one I think you are one of the few people that will get how big this is for me. Your 5Rhythms class was the start of this healing for me.

Much gratitude and Metta,

Dan

This letter exemplifies one man's journey toward freedom. He stands as a testament to the healing power of this path. By melting some of the layers of the ego and the self, he was able to find liberation from his past. He was able to accept, forgive, and let go. He said to me after that he was able to feel the love of his wife and daughters for the first time since the war.

The Rhythms themselves represent the primary states of being in life. We look at them as a mirror to life. In turn we can see what is reflected back to us as we practice. Where are your strengths and where do you need strengthening? In Dan's case, he needed to balance the softening with the strength. We are much like a tree. The more flexible we are, the stronger we are to withstand the winds. The more rigid we are, the less strength we have because we become brittle and snap. If we learn to balance the yin and yang, the feminine and masculine aspects of human nature, then we will have the full potential of our strength and power.

5Rhythms Movement Meditation

The 5Rhythms is a moving meditation practice that maps how energy moves. The founder, Gabrielle Roth, dedicated her life to mapping the human experience. Before her passing in 2012, she left us a series of maps that outlines the path to freedom through the vessel of the body. If we become fascinated with where we reside, who we are, and how we move in this world, then it is possible to find peace. Gabrielle was a wisdom warrior. From her own shamanic dance, she called us out of our heads and into our bodies. In stilling the monkey mind, she taught us to feel into the stillness of silence. She inspired us to move our feet and land in our heart.

We offer 5Rhythms in the format of classes and seminars. A class usually lasts two hours and includes a 10–30 minute discourse and 1.5 hours of guided moving meditation in which you dance alone, with a partner, and as a group. The class will end with an integration period of stillness. A seminar can last from one day to one month. During longer courses the focus rests on practice, philosophy, and embodiment.

The 5Rhythms is taught in 47 countries around the globe. We have a non-profit organization called 5Rhythms Reach Out. This branch of our organization brings free classes and seminars to children, teens, refugees, AIDS patients, incarcerated men and woman, addiction centers, elders, and Alzheimer's patients. We have committed to bringing this work across all borders, to those at the center of society and those on the far outskirts. We were born to dance, and through dancing mindfully and engaging our creativity, we bring integration, balance, peace, and happiness into our lives.

The 5Rhythms practice moves through five phases, or rhythms. Music accompanies these phases, and participants follow their own improvisational dance while being guided by a certified 5Rhythms teacher. The music varies greatly, from rock 'n' roll, to cello, from "drum and bass" to opera, depending on the teacher's choice. Each person dances according to their individual physical capacity. Because of this, the practice is accessible to everyone including those with all kinds of physical limitations.

The first rhythm is Flowing. This is the yin energy, the aspect of our nature that knows how to receive. The second rhythm is Staccato, the yang energy. This is the aspect of our nature that gives. The third rhythm is Chaos. This is the holy union of the first two rhythms. Chaos allows us to break open and surrender. Chaos moves us and naturally delivers us into the state of Lyrical, the fourth rhythm. Lyrical is a state of being in which everything is free to reform, shape-shift, morph, and change. Lyrical empties us unto the fifth rhythm, Stillness. Stillness is the state of being that allows us to integrate and unify. Stillness is the realm where the normal veils of separation are lifted. It is here that one can experience connection to oneness in ourselves, each other, the *sangha*, and the divine.

> These rhythms catalyze motion deep in the psyche. Each is a practical tool of awakening that will release us to dance on the edge, to be outrageous, to transform suffering into art, and art into awareness.[3]

Gabrielle instructed us to take inspiration from every aspect of life—both peaks and valleys. If we can let go into the larger energy as it moves us, then there is no clinging, craving, or aversion. There is just energy.

She taught that spirit is breath and energy in motion. We are not fixed beings. We are alive with the truth of impermanence and change. From birth to death, we are asked to let go again and again to all the inevitable changes of existence. All we have to do is look to the body to show us this truth.

Our challenge is not just to be where we are. It is also to move through the changes. In order to learn how to better move with these changes, one can contemplate the word grace. To me, grace is free of all resistance. To learn how to dance through life with grace is a sacred task that we are entrusted with at birth. If we learn to embody grace, then life fills us with effortless ease, gratitude, and appreciation. Each present moment then becomes a precious gift, a blessing.

Dharma

When I came to the Dharma to sit down in meditation, I came out of pure desperation. I was not seeking enlightenment. I was not seeking eternal bliss. I simply wanted to be free from a broken heart and a beat down soul. It has been a very strange and intense journey, but one full of richness. I see the process of the Dharma much like an aikido move. We transform the negative force into a positive, one that works for us rather then against us. We take the worst life has delivered, and we make it into our biggest gift. So this is where we begin.

The Four Foundations of Mindfulness are four practices from the *Satipatthana Sutta* that outline present time awareness and are fundamental aspects of Buddhist meditation.

They can also be applied in moving meditation. The Four Foundations of Mindfulness are:

- Mindfulness of the body (*rupa*)
- Mindfulness of feelings/sensations (*vedana*)
- Mindfulness of mind or consciousness (*citta*)
- Mindfulness of mental objects (*dhamma*)

The Buddha referred to these Four Foundations as a "direct" or "one path" to liberation (*nibbana*). These practices are taught throughout Theravada Buddhist traditions, both East and West. They are the essentials of practicing all forms of meditation, both moving and sitting. This is the foundation that the rest of your practice can build from.

The next step for me came in the form of practicing the *Brahma Viharas* in motion. It is here that practitioners can open the gateway of the body for the heart and mind to follow. These practices have acted as a poultice to the wounds of my heart. I see them as the antidotes to suffering. They are the practices of loving kindness, compassion, sympathetic joy, and equanimity. They are high states for anyone to attain. Practicing these qualities in moving meditation can make them more accessible. As we move with the volition of compassion, equanimity, joy, and loving kindness, the body teaches the mind how to open to these states. They are no longer merely concepts. They become an embodiment, a living, breathing state of loving kindness, generosity, forgiveness, joy, equanimity, and compassion.

The Buddha's path is one of purification. The path of the 5Rhythms is also, literally and physically, a process of purification. When the body moves, it sweats. As we breathe, we pump oxygen and new life into every cell. The skin is the largest organ in the body. We are sweating out all that we no longer need. We are breaking old patterns down and creating new ones. As we move our feet and body in mindful awareness, we create new neurological pathways in the brain. We are excavating the past so we can live fully in the present.

Science shows that the body sends messages to the brain. By shaping our body, we are shaping our mind and our reality. If you seek forgiveness, then practice the movements of forgiving. If you desire freedom, then practice the movements of freedom.

In Buddha's first meditation instructions, he advises an upright, seated position. This is a posture of balance. The spine aligns to the hips, head aligns to the spine, and the chin is level. Putting the body into the shape of equanimity, we then begin. It is not hard to take the position physically, but it is very hard to experience balance and equanimity mentally. Thus, we practice.

When I began seated meditation, I was instructed to sit still as a witness to the impermanence, the arising and passing. That sounded easy until I tried. I always thought I had to do something with it. I did not realize there was nothing I had to get through; it is just now as it is. Each moment requires of us just one thing, to be present with what is. That's it.

As a dancer, it was revolutionary for me to learn how to be rather than do. It was then that I realized what I had been missing from Gabrielle's teaching all of these years. She was pointing to "being" the whole time, but I did not understand what that actually meant until this moment. Staying present with the meditation sometimes felt like standing in a fire and letting it burn me. But as I have learned to be there, a more powerful part of myself was born from the ashes. Gabrielle describes this as turning our suffering into art, and our art into healing. The art is the meditation. The meditation is the healing.

Safety: Body and Practice

Meditation practice helps us to develop skills that can be applied in daily life. In effect, these skills assist us in becoming more fluid and less resistant. Without the resistance, we have much less suffering. As a result, meditation can teach one to be a more skillful athlete of life.

As we learn to extinguish the unskillful fires, we can also learn how to cultivate skillful behaviors that propagate happiness, joy, and loving kindness as mentioned above. The practices of meditation and movement are the creative cultivation of a peaceful life. They themselves are acts of generosity and loving kindness towards yourself and others.

Lucia Horan, 2014. Photograph by Lea (lestudionyc.com).

As humans our pain and suffering is experienced through the body. The body holds a cellular memory of life. We are shaped by our fear, sadness, anger, joy, and compassion. All you have to do is look at someone's spine to get an idea of how "up" or "down" they are. Look and see, the spine and the whole body tell a story. Through false smiles, we see the body betraying the truth of one's past and present reality.

For many people, it is very painful to be asked to pay attention to their body. When asked to be mindful of their hips, a story comes. When asked to move their shoulders, an image is there. For some, these stories hold deeply painful memories. For some, the body is the most unsafe place in the world. To be asked to pay attention for longer then a few seconds is almost impossible.

My job is to help people integrate their past and re-establish a safe and loving relationship to their body. In some ways it is like seducing the mind back into the body from wherever it had to go to survive. The problem with the human survival strategy is that when a person returns, they are usually fragmented in some way. They have to remain hyper-vigilant to their environment, constantly tracking where the threat may be coming from. Sadly, this kind of trauma is all too common.

As a person begins to move and sweat, presence is established in the body. The result of embodied presence is a calming of the mind and the nervous system. Once a person has stabilized, they can find a sense of safety. If we begin here, then success in meditation is possible.

Embracing Freedom

In this lifetime, I was lucky enough to be born into the family of 5Rhythms. Gabrielle Roth was the mother of my half-brother. We grew up in a unique way, as our mothers were very close. I was fortunate to have my spiritual teacher provided for me. As I came to understand the Dharma, I came to know that is what Gabrielle was essentially teaching: the embodiment of the Dharma, Tao, the truth, the way, the direct path. And so it made sense that Buddha has also become my teacher.

Both maps of Dharma and 5Rhythms give us directions out of isolation and into connection. They show us how to transform fear into fearlessness and anger into forgiveness. Forgiveness, in turn, can bring lessons on compassion. As I have turned towards my own suffering, I have come to more deeply understand the suffering of others. An expanded capacity to be with my own vulnerability has aroused in me an increased compassion for others. I have learned that simply being present is enough.

You are the authority in the house of your body. You will know if it is good, because it will work. There is not just one dance in life, there are thousands. Be gentle, be kind, and know that you are not alone in your fight for freedom. Those who have come before you have worn a clear path for you to follow. Listen to your feet and see where they take you.

Remember it is not enough to just sit. It is not enough to just dance. Establish a mindful balance between these two poles. Commit to the discipline of your practice. Keep showing up to do the work. In doing so, you will make the whole world into a practice lab for awakening, enlightenment, and freedom.

NOTES

1. Noah Levine, *Against the Stream* (New York: HarperOne, 2007), 124.

2. Against the Stream Buddhist Meditation Society was founded by Noah Levine, author of *Dharma Punx*, and includes a focus on social action through working with prison populations and people in recovery.

3. Gabrielle Roth, *Sweat Your Prayers: Movement as a Spiritual Practice* (New York: Tarcher/Putnam, 1997), back cover.

Ordinary Miracles
Tibetan Yogic Dance

Rose Taylor Goldfield

Beyond location and direction
Is the immeasurable palace of sacred play,
Where yogis and yoginis dance.
Come here, and throw your thoughts of past, present, and future
Into the timeless expanse.

—From *The Dance of the Nectar of Great Bliss*,
Khenpo Tsültrim Gyamtso Rinpoche[1]

In the dream I remember most vividly and with the strongest sense of pure sensory delight, I was dancing. I was one of a group of dancers filling a large hall, leaving just enough space between each of us to allow freedom of movement without sacrificing connection. We reveled in our miraculous dream bodies—devoid of matter yet vividly appearing—and we moved together as an intimately connected whole, effortlessly riding the energy of our dreamlike world.

Both of the above experiences of dance reflect the spiritual dance practice in which I trained and teach. For the Karma Kagyu lineage of Tibetan Buddhism, spiritual dance is a practice vehicle—from the freeform, naked dances of the lineage forefather Milarepa[2] in his Himalayan mountain retreats, to the intricately choreographed ritual dances performed by the monks of Tsurphu monastery in Tibet, which are still practiced to this day. Khenpo Tsültrim Gyamtso Rinpoche, my main teacher, composed this song that expresses his personal connection to dance, making a strong statement about the efficacy of dance as spiritual practice:

The buddhas surely do sing and dance,
To sing and dance is surely profound practice,
By practicing profound song and dance,
We reach enlightenment—how amazing![3]

Pith illumination is also found in these lines from Jamgon Kongtrul Lodro Thaye's "Song of Mahamudra":

Our wheel in samsara turns and turns,
While turning, our core remains unstained.
Appearance is empty of real effect,
Appearance is kayas' richness manifest.[4]

73

These lines beautifully express the principles of Tibetan Buddhist yogic dance, which make it a path for enlightenment. Our daily experience is one of turning through a variety of dualistic cycles—cycles of inhalation and exhalation, temporal beginnings and endings, of day and night, of the stages of relationships, of thoughts and emotions, of life and death. And yet in the center of all that cycling movement, there is our unstained core of deepest stillness. This core is beyond all duality, and yet it gives rise to apparent duality, a dance featuring movement and stillness. When we connect with our core, we notice how the fluctuating appearances of life—dynamic in their dualistic tensions—are soft, dreamlike and filled with richness. In this way, we can experience the ordinary features of our lives as miraculous. All life's movement can be experienced as dance.

With training, we can feel into and experience this for ourselves. As Khenpo Rinpoche puts it,

> Every time your body moves around, it is vajra[5] dance,
> All your speech is vajra mantra, all thoughts are luminous clarity—
> Everything appearing is Mahamudra's[6] play.[7]

In this essay, we will first explore the three kayas, or three enlightened dimensions, which describe the awakening that blossoms within the Buddhist dance experience. Next, we will visit three forms of dance practice that help move us into direct experience of these enlightened dimensions.

The Three Enlightened Dimensions (Kayas) in Dance

Deeply connected with our unstained core, and ready to manifest in sacred dance, are the *dharmakaya*, *sambhogakaya*, and *nirmanakaya*—described as the three dimensions, aspects, or bodies of enlightenment.

"*Kaya*" in Sanskrit literally means "body," and when we understand the profundity of the word body, we see why *kaya* is also translated as "dimension of enlightenment." Our body is our vehicle for moving towards enlightenment, and it is the locus for enlightenment itself. The body is a microcosm of the universe. The external location of the Buddha Shakyamuni's enlightenment was in Bodhgaya, India, at the base of the Bodhi tree—the tree of life, representing the entire universe, growing at the world navel. The practitioner deep in meditation at the world navel is "the umbilical point through which the energies of eternity break into time."[8] Internally, the tree of life is the subtle body's central channel running from the pelvic floor up to the crown of the head. The world navel is mirrored in the body as the origin point, located just below the superficial navel, deep in the center of the experiential body.

The *kayas* are experiential realms. The more we can flow with our experience, rather than freezing it into objects, situations, and relationships that feel solid, disconnected, or overwhelming, the more fully we experience these enlightened dimensions.

The *dharmakaya* is the open dimension of pure awareness. As such it is a body without form, free from form's limitations. It exists in what is known as the fourth time, the timeless expanse, beyond the three times of past, present, and future. It is invisible in that it is beyond the world of physical matter, beyond that which the senses can perceive. It is the open ground of awareness and creativity that forms the basis of our dance practice.

The *sambhogakaya* is the energetic and pulsating flow of experience taking shape as patterns and symbols. It is more tangible than the *dharmakaya*, and yet still subtle and difficult to pin down as being "this" or "that." It includes not only the speech of the buddhas, but all forms of communication: verbal, nonverbal, and symbolic. Tsangpa Gyare[9] captures this type of symbolic communication, which points us back to the basic truth of the *dharmakaya*, in these verses:

> When you look at the clear bright ocean,
> And the waves rise up and dissolve back down,
> Don't you know this is the lama teaching you
> That thoughts are dharmakaya?

> When the springtime sun starts to warm the earth,
> And the ice melts down into water,
> Don't you know this is the lama teaching you
> Samsara is nirvana?[10]

The *sambhogakaya*, like the *dharmakaya*, is always present. *Sambhogakaya* manifests as our subtle body—our felt experience that arises in the meeting between the physical body and awareness. Thus, all our experiences are suffused with the energy of the *sambhogakaya*, full of profound meaning, which we can access at any moment. We connect with the *sambhogakaya* when we open to feelings, sensations, and patterns of energy in the physical body. Doing this, we find that our felt sensations often do not reflect the measurable physical body. Some sensations feel as tiny and sharp as a pinpoint, while others feel vast like space, or like deep valleys, or mountaintops. We feel patterns twisting and pulling in ways that do not necessarily reflect the tissues or position of the physical body. This is the realm of the energetic quality of our dance practice that forms into patterns of movement.

The *nirmanakaya* is the dimension that is most easily understood by conventional mind. It is the realm of measurable objects and events within the framework of conventional time and space, whose enlightened quality is a continually vivid variety of unique experiences. It is comparable to our physical body—our visible, tangible aspect that we can see at work in our lives. It is our more obvious way of engaging with the world: not only are we ourselves aware of it—as with our mind's awareness, and subtle body—but others can perceive it also. It exists within the confines of time and space—in one point in time, one location in space. In our dance practice, this is each specific movement we use, the timing and the gestures we form.

The ultimate reality of awareness (*dharmakaya*), the subtle body (*sambhogakaya*), and the physical body (*nirmanakaya*) is that they are inseparable. As the Indian yogi Dombe Heruka sings, "Body and mind—nonduality/Spacious and relaxed transparency."[11] This leads us to a very different view of the body: the body is like light or a rainbow, inseparable from awareness and suffused with wisdom. As the Hevajra Tantra states, "Great wisdom lives in the body: Completely free of all thoughts."[12]

Thus the body, free of thoughts, and free of particles of matter, is the dance and play of mind's native luminosity. As Orgyenpa[13] sings,

> All phenomena are like reflections
> To think that they are real is missing the point
> All of existence is mind's dance and play[14]

When we open to this reality, the body's wisdom manifests itself to us. Our experiences begin to flow like a dance. In three *kayas*' terminology, upon realizing that all apparently ordinary experiences are imbued with the awareness of the *dharmakaya* and the energy of the *sambhogakaya*, the ordinary world becomes the dance of the *nirmanakaya*. This is the union of our open awareness of mind, our subtle body energy, and our physical body.

When we practice yogic song and dance, we engage all these three aspects of our being. Our physical body is engaged in movement, and we connect with the subtle body by joining our awareness with the felt experience of the body. We notice the sensations that arise and feel how it is to move—not as a solid, heavy body, but as a feeling body of awareness-energy.

Dancing from the Origin Point

The "origin point" is your own personal connection with the *dharmakaya*. It is located four finger widths below your navel, in the very center of your body. You feel into the origin point by breathing down into your lower belly and letting your awareness settle and ground in the center of your being. In yogic dance, we move while centered in this awareness.

For the physical body, the origin point is our center of gravity and the spot from which we first developed—where our father's sperm entered the center of our mother's egg. We grew around this point while nourishment from our mother entered through it. The fetal position curls around this center like flower petals. Our earliest movements were all organized around the central hub of the origin point, radiating out from it and contracting back into it.

This process of growth sees our human form take shape through the *kayas*. We begin in the undifferentiated state of the *dharmakaya*, indistinguishable from our environment. Gradually we take shape and form as energetic patterns coming together in the realm of the *sambhogakaya*. Then we develop our solid, earthbound form in the realm of the *nirmanakaya*. This process is not concluded at our birth but continues through the first seven or eight years of life.

In terms of the subtle body and mind aspects, the origin point is more than just the creative source for the body; it is the source of all confusion and wisdom, the source of *samsara* and nirvana. Everything in experience arises from this center and dissolves back into it. It can be described as a small *bindu,* or "droplet of energy," but is capable of holding all reality; it is minutely vast. It is beyond our conceptual mind's ability to understand how this could be, but we can experience it through our yogic practices.

This point that holds all reality is, therefore, a great center of energy in the body. When mind focuses on it during movement, the subtle energy and mind gather in our body's core rather than being scattered. Concentrating ourselves in this way helps us to clarify our practice and makes it effortlessly energetic. Energy gathers at this center and radiates out from it. This creative energy is grounded and centered, so it flows smoothly and ceaselessly: we harness it for our yogic dance practice.

My most intense experience of the origin point in all its profundity was during my pregnancy and while birthing my son. Birth is one of the creative processes that so clearly arises from the space of the *dharmakaya*, mysteriously resulting in a conscious being's manifestation from a sperm and an egg. As I moved through the months of my pregnancy, I found myself disconnecting from the definable world's limits of time and space. My experience of time noticeably shifted. When organizing meetings, I would suggest dates that had already passed, and I could not quite wrap my head around why that was problematic!

Song and dance were important supports throughout my pregnancy and labor. My body was changing at such a rapid rate and I did not feel well enough to exercise, but it felt good to get to know my body each day by just playing some music, listening to the *sambhogakaya* level of my body's response to the music and simply moving while meditating on my sensory experience. In birthing, it took a long time for my cervix to dilate. I had prepared different playlists for birthing, some more energetic, some more meditational, and I moved to them and encouraged my cervix to open.

It is difficult to describe but during pregnancy and birthing, I simply felt myself in touch with a world that was outside the restrictive rules under which people ordinarily operate. I found myself entering, deeper and deeper, into a liminal space from which it was hard to communicate with others. This experience grew until the time I completely withdrew from the ordinary world and entered what felt like an internal cave in order to meet and return with my son. I birthed at home, and although my birthing team was with me, I felt completely alone in this other world. After twenty-five hours of labor, Oliver was born, but he was in need of resuscitation while I hemorrhaged beside him, which was particularly fraught because I was anemic.

Although recalling this now it seems dramatic, and it looked so with blood soaking the bed and floor, at the time I felt perfectly peaceful. My mother, husband, and I sang Milarepa's and Khenpo Rinpoche's songs to Oliver to welcome him into the world and encourage him to stay with us. My husband and I had to decide whether to transfer to the hospital or not, and we both knew instinctively that we should stay at home. At this present time, I cannot believe how easy it was to make that decision. I just felt deeply connected to the intuitive sense of the origin point and to my child and husband.

Gradually over the subsequent weeks and months I became more attuned to the regular world, the time and space of the *nirmanakaya*, but there were many strange twists and turns along the way! It was a prolonged and moving experience of shifting between the experiential dimensions of the three *kayas*. And as I returned to this more physical world, Oliver also established himself more and more fully in the *nirmankaya* realm. Now, my husband and I regularly sing and dance with Oliver: it brings us into the present, enlivens routine, and brings us all joy.

Three Modes of Dance That Access the Three Dimensions of Enlightenment

There are three forms of dance I practice. While they all connect with all three dimensions, each emphasizes one in particular.

Form: Embodying the Female Buddha Tara

These are ritualized deity dances and songs wherein we, as the dancers, connect with the energy of a particular Buddha, or deity, such as Tara, renowned for her abilities to protect sentient beings from fear and to help them accomplish their aims in harmony with the Dharma (she is also known as the "Noble Liberator"). We may dress as she is depicted in sacred art works and we use prescribed movements that include the symbolic hand gestures known as *mudras*, each of which holds a specific meaning. Form dances are connected with the *nirmanakaya*: the world of manifest appearances.

In form dances, we become a reflection of Tara's enlightened image. By doing this while moving in the deity's ritualized fashion, we begin to arouse our internal Tara energy. At the same time, we understand that her form is not a truly existent entity; rather, it arises from emptiness and dissolves back into emptiness at the end of the dance. The practice often begins with reciting the origin story of Tara, to help us connect with her energy. Because we are working with specific movements, this practice helps to focus the mind in a way similar to *samatha*, calm-abiding meditation.

I find this to be a powerful practice, particularly when I feel bothered by interactions with people I am having difficulty with. While I do seated meditations of compassion for the person I am angry with, I find my conceptual mind often runs off on storylines or defensive tactics, or I just get distracted. Performing the Tara dance, I find I can maintain my focus more easily and I feel Tara's power of compassion helping me find my own internal sense of softness and acceptance both for the other person and for my own experiences of anger and hurt.

Subtle Form: Dancing the Five Energies

In describing the *sambhogakaya*, Traleg Rinpoche states, "It has to do with mental powers, with the ability of one's mind to manifest in relation to the five wisdoms."[15] In the subtle form song and dance practice, we evoke these five wisdoms energetically through specific styles of movement and music. Each wisdom is associated with different environmental and psychological qualities, which together form a "family." These are: the all-encompassing wisdom of the Buddha Family; the mirror-like wisdom of the Vajra Family; the wisdom of equality of the Ratna Family; the discriminating wisdom of the Padma Family; and the all-accomplishing wisdom of the Karma Family. It is possible to get a sense of the unique energies of these families just by reading this table:

Family	Buddha	Vajra	Ratna	Padma	Karma
Wisdom	all-encompassing	mirror-like	equality	discriminating	all-accomplishing
Element	space	water	earth	fire	wind
Season	none	winter	autumn	spring	summer
Color	white	blue	yellow	red	green
Disturbed Aspect	ignorance	anger	greed	attachment	jealousy
Mudra	teaching	earth-touching	bestowing	meditation	protection
Symbol	wheel	vajra	jewel	lotus	sword
Beings	god	hell	hungry ghost	human	jealous gods
Direction	none	east	south	west	north
Animal Seat	lion	elephant	horse	peacock	garuda

When in a group, we start the practice by discussing the qualities of each wisdom family and then meditating on the family's element, as that is an easy way into the visceral sense of the family's energetic style. Then we perform group exercises with music and actions that evoke the family's style of movement. For example, all-accomplishing wisdom is focused on a particular goal. It is directed, moving in straight lines for the swift accom-

Students dancing with the five energies, at this point moving with the energy of the Buddha Family, Sukhasiddhi All-Sangha Residential Retreat, San Rafael, California, June 2012. Photograph by Leslie Shelton.

plishment of its purpose. When we move in space with others, this energy flows and engages others in the room in a particular way. The quality of this aspect is illuminated by the animal associated with this energy, the garuda, a mythical bird with a vast wingspan. The ability of this bird to soar gives it an overview of the whole situation—it has a clear vision and can see the pattern of movement that accomplishes its aim. A practitioner embodying this energy moves through the group with open compassion but also with a one-pointed and undistracted intent. This energy is associated with nature and karmic order. It is in accord with the group energy and fits in like cogs accomplishing their particular purpose of moving the clock's hands.

A very different energy is that of all-encompassing wisdom—it is more circular and softer in its motion. It has no direction or goal; it encompasses all directions. The dance of the whirling dervishes evokes this type of energy. For this movement the practitioner needs to be tuned into the space between the practitioners. The spinning makes us lose track of our fixed locality and formed ideas. We lose our separated individuality and become part of a mass of swirling energy.

In subtle form dance there are initially some prescribed group movements and songs, and as the energy of a family is roused in the room we move into freestyle dance to a piece from the repertoire of the family's music. In this way, practitioners get to manifest their personal connection with the energy. This subtle dance form powerfully attunes us to the five wisdom families and the *sambhogakaya*. Although I practice this alone, I feel it has the most potency in a group, where the energy in the room becomes palpable.

On one five-day retreat in Fairfax, California, we worked through a wisdom family a day in the order of their elements, from the subtlest (space) to the coarsest (earth). The space element gave people a chance to take a breath after concluding their daily life activities to enter retreat. Then we moved into wind, a more active energy, and, at the mid-point of the retreat, fire. It was fascinating to see how the group seemed almost intoxicated and slightly mad at this point. The energy had really heightened, with the potential to get out-of-control, like a forest fire. The Padma Family can have this quality of intoxication and one of the foods associated with this family is alcohol. It was exhilarating to be teaching and riding this energy of forty participants manifesting strong Padma energy. Then the next day, the craziness subsided as we continued with water, a downward flowing energy, in opposition to Padma's rising energy. The program ended with earth energy, the harvest at the end of the season, where we enjoy the richness we have evoked. By the end of the retreat the atmosphere was more grounded, but with a full and ripe sense of the energetic journey we had all been on together and the jewels of insight into what we had discovered about our personal relationship with these energies.

Formless Dance: Heart Essence Dance

Formless dance practice emphasizes experience of the *dharmakaya*. Here your movement is not guided from the outside, but by looking deeply within and listening to your body and how your body feels like moving in the present moment. This sounds simple, but being the subtlest it can be the most elusive of the dance practices to actually connect with. It requires us to drop all our preconceptions and judgments about our bodies, movement, music, and being with others in movement; and to simply rest in our experience as it is in the moment. From that place, we move.

When I practice in this way, I begin in meditation, either seated or lying on the floor. I drop any idea of creating something, doing something, or accomplishing anything. Breath comes into my body and stirs sensation; I watch it subtly shift energy in my lower belly, around my origin point. Breath leaves my body and stirs sensation; I notice my intimate connection with my environment, without boundary. Flickers and flirts of sensation arise in my sensory field. At some point, my attention is taken by one of these flickers of sensation, and my body begins to follow it. I curl in around it on my left side, while my right extends. Like pebbles thrown in a lake, these movements create ripples of further sensation to explore. I simply follow. If my mind gets taken by thought, I return my attention to the breath in my lower belly, and to sensation, and let the movement resume once more.

Although we are working with relaxing the thinking mind, we do not want to block any feeling that is arising, for when we battle with our experience, we remove ourselves further and further from the direct energy of our experience. So if judgment arises, rather than judging the judgment, we try to cut the narrative or snowballing effect of that thought, and stay with the tangible energy beneath the judgment. With warm acceptance, we allow that energy to be just as it is in this moment.

This verse from Maitreya's *Treatise on Buddha Nature* is an excellent guide for this practice:

> We don't need to get rid of anything,
> We don't need to add anything.
> Simply experience directly what is actually there—
> This authenticity will liberate you.[16]

This is the type of song and dance that Milarepa was engaged in, and that he sang about in this verse:

> Since the trulkhor comes from what I am, it feels extremely good
> To leap and run about is dance, feels even better still
> To be a king of speech, with a treasury of song feels good
> That the words are like the buzzing of bees, feels extremely good
> That the sound it makes is merit collecting, feels even better still
> The bliss is good in the expanse of the confidence of strength of mind
> What develops on its own by its own force, feels extremely good[17]

Trulkhor is a set of specific yogic exercises that are practiced in the Karma Kagyu tradition. However, what Milarepa is singing about here is natural *trulkhor*, which has no specific movements. This *trulkhor*, or dance, develops "by its own force." It comes from the power of resting in your true nature, your direct experience of the three *kayas*. When you rest there, you do not drop into a void of stillness; rather, there is energy and movement. In formless dance, you follow that movement.

Dance in Life

These dance practices can be both profound and enjoyable, and at the same time the point of these practices is to learn to dance within our daily lives. We look for the still point in the turning world, without being afraid of the world's turning. This is what Lodro Thaye is pointing to when he talks of appearances being the "*kaya's* richness manifest." Our daily lives are simply the miraculous dance and play of these three dimensions of experience.

Khenpo Rinpoche would have me spontaneously dance in all sorts of situations: from crowded tourist spots to airports, from the busy streets of London to the secluded mountains of Bhutan. This taught me not to leave dance practice in the meditation hall but to take it into my daily life, for this is where it is most needed. Throughout the day, we can drop into the present moment, feel our sensations, feel our breath coursing through our body, and just allow the body to begin to move. We can follow the movement in subtler ways if that feels more appropriate, or we can make the movements bigger. This helps us to connect to the dancelike nature of our daily life experience, and the richness, subtlety, and flow of our embodied being.

NOTES

1. Gyamtso, Khenpo Tsültrim. (1998). Unpublished poem. (Ari Goldfield, Trans.)
2. A founder of the Kagyu lineage of Tibetan Buddhism, Milarepa (1040–1123) is revered for having persevered through terrible hardship and austerity on his journey to enlightenment. He is famous for his many songs about his experiences and realization.
3. Gyamtso, Khenpo Tsültrim. (2009). Unpublished poem. In possession of Rose Taylor Goldfield.
4. Lodro Thaye, J. *Phyag rgya chen po'i rdo rje'i mgur* [Song of Mahamudra]. (Ari Goldfield, Trans.)
5. Adamantine or indestructible.
6. "Great Seal." A profound set of instructions that describe the true nature of reality as clarity-emptiness or bliss-emptiness, and how to meditate upon this true nature. The key Mahamudra meditation instruction is given by the bodhisattva Maitreya in *The Treatise on Buddha Nature* (quoted below in my chapter).
7. Gyamtso, Khenpo Tsültrim. (2005.) Unpublished poem. In possession of Ari Goldfield.

8. Joseph Campbell, *The Hero with a Thousand Faces* (Novato: New World Library, 2008), 32.

9. Disciple of Lingchen Repa Pema Dorje, 1161–1211.

10. Khenpo Tsültrim Gyamtso, unpublished poem (2009). In possession of Ari Goldfield.

11. Quoted in Wangchuk Dorje, lhan cig skyes sbyor gyi zab khrid nges don rgya mtsho'i snying po phrin las 'od 'phro [The Profound Instructions on Connate Union: The Radiant Activity at the Heart of an Ocean of Definitive Meaning]. Translated by Ari Goldfield. Accessed May 6, 2015. www.dharmadownload.net/pages/english/Texts/texts_0051.htm.

12. *Hevajra Tantra*. Translated by Rose Taylor Goldfield. Accessed May 6, 2015. http://tbrc.org/link/?RID=O1PD92753|O1PD927531PD92757$W20866#library_work_Object-O1PD92753|O1PD927531PD92757$W20866.

13. Disciple of Gotsangpa Gonpo Dorje, 1230–1309.

14. Quoted in Dorje.

15. Traleg Kyabgon, "Karma Triyana Dharmachakra," Oral teaching given in Woodstock, New York, November 1989.

16. Maitreya, *theg pa chen po'i rgyud bla ma'i bstan bcos*. [The Treatise on Buddha Nature]. Translated by Ari Goldfield. Accessed May 6, 2015. http://www.dharmadownload.net/pages/english/Texts/texts_0015.htm.

17. Tsang Nyon He-ru-ka, *rnal 'byor gyi dbang phyug chen po mi la ras pa'i rnam mgur* [The Life and Songs of Milarepa, the Great Lord of the Yogis] (1488). Translated by Jim Scott, Accesses February 7, 2015. www.tibet.dk/pktc/tibdtexts.php.

Dance as Dharma Practice in the Twenty-First Century

LALITARĀJA

"The undeniable fact that the Buddha and his enlightened disciples could appreciate and enjoy the beauty of nature and of art, and that they could even add to the sum of that beauty by their own aesthetic activities is, we believe, sufficient proof of our contention that religion and art both are manifestations of the same movement of self-transcendence, and that the genuine devotee and the true artist travel along ultimately convergent paths."

—Sangharakshita[1]

What does it mean to bring a dance practice to the core of an attempt to live a Dharma life? I want to reflect on how I got here, on some of the core teachings that have influenced my path, and how I seek to come into relationship with those teachings in a meaningful way.

As an ordained Buddhist, I am the recipient of the beneficial influences of a great many practitioners, Buddhists and artists alike, and especially those who are both. I am a disciple of Sangharakshita, a Buddhist teacher who, having discovered that he was a Buddhist at age sixteen, subsequently spent more than twenty years in Asia as a monk, studying and becoming friends with a number of Buddhist teachers from Theravada, Tibetan, and Chinese origins. Eventually he returned to the United Kingdom in the mid-sixties and set up an order and movement, which made possible my contact with the Dharma. His own appreciation and practice of the arts encouraged me to explore the Dharma and his teaching more deeply. Even though my direct contact with him has been limited, the impact of his teaching has changed the course of my life to the extent that I eventually joined the Triratna Buddhist Order, an international order that evolved from Sangharakshita's emphasis on living the Dharma life fully.

My dance teachers have had no less of an impact on my life, even though they have not all had the same intentions and their various teachings have come from many different directions. Nonetheless, from my earliest ballet teachers to my more recent teachers of Contact Improvisation, the best of them gave me openings into the same realms as my Buddhist practice.

Finding the Dharma Amidst the Ballet

When I first encountered the Dharma through Sangharakshita's teaching, I was working for Peter Darrell's Scottish Ballet (a fellow dancer in that company took me to my first meditation class), slowly working my way up the ranks and learning my trade as a performer. We did a lot of performing and that is exactly what I wanted. I loved touring. Living out of a suitcase on tour allowed me to have a simpler life than I would allow myself at home, and I found myself easily settling into routines of yoga and meditation before going into the theater each day.

At the Glasgow Buddhist Centre,[2] I found that my dance training had given me a basic foundation in body awareness. This didn't necessarily make meditation easy, but it meant I was able to sit, and that, in turn, seemed to allow me to enjoy the practice even when it wasn't going well. On stage it was the practice of loving kindness that I engaged in most strongly. Preparing to go on stage by cultivating loving kindness to all beings, and then trying to maintain that through a performance, is a delight, and was particularly enjoyable amongst the sequins and baubles of the second act of the Nutcracker! It kept me grounded and provided a large group of people in the audience to send my *metta* (loving kindness) to. Cultivating a sense of being less self-centered also deepened my understanding of how to be in an ensemble. In a company of forty dancers, my circle of friends increased from a half dozen to just about all of them.

However, in my heart of hearts I knew that ballet wasn't for me; the romantic sensibility didn't sit with my values and tastes. I had loved my time at Scottish Ballet, but if my practice of this art form was going to connect with my Buddhist life, then I needed to practice in a way that came closer to expressing my values.

There followed some years of experimenting with other kinds of dance, working with single choreographer companies and touring the world, eventually being introduced to somatics and taking up improvisation and Contact Improvisation. Settling into improvisation as my core practice coincided with my requesting ordination into the Triratna Buddhist Order, and between these two streams in my life a whole new phase opened up.

Dance and "the Religion of Art"

In London I met members of the order who were committed artists and I was introduced to *The Religion of Art*, a small book of essays written by Sangharakshita in the 1950s. In it I found affirmation that I could practice this path fully without dropping the artist in me. Some of the statements I found incredibly inspiring, such as "Every genuine work of art enlarges the circle of our consciousness"[3]; "Religion and art are manifestations of the same movement of self-transcendence"[4]; and "The religion of art may therefore be defined as conscious surrender to the Beautiful … as a means of breaking up established egocentric patterns of behavior and protracting one's experience along the line of egolessness into the starry depths of reality."[5]

I felt a certain amount of tension, though, with the presentation of some of Sangharakshita's ideas about art. He uses a lot of examples from poetry (he is a poet after all) and that is not an art form I'd investigated in any depth, except by playing Patti Smith's *Horses* album over and over again. There is also an emphasis on refinement and beauty that, having grown up on the punk rock of the 1970s, sounded somewhat too conservative to my mind. His definition of art as "the organisation of sensuous impressions into pleasurable formal relations that express the artist's sensibility and communicate to his audience a sense of values that can transform their lives"[6] aroused both inspiration and resistance. I gravitated toward the sense of connection and communication and possibilities of transcendence, but felt distant from the language of "pleasurable formal relations" as notions of "mere" beauty.

I have seen a lot of choreography that was "merely" beautiful. Some choreographers appear to become intoxicated with having beautiful dancers to work with. Some seem to simply produce and re-produce beautiful but empty spectacle. I wanted more than this kind of beauty, more than "pleasurable formal relations." I wanted to engage my ethical and artistic sensibilities in a creative path that could support and express my Dharma practice, ideally offering a vehicle for exploring the overlap between them that could become the working ground for my practice.

In encountering improvisation and Contact Improvisation, I found that both require a strong present moment engagement. Performing real time composition requires a deep and broad awareness of what is happening in the performance while at the same time being very relaxed and open. The fact that these sound like meditation instructions strikes me as more than a coincidence. I felt that dance and meditation were coming much closer together as practices and becoming much more mutually supportive.

Contact Improvisation eventually worked its way into the heart of my movement practice. There are many reasons for this, ranging from the strong *sangha*-like community that has formed around this modality to the meditative practices within it, like the "small dance." I saw Steve Paxton (Contact Improvisation founder) as putting the body into a state of inquiry. This represented a fundamental shift in my dancing, a shift from aesthetic concerns into functionality. Describing the dance, Paxton says:

> At first, there seemed to be only two options—trying to follow the flow of communication or resisting it. Each dance is a series of on-the-spot decisions. And they are on the spot. The soft skin is alert to the points of contact, signals telling the dancers where they are, orienting them to their partner and the floor.
> Their perceptions are stretching. They are adrenalized. Inside their minds, the many touch events and constantly changing relationships blend into a continuity of moving masses which creates a logic reached only in the heat of the dance. A logic as secure as that found when standing alone and watching the reflexive dance of one's bones.[7]

I had been aware of the Buddhist teacher Chögyam Trungpa Rinpoche through some of his books, and as I found out more about improvisation, I became aware of his Naropa Institute and his encouragement of the arts and artists within that program. Notably, I read about the work of Barbara Dilley, a member of the Grand Union dance improvisation group. It was through Dilley that many of the first generation of contact improvisers had come to teach at Naropa. I never had the opportunity to study with Dilley, but once I was introduced to her Contemplative Dance Practice[8] it became another core element in my movement practice for many years.

I continued to seek out the kind of work that would fit with my practice. I performed for various choreographers such as Laurie Booth, Yolande Snaith, and Fin Walker in both set and improvised work, and also started to make my own choreographic contributions. I even performed the night before I left for the four-month retreat on which I was ordained into the Triratna Buddhist Order.

Unraveling Post-Ordination

Coming back from that retreat, I tried to carry on as normal. I went back to choreographing but I wasn't the same. I had taken some big strides forward in my Dharma practice but there were parts of me—both as a Dharma practitioner and as an artist—that needed to catch up. I created improvised work that I'm still proud of, but all my efforts to make set choreography seemed to come out wrong. As I entered my forties with the choreographic endeavours not working out as I hoped, combined with two close bereavements and the end of a relationship, I went through something of a mid-life crisis.

It was a painful time, but I had a clear sense of what was happening to me. I felt that it was imperative to treat this as an opportunity to deepen my Dharma practice. I felt that I needed to have this experience, and have it fully, in order to learn from it—and believe that I did just that. By the end, I felt that I had sufficiently caught up with those parts of myself that had got left behind or put to one side in the course of my life. I don't think I had much choice—these parts were insisting!

In meditation, in the studio, in all areas of my life, I was being called to a deeper authenticity. The call had come from the retreat but it took time to hear, and more time to respond. I embarked on integrating psychological material that had been around most of my life. I worked on my own in meditation and in the studio, as well as with a therapist. As a result, I was coming into a different relationship with pain and difficulty and gained some clues as to how I could move into the next stage of my life.

As things began to calm down, I decided to do a masters program in choreography. When I left school at age sixteen, I had no interest in studying. Now I found myself exhilarated by it. I read a lot, I watched a lot, and I discovered that I could enjoy writing. It was a time to reflect as well as study, and I tried to get some sense of how to move forward. I wrestled with the question of what kind of work to make. I created a variety of dance, I wrote essays, and I tried to think my way to a conclusion. Ultimately, I found myself wanting to articulate something about my attempts to live a Dharma life as a dance artist.

From Mere Beauty to the Egoless Sublime

I was still wrestling with ideas about beauty as an aesthetic value to work towards. In contemporary culture, beauty has become a cliché, whilst the means of its production have become commoditized and shifted away from the fine arts and into mass culture. I reflected a lot on Yvonne Rainer's text "No Manifesto." It begins with "No to spectacle, no to virtuosity…."[9] This set up a creative tension in me. On the one hand, I felt that I had enough of superficial spectacle that had little to say, but on the other, I had spent many years training in technique and developing particular skills to develop virtuosity. I became interested in the idea of a virtuosity of simplicity. I allowed myself to disagree with some of Rainer's clauses while resonating strongly with others. In a similar vein, there was Guy Debord's *Society of the Spectacle*, which spoke to me of the alienation in our culture from real communication and authenticity. Debord quotes Feurbach: "But for the present age, which prefers the sign to the thing signified, the copy to the original, representation to reality, appearance to essence … truth is considered profane, and only illusion is sacred."[10] It seemed that there was an overlap between Rainer and Debord that spoke to the need for authenticity, an authenticity that would not be achieved by shouting louder, jumping higher, or dazzling the audience in other ways.

In seeking a more relevant model of aesthetics to aspire to, I turned towards the potential of the sublime—the magnificent, awe inspiring, and boundless sublime that is beyond the reach of our conceptual readings, and in which the multiplicity and inherent instability of the world can be approached. Perhaps in the awe and wonder invoked by the sublime, there lay a more direct path to waking up to the reality of things. I had been recommended Susan Broadhurst's *Liminal Acts*, in which she writes of the emergence of a "liminal theatre" and presents Lyotard's conception of the sublime in a way that would allow for "the unrepresentable in presentation itself."[11]

I felt that in the sublime, there is an encounter on some level with the fact that we are each a small moving nexus point in an infinite and complex network of causes and conditions. For me, seeing the world in this way echoes the Buddhist notion of Right View, or Perfect Vision, the first step on the Buddha's Eightfold Path, which is sometimes characterized as understanding that everything is impermanent, lacking in self-hood, and essentially unsatisfactory.

But this doesn't really do it justice. For many people who take up Dharma practice, it's not just an understanding. "It is a *vision*, and as such something direct and immediate, and more of the nature of spiritual experience than an intellectual understanding."[12]

In dancing Contact Improvisation, a deeper connection with others is always available and one is focusing on a perceptual field that is always changing. For me, being ready for connection and ready for change in this way can be an expression of Right View. To turn vision into transformation, one must attend fully to that vision in the dance. Mindfulness must be engaged in point-of-contact connectivity, as well as the constantly changing subject-to-subject relationship. Beyond mindfulness of the body, mindfulness of connectivity and change can open up an immediate experience of impermanence and lack of being a separate self. All this requires attending to a broader field of experience. In surrendering fully to the awe inspiring, constantly shifting complexities of connecting with another being in the contact dance, I can find glimpses into the transformative possibilities of the sublime dance.

In this period, I changed the way that I approached making work. Letting go of the rules somehow allowed me to be more simple and direct. I had a tendency to overthink things, and in attempting to direct myself toward the sublime I needed to let go, to drop into a bigger perspective where it seemed important to do less. I sought a middle way between improvised and set work by improvising with a much stronger score than I had used in the past. I borrowed from Deborah Hay[13] the idea that a score is a practice, not just a set of instructions. In the process, I felt that something of Sangharakshita's teaching on egolessness was starting to come into play.

I went back to *The Religion of Art* and some key themes struck me more forcibly than before. In defining the terms he will use, Sangharakshita says of religion, "The truly religious life is the life of egolessness; and genuinely religious beliefs and practices are those by which the realisation of egolessness can be achieved."[14] In framing his use of the word ego he says, "The ego does not really exist; it is not a thing but a thought; not a metaphysical entity but an epistemological error."[15] Later, he develops this theme: "Religious art is that kind of poetry, music, or any other species of art, which conduces to the experience of egolessness."[16]

The Religion of Art also goes much further than "mere beauty" in its conception.

Lalitarāja dancing in "We don't know…" Conceived and performed by Anna Jussilainen and Lalitarāja at the Michaelis Theatre, University of Roehampton, March 2013. Photograph by Eulanda Shead.

Invoking the ancient Indian poets he says, "The essential quality of Beauty is that it remains from moment to moment ever new."[17] He proposes an "Absolute Beauty ... whose demands upon us are inexhaustible, which never allows us to rest in any perfection, and which even beyond what seems to us the highest transformation calls for another higher still."[18] The work that I was making was less conventionally beautiful, but was certainly new each time it was performed.

Taking the Work Forward

After finishing my masters program, I continued to perform dance for others for a few years while also spending time in the studio on my own trying to discern my artistic direction. One thing was clear—I had lost the stomach for writing funding applications. Trying to be an independent artist requires getting support in order to pay dancers, and I always had the feeling that I was trying to justify my existence on paper. Perhaps there were other ways to keep making work and to support myself and my dancers without relying on public subsidy.

In the meantime, I took a job in the Dance Department at Roehampton University, and happily I'm still there! I'm lucky to be part of a wonderful team and to develop my teaching practice while continuing to make and perform work as I am inclined. Importantly, I feel able to continue to blend Dharma and dance into a coherent path for myself.

Contact Improvisation is the dominant form in my current practice. In teaching Contact, I'm struck by what it offers students in terms of broad life lessons—in presence, connection, trust, confidence, and ability to take risks (on top of whatever dance skills they may cultivate). My own relationship to the form is, I hope, maturing, and I am finding the opportunities for making it more a part of my path.

In thinking about the transformative possibilities of the sublime dance of Contact, I find a resonance with classical models of *vipassanna*, or insight meditation, where it is recommended to first develop *samatha,* or calm abiding, to the point that one can engage with the penetrative seeing that is *vipassanna*. In becoming absorbed (or finding a calm abiding) in the dance, there is less "I" and "me" invested in how it might look or how spectacular the dancing might be. In this state, I am with my experience as a flow in a way that is very similar to sitting on a cushion and being with the flow of experience. In both *vipassana* practice and contact dance, experience is constantly arising and passing away, with no fixed self to grasp at it, exposing the lie of the "epistemological error" that is the ego project.[19]

My personal Dharma practice has always tended to revolve around meditation, and this continues. In the midst of a busy life I remain stubborn about meditating every day. Even if done briefly, my daily sit is an affirmation of the importance of practice. I continue to contribute as much as I can to my local Buddhist center. One way or another, I've been involved in supporting, and then leading, classes for twenty-five years. On the one hand, it's great to be able to share and give back to the community, and on the other, I continue to learn humility from the folks that come along. They always seem so grateful, yet I feel that I am learning as much as them in the exchange.

Some years ago I was in a workshop session for Contact teachers with Martin Keogh, exploring what our subtext for our teaching was—what were we always teaching, no matter what the content of the class was. At the time I articulated that I was always teaching awareness—whether in the dance studio or at the Buddhist center, this seemed to hold true. I've found it helpful over the years to keep track of how this changes. My current version, which emerged in dialogue with students who were seeking to understand where I was coming from, runs something like, "I'm trying help you focus on getting good at being who you really are," and then I say, "you may as well get started, it's a lifetime's work."

NOTES

1. Sangharakshita, *The Religion of Art* (Glasgow: Windhorse, 1998), 52.
2. At the time the Glasgow Buddhist Centre was part of the friends of the Western Buddhist Order, now renamed the Triratna Buddhist Order to reflect the international nature of the movement.
3. Sangharakshita, *Religion of Art,* 35.
4. Sangharakshita, *Religion of Art,* 52.
5. Sangharakshita, *Religion of Art,* 93.
6. Sangharakshita, *Religion of Art,* 84.
7. Steve Paxton, "Fall after Newton," in *Contact Quarterly Omnibus*, ed. Nancy Stark Smith and Lisa Nelson (Northhampton: Contact Editions, 1997), 143.
8. The contemplative dance score consists of equal periods of sitting meditation, warming up, a period of open dancing, and finishing with a short sitting meditation.
9. Yvonne Rainer, "A Quasi Survey of Some 'Minimalist' Tendencies in the Quantitatively Minimal Dance Activity Midst the Plethora, or an Analysis of Trio A," in *Twenteith Century Performance Reader*, ed. Michael Huxley and Noel Witts (London: Routledge, 1996), 293–294.
10. Guy Debord, *The Society of the Spectacle*, trans. Black and Red. 1967. Accessed April 8, 2015. http://library.nothingness.org/articles/SI/en/display/16.
11. Susan Broadhurst, *Liminal Acts: A Critical Overview of Contemporary Performance and Theory* (London: Cassell, 1999), 60.
12. Sangharakshita, *The Buddha's Noble Eightfold Path* (Glasgow: Windhorse Publications, 1990) 14. Accessed April 9, 2015. http://www.sangharakshita.org/_books/Noble_Eightfold_Path.pdf.
13. See Deborah Hay, *My Body the Buddhist* (Hanover: Wesleyan University Press, 2000).
14. Sangharakshita, *Religion of Art,* 80.
15. Sangharakshita, *Religion of Art,* 85.
16. Sangharakshita, *Religion of Art,* 81.
17. Sangharakshita, *Religion of Art,* 94.
18. Sangharakshita, *Religion of Art,* 94.
19. Sangharakshita, *Religion of Art,* 81.

Contemplative Dance Practice
A Dancer's Meditation Hall,
a Meditator's Dance Hall[1]

Barbara Dilley

In 1978, at Sacred Heart School on Fourteenth Street in Boulder, Colorado, Chögyam Trungpa Rinpoche teaches Dharma Art. He says that Dharma Art isn't about Buddhist iconography but rather it is an art that "springs from a meditative state of mind." My longing to bring meditation and dancing closer together is stirred. For me, Buddhadharma illuminates the mind body process like nothing else. The vocabulary of mindfulness/awareness feels like a natural connection, but I'm not sure how to proceed.

Contemplative

In the Buddhist teachings, the practice of contemplation is often associated with the three *prajnas*—hearing, contemplating, and meditating. *Prajna* is "best knowing," that deep, expansive awareness giving rise to insight into the way the world works and compassion for oneself and others. The three *prajnas* are active and, like a mobius strip, they circulate in and around one another. They move across many layers of awareness within the singularity of an experience. This experience of many layers is rich to me. First we hear about the way mind body works, then we reflect on what we have heard and explore our experiences, and, along the way, we practice meditation within this field of attention created by hearing and contemplating. It is intimate.

My favorite Western definition of contemplation is garnered from several dictionaries.

Contemplation: L. *contemplari*, to observe, consider, to gaze attentively; *con-templum*, an open space for observation marked out by an auger with his staff,
a temple; akin to the Greek "temenos," sacred precinct.
contemplatio, surveying.
Contemplation: to think about intently, to consider; to meditate on, to study, to ponder.
Contemplative: given to contemplation or the continued application of the mind to a subject; thoughtful.[2]

My eye catches the phrase "open space for observation." This is what I experience in meditation halls when I sit together with others, breathing and watching our minds rise and fall, then walking together, feeling the sole of each foot touch the floor. This is the most expansive place of observation and I return again and again.

> MEMORY: During a meditation retreat, I look forward to walking meditation. The instructions are simple: Bring attention to each foot as it touches the floor—heel, then sole, now toes. Notice thinking, and then come back to the lift, swing of leg, placement of foot. Within this repetition and simplicity, I drop into layers of movement studies visualizations. (Is this entertainment?) In my mind's eye I see bones and lungs and the roof of my mouth. As I make my way around the meditation hall, I see gravity falling down the back.
>
> (breathe, swing, step)
> head floating like a balloon on a string
> (breathe, swing, step)
> energy flowing up the front
> (breathe, swing, step)
> tail bone dropping toward the center of earth
> (breathe, swing, step)
> root of the tongue softening
> (breathe, swing, step)

Synchronizing Body and Mind

In the Dharma Art teachings, Trungpa Rinpoche speaks of synchronizing body and mind. The weaving together of body sensations and thoughts underlies these early experiences of sitting and walking meditation. Rinpoche describes this process as noticing that our mind is too long and body too short. It is so poetic and I recognize what he is expressing right away. It is a disconcerting sensation, to say the least. Also, I know moments when body mind arrive together, right here, right now. Breathing and moving and thinking are somehow in the same space of awareness, but I only know this when it is gone. The image of body mind synchronized, of finding this in our kinesthesia and losing it and finding it again, is a central view of Contemplative Dance Practice.

A Dancer's Meditation Hall

After teaching during the first summer of Naropa in 1974, Trungpa Rinpoche invites me to come and create a dance program. Because Naropa University is a place of contemplative learning, I wonder about how to shape a student's journey with just enough experience of the view and practice of meditation. Contemplative Dance Practice evolves after the Dharma Art teachings and grows from my ongoing meditation practice and study. It invites students to find a personal view of body mind through direct experience.

Contemplative Dance Practice is a dancer's meditation hall and also a meditator's dance hall! The form is adapted from *nyinthuns,* a Tibetan Buddhist day-long group meditation practice. When we first did the practice, it lasted for three hours because *nyinthun* sessions last this long.

During a summer session at Naropa in 1980, Contemplative Dance Practice (CDP) was offered for the first time. It was part of a four-week curriculum mingling "American contemporary dance training with meditation practice." During each week, participants took classes in technique, improvisation, and experiential anatomy. We explored meditation together and attended a weekend of Shambhala Training meditation created by Naropa's founder, Trungpa Rinpoche. On Wednesday mornings we gathered for three hours of CDP. Alone and together, using everything we were learning and what we already knew, we explored body mind, first on the cushion and then in the middle of the space.

The inner monologue might sound like this: *What are thoughts? Are my thoughts different when I practice meditation? Are they different when I move and stretch and feel?* Sometimes we find a sensation of Nowness that we learned about in the Shambhala teachings. *Can I think about the past and be in the moment?*

The practice seems to nurture us in a simple, open way. It supports our artist-being, our lives as teachers, therapists, students, parents, and friends. Everyone wants to keep practicing. *What is a meditative state of mind? Is it a state I fail to find? Is it part of experience because I sit? How do I feel after sitting for thirty minutes? When I move out onto the floor what changes?*

Zen Mind, Beginner's Mind

Suzuki Roshi's book, *Zen Mind, Beginner's Mind*, informs my learning about meditation. I take the book with me on a solo retreat. His wry wit, deep and surprising with wonderful poetic metaphors, sustains my days of solitude. His instructions give me encouragement. In meditation my inner thoughts are strong: *I am sad but I don't know why. Wait, where did that feeling go?*

Over the years, a quote from this book becomes part of a handout for Contemplative Dance Practice. In summer CDP sessions I use his phrase, *Not Two/Not One*, as the title.

> This is the most important teaching;
> not two and not one.
> Our body and mind are not two and not one.
> If you think your body and mind are two that is wrong;
> if you think they are one, that is also wrong.
> Our body and mind are both two and one.[3]

The Zen Buddhist form of placing meditation cushions close to the wall and facing the wall influences the way I set up the room. Because we move from the cushion into the room, we face toward the middle of the room. CDP needs a nice, open space the way meditation halls are spacious and dance studios have room to lie down on the floor. It's good to have not only cushions, but also chairs or perhaps a bench, so everyone can sit together with ease.

The Practice

Each practice session has five parts: Introduction, Sitting Practice, Personal Awareness Practice, Open Space, and Closing Circle. A small bell marks beginnings and endings of the sections. Perhaps there is a little table for a simple shrine of candles, flowers, possibly incense.

I. Introduction

Sitting together in a circle we say our names, especially if people don't know one another, and share something about why we are here. I speak a bit about the practice we will do, then invite everyone to find a seat along the edges of the room. We use meditation cushions if they are available, or blankets, pillows, yoga blocks, even chairs.

II. Sitting Practice

I give simple instructions: an upright, relaxed posture, noticing sensation of breath moving, and letting thoughts come and go. I invite people to find micro-movements in the posture, those smallest of sensations because of breath and heartbeat and the settling of bones under gravity. After about 20–30 minutes, I announce "Personal Awareness Practice."

III. Personal Awareness Practice

In Personal Awareness Practice, the invitation is to explore how to bring meditation awareness into movement. I encourage stretching out from the sitting posture and then moving out into the room. Often the instruction is to listen for the voice of body mind, and to use everything you already know. It's a time for self-care, research, and courting the unexpected. I encourage "kinesthetic delight," that felt sense of simple goodness in being alive. Inner thoughts may be something like this: *What does "not two and not one" mean? I could stay here on the floor like this for a long time. Am I supposed to move around?* Near the end of this section, I call people back to their spot for a short moment or two of sitting meditation then announce "Open Space."

IV. Open Space

In Open Space, everyone begins sitting and then enters or exits as they choose. It is an open time, an invitation to host this body mind moment as a guest and to play with others who also enter. Open Space holds each of us just as we are. It's a big moment to decide to enter. Fear arrives in its many guises. We may be alone out there with everyone watching. It is rigorous because awareness keeps shifting between inner and outer noticing. Sometimes the space is empty for a while. Sometimes everyone decides to come in! Who knows what will happen? There are two rules: take responsibility for personal experience and don't cause harm. We discuss this in the ending circle. Thoughts we have may be something like this: *What changes when I move out into Open Space with others? What do I do when someone touches my arm? Do I have to respond? I want to go back to my cushion.*

Sitting around the edge of the room, I invite everyone to become a Well-Wisher and On-Looker. There is enjoyment of the presence of others and the room and the light. There is no judgment or comparison, only appreciation and curiosity. Often people bring notebooks and write about wonder and sorrow. I always encourage resting. At the end of this time there is another short period of Sitting Meditation Practice.

V. Closing Circle and Conversation/Discussion

As we sit together I invite comments and discussion. I suggest that we speak from two places—"what I experienced" and "what I saw." Sometimes there is a lot to say and sometimes not much. Then there are announcements of the next session and perhaps an ending bow.

Variations

Over the years, CDP has developed many variations. I have encouraged everyone to adapt the form to fit the place and time and particularly the folks who show up. There

Contemplative Dance Practice retreat with Merian Soto, Polly Motley and Lisa Kraus, SILO at Kirkland Farm, Pennsylvania, 2013. Photograph by Asimina Chremos.

is the original three-hour session, a two-hour practice, and a one-hour form. The one-hour CDP is affectionately called TwentyTwentyTwenty—twenty minutes sitting/twen minutes Personal Awareness Practice/twenty minutes Open Space. It is often used t start a day of classes or before a rehearsal.

There is another variation called Sanctuary. It lasts about a half hour and sittin, meditation is optional. Sanctuary practice mingles personal movement time with Oper Space and often includes a sound environment. We start in a circle, bow in, and someone agrees to track the time by calling "middle" and "finding an ending." Sometimes structures for improvisation like a Grid are called into the room. Sometimes I coach various approaches to movement research. Sometimes I read a poem or text about awareness, about being human.

There are day-long retreats with CDP in the mornings, then afternoons engaged in various approaches to improvisation and composition. Sometimes at the end there are offerings of solos, duets, and group scores in celebration of the time together.

CDP practice has evolved over the years in an organic and heartfelt way. I love receiving another announcement of a group forming. I encourage leaders to trust themselves and follow their longing and delights. CDP is a simple practice: sitting to enter the silence, then personal moving to integrate body mind in the moment, and finally sharing these moments together in Open Space.

NOTES

1. Based, with permission, on parts of Barbara Dilley's *This Very Moment: Teaching Thinking Dancing* (Boulder: Naropa University Press, 2015).

2. *Merriam-Webster Dictionary*, 1998. *Oxford English Dictionary*, Volume II, C. Oxford University Press, 1978.

3. Shunryu Suzuki, *Zen Mind, Beginner's Mind* (New York & Tokyo: Weatherhill, 1975), 25.

Zenful Dance
Breath Movement Meditation

Leah Joy Malberg

Bringing Zen to the Dance Floor

In an effort to find balance at a time when I was searching for meaning in my life, I began playing around with a practice that combined breath and movement. This idea first arose one day during my daily seated meditation practice. I remember chuckling to myself while seated at home on my cushion and thinking, "How ironic! This idea has come to me as I'm sitting here practicing letting go of my thoughts … ha!" In 2006, I came up with the name Zenful Dance to reflect this emerging combination of my then-somewhat established Soto-Zen Buddhist meditation practice and my 20-plus years as a dancer/choreographer/teacher.

I began dancing at the age of three, and dance defined me from this early age onward. I was a classically trained ballet dancer without a ballet dancer's body. Heartbroken at the dim prospects of becoming a professional ballerina, but determined to find a place to call home, at sixteen I left ballet to explore jazz, Congolese, hip hop, Samba, Israeli Folk, belly dance, and eventually ballroom dancing. My dad strongly suggested I major in something other than Dance, and so I majored in Business Administration. I also did a minor in Dance, studying at the College of Marin and then San Jose State University's Ballroom Dance Club. During this time I completed my ballroom dance teaching certification at the Fred Astaire Dance Studio in Santa Clara, California.

With this training under my belt, I launched Dance4Life Productions (later, the LJM Agency) a dance and music performance/education contracting company. Over the next thirteen years, this career took me to places like the Silicon Valley campuses of Applied Materials, Novell, NASA, and Cisco Systems. In 1998, I traveled to Harare, Zimbabwe, and helped organize an exchange program with Clayton Ndlovu (Zimbabwe College of Music) and Irene Chigamba (National Ballet of Zimbabwe/Mhembero Dance Troupe), teaching American style ballroom dance to its corps de ballet in exchange for training in traditional Zimbabwean folk dance. These relationships later helped me to launch programming for both San Jose and Emeryville, California, Unified School Districts to provide dance education to elementary and secondary school children in over 15 different dance styles. Amidst these larger collaborations, I also maintained a full schedule of teaching (both private lessons and workshops) and performing throughout the United States.

Several years into what many would define as a successful dance career, I felt like something was missing. I knew I was providing a great service of dance entertainment, recreation, exercise, and education, but I felt a lack of fulfillment in my work. It was at this point that I knew a shift was necessary in order to keep my passion moving forward.

A friend at the time had introduced me to Zen meditation at the Tassajara Zen Mountain Center in Marin, California. The practice of *zazen* had an incredible impact on my life. It opened my mind up to the belief that thoughts are just things, and that amidst the (small or monkey) changing mind that assigns certain levels of importance to thoughts I hold and decides when I let go, what is more substantial is the breath. I found this notion profound—when I stripped away all thought, only the breath remained and this breath connects with the breath of all other living things.

I continued my practice at the Berkeley Zen Center and the Sonoma Mountain Zen Center. After a while I began integrating the practice of Zen into my work. This quickly brought my teaching experience to a new level. Being present with the breath was a huge "aha" moment for me. All the expectations I had layered on top of what dance should and should not have been began to peel away. For the first time since I was a kid, dance was all those things I remembered it being: beautiful, non-judgmental, safe, charismatic. Whatever it was in the moment, it was exactly right. The students noticed a difference in my teaching style right away. It was as if, overnight, my job as a dance teacher was elevated back into a passion. It was less about the end goal (i.e., technique, performance, competition) and more about the exploration of oneself through breath movement. My students were most present when they connected their breath to the dance.

From Dancing with Zen to Zenful Dance

In 2007, I suffered a neck injury which prevented me from continuing a professional dance career. I nonetheless continued my work with Zenful Dance, as it was a physically gentle practice that encouraged self-acceptance. I sensed there was important work to be done through this vehicle.

Zenful Dance is a breath movement meditation practice based on the *Anapanasati Sutta*, a teaching the Buddha gave focused on awareness of breath flow. *Anapanasati* has been described as "one of the most universally-applicable methods of cultivating mental concentration,"[1] and is practiced by bringing attention to the breath, without need to breathe in any certain way. "This, unlike the Yogic systems, does not call for any interference with the normal breathing, the breath being merely used as a point on which to fix the attention, at the tip of the nostrils."[2] In Zenful Dance, such awareness of the breath, combined with basic movement, is used to accentuate or create a visual extension of the natural breath, so that the qualities (i.e., natural inconsistencies or unevenness) of each breath are clearly apparent to the practitioner. The practitioner can then begin to build upon the foundation of mindfulness though breath movement.

Zenful Dance is practiced in three sections: alone, with a partner, and then in a group. In total, there are seven parts of Zenful Dance: the first five parts, done alone, are Breath Watching, *Zazen* (seated meditation), Stand, *Kinhin* (walking meditation), and Dance. Part six is the Dance in partnership, and part seven, the Dance in a group, is practiced in a circle formation. In addition, it is important to note that the seven parts of Zenful Dance are aligned with the *Anapanasati* Seven Factors of Enlightenment, as shown by this table:

3 Sections of Zenful Dance	7 Parts of Zenful Dance Breath Movement Meditation	Anapanasati 7 Factors of Enlightenment (terms written in Pali with English translations)
Section One: Alone	1. Breath Watching	1. *Sati* (mindfulness)
	2. *Zazen* (seated meditation)	2. *Dhamma vicaya* (dharma or analysis)
	3. Stand	3. *Viriya* (persistence)
	4. *Kinhin* (walking meditation)	4. *Piti* (rapture)
	5. Dance	5. *Passaddhi* (serenity)
Section Two: Partnership	6. Dance with a partner	6. *Samadhi* (concentration)
Section Three: Group	7. Dance in a group	7. *Upekkha* (equanimity or letting go)

The Seven Factors of Zenful Dance

The seven parts of Zenful Dance are aligned with the *Anapanasati* Seven Factors of Enlightenment. The first part, Breath Watching, is aligned with mindfulness, or *sati*, as described in the Pali Canon. Mindfulness is the foundation of most meditation practices and breath watching cannot be performed without it. The second part is *Zazen*, seated meditation aligned with Dharma, the analysis of the nature of all things. I love that *Zazen* offers an opportunity to sit completely still while being mindful of all things, both outside the body and inside. Through such analysis, practitioners can begin to see the body's nature as part of a much larger whole. The third part is Standing and is aligned with persistence, or *viriya*. Standing meditation requires balance and persistent concentration. When standing, practitioners are mindful of both the outside environment and sensations inside the body. The fourth part is *Kinhin*—walking meditation—and is connected with rapture, or *piti*. This is the first part of Zenful Dance in which practitioners move about the floor, and there is joy and freedom in that.

The fifth part is Dance alone, which is aligned with *passaddhi*, or serenity. I present four basic movements, and invite practitioners to attune the pace of these movements with the rhythm of their breath. This part provides practitioners the first opportunity to really sense a physical extension of their breath through movement. It brings a quiet realization (and some humor) of how to accept oneself for who we are and who we are not, and this can provide a sense of calm and peace. The sixth part is Dance with a partner and is aligned with *samadhi*, or concentration. Practitioners pair up and perform one of the four movements while facing one another. Since the task is to continue to follow one's own breath as the leader for the movement, it requires concentration not to get too caught up in the tempo of the partner's breath. I love this part because it teaches empathy without codependency. As in life, sometimes we are in sync and often we are not, but we can coexist peacefully through the breath. The seventh part is Dance in a group, which is aligned with *upekkha*, or equanimity. This final part teaches the ultimate practice in letting go. The group forms a circle, with everyone dancing one of the four movements. With many others dancing in full view, practitioners experience their lack of control over the movements around them, and continue to focus on their own breath to set the pace for their movement.

Leah Joy Malberg (far left) leading a group in Zenful Dance on a rooftop in Astoria, New York, with view of the Queensboro Bridge in the background, July 2014. Participants from left to right: Jeff Taylor, Paul Bacher, Kelly Doherty and Valerie Gurka. Photograph by Chris Marksbury, CM Photos.

Breathing Zenful Dance into an Expanding Sangha

The Zenful Dance curriculum and structure has changed over the years through trial and error, and the journey has been truly awesome so far! I offered Zenful Lunch, a 30-minute class with tea and fresh fruit, weekly over the course of many months to the corporate community of Englewood, New Jersey, in an effort to provide meditation services to busy professionals on their lunch hour. I also taught hour-long classes at no charge on the weekends to folks in Manhattan looking to try out breath movement meditation for the first time. I have led a two-hour format throughout California and northern New Jersey for students looking for an intensive practice allowing more time to breathe through each of the seven parts of Zenful Dance. Students Buddhist and non-Buddhist, male and female, and of all ages have come to practice Zenful Dance. Over the years, I've held classes in dance studios, Zen centers, yoga studios, and wellness centers, and even outdoors, weather permitting of course.

The purpose of Zenful Dance is to bring about self-awareness, joy, dedication, compassion, empathy, peaceful resolution, and ultimately, the release of oneself from suffering. It has brought many honest and inspirational discoveries over the years and has enabled both peace of mind and a gentle certainty that connects us all to our communities and ourselves. I have seen numerous students' faces leave lighter and their bodies breathe easier. I have witnessed dropped levels of stress in my own body and mind that are much more sustainable throughout the day.

I often ask my students for feedback on their experiences and would like to end by sharing a couple here.

"Time slowed down. I was present and it felt wonderful! Thanks for creating such a peaceful space to be mindful."—Zenful Dance student, 2014

"Leah Joy, your mediation dance class was very refreshing. My breath calmed my movements and thoughts. What a great intro to meditation for busy New Yorkers!"—Zenful Dance beginner, 2014

NOTES

1. Francis Story, *Dimensions of Buddhist Thought: Collected Essays* (Sri Lanka: Buddhist Publication Society, 1976), 276.

2. Story, 276.

Performance

Co-Creating with Space
Space Is Solid, You Are Empty

Lee Worley

I began my journey as an actress with big ideas about saving the world through theater performance. In 1962 I was fresh out of college, studying at the Neighborhood Playhouse in New York City and dissatisfied, not with acting, but with scripts, scene study, and having to browbeat my scene partners to get some acting from them. For some (in my opinion) unfair reason I was often saddled with apathetic fellow students not hungry to be brilliant. Thus, when Joe Chaikin, who later founded New York's Open Theater, invited me to visit a workshop where he and some acting students were exploring improvisational forms, I leapt at the opportunity to work with more professional people and innovative ideas.[1]

Eventually my passion for pursuing big ideas led me to Buddhism, or more precisely, to study under the direction of the renowned Tibetan Buddhist meditation master Chögyam Trungpa. In 1972 I received an invitation to attend a theater conference hosted by a group of Trungpa's students, who referred to themselves as the Mudra Group. At the time, I could not have guessed that this funky weeklong Mudra Theater Conference would launch me on a lifelong investigation into how Buddhism and theater could and would mutually inform one another.

In the summer of 1974, a member of the Open Theater who had attended the Mudra conference was at the last minute unable to teach at the Naropa Institute, inviting me to teach in his place. Thanks to this auspicious coincidence and the generosity of my teacher, Chögyam Trungpa, I have spent the last four decades combining my desire for a clearer understanding of the study and practice of Buddhadharma with my love of living performance. This essay traces that journey.

The Open Theater

In the early days of the Open Theater, I participated in an ensemble consciousness that I had been yearning for without having any name for it. While we explored many styles and techniques of acting, I was most influenced by our work to find ways to communicate beyond the "talking heads" approach popular in the theater of the 1950s, an approach that had lingered in acting studio training and on Broadway. In contrast, the exercises of the Open Theater relied on body-centered messages and rhythmic repetition to hold the group's communication together, creating an ability to stop and start as one organism, abruptly falling apart into individual solo riffs, unexpectedly sliding back into unison like a jazz ensemble. Some of the Open Theater workshop exercises led to novel performances, capturing the imaginations of off-off Broadway audiences and other experimental artists.

Decades before the term "physical theater" was coined, the Open Theater sought a body-based performance style. To some audiences, we might have seemed more like dancers than actors, except that Chaikin and other playwrights, such as Jean Claude van Itallie, were intent on shaping meaning through improvisational and scripted forms.[2] Our ensemble experiments—for example, exploring whether a feeling like lust or anger might lurk underneath a character's outer behavior—also made for good entertainment. One of our signature exercises (dubbed "Insides") began with a seemingly innocuous "outer" activity such as a church meeting or visit to the dentist's office, morphing into a physical and vocal "inside" expression of the hopes, fears, desires, or revulsions seething within. Without missing a beat, the ensemble's "insides" ceased, and the outer scene picked up exactly where it had left off.

Though we did not know or use the terms *mindfulness* and *awareness*, the practice of mindful awareness was central to our ensemble work. Twenty years later, the Open Theater was invited to a reunion at Kent State University, where, having lit upon the idea at a party the night before, we played "Insides" during a panel discussion. The ease, harmony, and magic that emerged made the length of time since most of us had seen one another seem improbable.

Origins of the Mudra Theater

As in a family, the child in a company needs to go away in order to discover herself. I remember thinking that although I would probably never have such a wonderful group as the Open Theater to work with again, I needed to find my own approaches. I determined that if I wanted to make theater, I could do it anywhere. In truth, I had fallen in love with northern New Mexico and with being a mother. When my daughter was three months old, I moved to Santa Fe, which at the time was a culturally diverse small town with dirt streets, hot chili, and many newly arrived artists with similar desires to find a more relaxed life.

Still running on the adrenaline of a New York lifestyle, I started a little acting workshop in Santa Fe which had only been together a few months when I received an invitation to participate in the Mudra Theater Conference. The conference proved to be a chaotic mix of novice Buddhists, seasoned avant-garde performers, and an inscrutable host (Chögyam Trungpa), unperturbed by the egos flying around him. Prior to the Boulder conference, the Mudra Group had been reading Trungpa's plays, attempting to pour tea properly, and reciting mantra-style sound creations. The smug professionalism of the theater artists intimidated them, and they complained about the visiting actors' big egos. At the same time, my New York actor friends complained with equal self-righteousness about the rudeness of the Buddhists who didn't understand "art." As the conference progressed, chaos escalated.[3]

Despite, or perhaps because of, the chaos of the conference, new ideas about the possibility of theatrical performance not dependent on personality, talent, cleverness, and special effects arose in me. I began to sense that performance could emerge from the genuine authenticity of its actors and glimpse how theater could illuminate the suffering of humans and the earth and contribute to our mutual healing.

Following the conference, the Mudra Group continued meeting with Trungpa, who introduced a series of physical exercises that Tibetan monks used in preparation for a complex *sadhana* practice. *Sadhana* practice (literally translated as "means of accomplishment") is a Vajrayana Buddhist ritual that uses visualization and recitation as methods. Wearing heavy brocade costumes and headdresses, the sixty-four dancers hold large hand drums and oversized Tibetan *ghantas,* or bells, as they travel in a large circle in this extremely slow-moving twenty-four-hour nonstop dance.[4]

While the preparatory exercises are not athletically challenging, they are mentally and physically rigorous in undermining discursiveness of mind and body, revealing our inability to stay focused on one thing. Until we have a practice like meditation or an alarming task like driving on black ice, thoughts tend to flicker and flutter, appearing and vanishing rapidly, becoming strings of narrative locking us into unawareness.

In 1973, "space" as an elemental force was an unfamiliar idea to the Mudra performers who sometimes responded with hostility to the exercises, fearing annihilation unless they fought it. From time to time, Trungpa visited the group to make corrections or introduce further material. The transcripts of these meetings reveal that while students thought they were working to develop a contemporary Buddhist theater, Trungpa suggested that before they were ready to become stage actors, they needed to "re-member" themselves—to become authentic, integrated human beings.

Teaching Space Awareness

When the Naropa Institute began to offer a year-round curriculum in 1976, I moved to Boulder to start the theater program there. Until I saw Trungpa teaching, I had not imagined that words like *ego* and *space* could be brought to life. However, I found in Buddhism a vocabulary for experience and action that supported and refined my teaching and directing. Through my meditation study and practice, I could see how I and others were undermined by neurosis. Through Mudra practice, I learned that restlessness could be channeled into sound and movement exercises and that attending to the messages of my sense perceptions could serve as an antidote to "monkey mind."

As a teacher and director, I began to use Buddhist concepts and language to communicate with and shape training exercises for professional actors and actors of everyday life. I saw how disturbing emotions—especially passion, aggression, and ignorance—fuel our worldly actions and translate precisely into gestures, such as pulling toward, pushing away, or not noticing. My experience as Trungpa's student confirmed that what I'd learned through ensemble playing was indeed a truth of the human condition.

Although I was consistently practicing the Mudra exercises, I did not immediately incorporate them into my teaching. As with other forms of practice, the benefits began to crop up spontaneously, shifting my understanding of the nature of form and space. Typically, we refer to material objects as form and think of space as the emptiness which contains objects. Visual artists, for example, speak of figure and ground, while poets compose with a consciousness of words (form) and silence (space).

My contemplative approach to performance evolved at a volatile time when the cultural landscape was transforming through a myriad of forces—the use of psychedelic drugs, the moon landings, and photographs revealing the earth suspended in space—extending far beyond the experimental theater community. Not only was our experience of figure and ground shifting, but so was our understanding of inner or psychological space. The colloquial expressions "Give me some space" or "I'm so spaced out" point to these shifts in perspective. In addition, the insights of Western physicists were beginning to inform our understanding that all forms—trees, supermarkets, freeways, and people—are mostly comprised of varying densities of space. Trungpa's slogan, "Space is solid," encapsulates the view that we cannot escape from space.[5]

Before I introduce the Mudra exercises in the section that follows, I invite you to consider your experience of the "intensification" of space in ordinary life; for example, overhearing downstairs neighbors shouting at one another, witnessing a corpse, being asked for your hand in marriage, standing in front of an audience, or gazing at the television as an airplane approaches the Twin Towers. These intense, frightening, and sometimes exhilarating situations are, in themselves, neutral because space is neutral. Trungpa gently suggested that space could be seen as a challenge rather than an enemy.

While reading my descriptions of the Mudra exercises, keep in mind that while practitioners can generate energy for them by recalling intense life situations, the *feeling*, not the story, is important. Space, the element we live in, is not hostile. It can be experienced as a powerful support or as a threat. We are the actors who intensify space.

The Intensification of Space

The initial exercise in Mudra Space Awareness practice is called "Intensification of Space," a practice that starts by asking students to imagine outer space, the space outside our bodies. While lying on their backs in a simple but precise physical form, students are guided to mentally expand their sense of space, stretching their awareness in all directions while maintaining a connection to their passive bodies. The Shadow, a benevolent guide and timekeeper, coaches students to first stretch their minds out into the room, then into the larger space of the building, then outside the building, around the planet and so on, up and down into sky and earth until reaching a sense of vast and deep outer space. Once out there, the Shadow suggests that space is dynamically beginning to return, coming from all directions, approaching slowly, then more quickly, eventually pressing up against the backs of students who, as this power touches them, are instructed to "intensify back." In Mudra practice, the word *intensify* means to physically tighten up to match the *intensity* of the encroaching space. Similarly, the practitioner intensifies the front of the body in relation to the space pressing down from above, and finally space presses against all sides of the body. The physical body becomes as solid as possible.

Initially, students find that they can control some, but not all, of their muscles. The Shadow instructs students to try to intensify evenly so that the physical form remains in the same posture. The arms, for example, which are somewhat stretched out from the body, are not pressed in toward the waist when space presses from the sides because an equal pressure on the inner arm presses back. The mind must continually search for the places in the body that are not engaged or that have slipped from tightness, striving for

Intensification of the Limbs, Shadowed by Evelin Ebinger (standing). Foreground performers from left to right: Sabine Putze, Katja Paping and Alain Guillou, Mudra Space Awareness Retreat, Dechen Choling Retreat Center, France, April 2015. Photograph by Lee Worley.

an impossible "total rigidity." With practice, this tightening goes beyond muscle groups and deepens into an experience of rock-like solidity of space and body.[6]

The practice rekindles mind's natural flexibility by not allowing it to fixate, narrow, or become biased toward particular body parts or spatial directions.[7]

Relaxing into Selfless Space

Having observed neurotic tendencies in Western actors (playing into the audience's desire to laugh, ignoring the audience or the other performers, becoming robotic or a talking head, or forgetting a panoramic awareness of the playing space), Trungpa introduced Mudra Space Awareness practice to cultivate authenticity both on and off stage. This crucial aspect of the Mudra work—using mental and physical effort to examine the origin of ego's development out of the nonduality of *shunyata,* or emptiness—sets the stage for the next aspect of space awareness practice to emerge: relaxation. Trungpa taught that 100% relaxation could only be approached through first tangibly experiencing intensification. After completing the intensification yet maintaining the posture described above, the Shadow instructs students to let go. At this cue, the student releases all mental tension and physical exertion, allowing the body and mind to open back out. As habitual clutching at "me" and "my body" dissolves, an empty but bright spaciousness appears, not unlike the experience that arises after strenuous manual labor or the completion of an all-consuming project.

Without first developing the body awareness that intensification cultivates, we can mistake relaxation for "spacing out" or "flopping" instead of actually removing the tensions that obscure pure awareness. Stretching into extremes and exercising these polarities enhances a performer's capacity for physical and mental imagination, moving toward an extended playing range. With practice, confidence in one's presence is strengthened, along with the ability to remain at ease and sustain one's intended communication under pressure.

Co-Creating with Space: Ensemble, Mudra and Meditation

Ensemble theater relies on a group actually willing to become an ensemble, whereas in choreographed forms, performers need not rely on a strong ensemble consciousness. Each performer knows what she is doing, requiring only simple awareness to cohere. However, improvisational ensemble works toward a sense that the whole is greater than the sum of its parts. Ensemble training must develop a person's flexibility of mind and body and extend her awareness so that she can attend to and interact with the whole (performers, audience, and even the theater space) while maintaining personal presence and integrity. In ensemble training and performance, an ineffable glue of collective awareness must be powerfully present.

Shamatha meditation practice, training the mind to focus on one aspect of experience such as the breath, is a fruitful support for ensemble training. With repetition over time, the practice of *shamatha* slows down torrents of thoughts, opening mind to the immediacy of the living moment. Ensembles that commit to group meditation practice increase the likelihood that at least one member of the group will be calm (if only momentarily), allowing others to tune in to this stability. However, performers are movers, not sitters. Ensemble awareness becomes possible when the performer's undistracted mind can rest calmly even while the body is moving, speaking, and interacting. Whether in movement or text-based work, on stage or in daily life, undistracted minds will remain open to moment-by-moment options and make fresh choices even under pressure.

Adding Mudra Space Awareness training to ensemble and meditation practices creates a firewall against ego and separatism, the hindrances to ensemble play. Mudra intensity is mindfulness on steroids, requiring the practitioner to constantly attend to and increasingly tighten up the physical body. Simultaneously, the Shadow reminds the practitioner of the intensity of space pressing against her, exposing and exploding any notion of "I" separate from everything else. With relaxation, this is even more apparent (and quite scary). With repetition, however, fear dissipates and a sense of wholeness emerges. In this context, ensemble members can take risks, protected within the bounds of benevolent space.

Awareness of inner body space follows naturally from developing awareness of outer space. As the intensity of space presses against all of the body and the solidity grows, practitioners may recognize deeper experiences of intensity and subsequent relaxation moving inside. Not only the muscles but the breath and organs and even the blood and bones begin to respond and come into awareness.

In a Mudra exercise called "Head, Heart, and Chest," the practitioner assumes a kneeling posture and works directly with this inner body space. Entering at the base of the torso, intense space gradually rises to fill the body's inner core, while the arms and legs remain relaxed. In this more fluid approach to intense space, the energy surges upward through chest to head and slowly lifts the body up and forward. While beginning students often struggle to experience their insides, with practice they are astounded at their growing sensitivity to the inner space of body.

Inner space awareness is also enhanced by meditation practice, which slows down the tendency for mind to busily jump around liking, disliking, pushing away, pulling toward the many perceptions bombarding us, so that we miss feeling the moment. With practice, we become aware of the extent to which we habitually live in imagination and projection. We also glimpse possible linkages between our experience of difficulty in practice with our struggle to maintain a fabricated story line of separate selfness as we try to match solid space with solid body. Once students are no longer seduced into thoughts *about* the practice, the experience of practice as painful often dissipates. Space becomes delightfully challenging, the body feels energized, and a flexible, open mind, balancing inner and outer experience, replaces resistance.

Meditation and Mudra awareness dissolve ego's protective barriers, reuniting us with a larger experience. Informed by these contemplative practices, our on stage and offstage interactions with others become more spacious, increasing the likelihood that we experience ourselves saying "yes" to whatever comes toward us, similar to the familiar acting improvisation exercise. With ego held in check, the total body can say yes.

Space Is Solid, You Are Empty

The subtitle of this essay ("Space Is Solid, You Are Empty") begins to emerge here, suggesting that you are empty of the self that always has to be protected. The phrase refers to seeing beyond a life dominated by conceptual mind and ego's attempt to maintain itself. While from ego's perspective, the totality of space and letting go of the illusion of a separate self are threatening, space-awareness students learn to have confidence in space, developing openness of mind and physical grace. Here, each individual's development merges into collaborative playing and a sense of the whole greater than the sum of the parts evolves.

At the beginning of the essay, I mentioned that members of the Open Theater demonstrated an ability to respond as a unit on stage, changing direction together as if by magic. Today, I am more awe-struck by ensemble-consciousness than I was then, having participated in many groups and gatherings—*sanghas*, committee meetings, family reunions, and college classrooms—where the potential for ensemble magic exists but does not fully manifest. In my experience, groups off- and on-stage that discover harmonies capable of catalyzing new insights and behaviors are rare.

Just as meditating together supports calm minds, a group trained in Mudra can move, speak, plan, and celebrate in a bigger awareness when one or two members hold a spacious mind. With well-developed space awareness, all movements of the group shape the ensemble. In the absence of shared training, the awareness of a single person co-creating with space can make a difference in a group. Chögyam Trungpa provided such an example. When this happens, it is palpable and profound. Words (mine included) fail or, at best, serve as fingers pointing at the moon.

In the past forty years of exploring space influenced by Buddhist practice and performance study, I have experienced glimpses of liberated energy that more closely resemble "space co-creating with itself" than "beings creating within space."

Dharma is the inconceivable truth of nonconcept, *shunyata,* or selflessness, a knowing beyond words. Dancing with Dharma evolves into *Dharma dancing,* making visible the truth of the emptiness behind, within, and beyond inherited, invented, and internalized dualisms.

How's that for a big idea?

NOTES

1. Eileen Blumenthal, *Directors in Perspective: Joseph Chaikin* (Cambridge: Cambridge University Press, 1984), 14–18.

2. Blumenthal, 104–106.

3. Fabrice Midal, *Chögyam Trungpa: His Life and Vision* (Boston: Shambhala Publications, 2001), 191–193.

4. Chögyam Trungpa, *Born in Tibet* (Boston: Shambhala Publications, 2000), 92–93.

5. For a helpful introduction to space from the Tibetan Vajrayana tradition see Chögyam Trungpa, *Glimpses of Space: The Feminine Principle & EVAM* (Halifax: Vajradhatu, 1999).

6. Midal, 193–196.

7. I describe a Mudra Space Awareness exercise from a first-person perspective in an online journal. Lee Worley, "Mudra Space Awareness," *Performance and Spirituality* 3.1 (Spring 2012). http://www.utdl.edu/ojs/index.php/pas/article/view/51.

Dancing in the Footsteps
of the Buddha

Wynn Fricke

It is easy to create suffering as artists. The sense of *self* which gives rise to this suffering is an intensely relevant subject for art-making, one that has repeatedly surfaced in my long career as a dance professional and *vipassana* meditator. At the heart of dance and our human experience is the essential study of tension and release. Dance can be the working ground for the investigation of suffering and the end of suffering—*the unshakable release of the heart*, as the Buddha described.

During my time as a dancer with Zenon Dance Company, and other Minneapolis-based companies, the contraction of *self* was well known to me. Sometimes a choreographer would ask me to perform in ways I found unflattering, and I had to work with the resistance that came up. Could I have the humility to be grotesque, sexually demonstrative, ridiculous, rageful? As an expressive dancer, it's part of the training to go there—to construct different characters and inhabit them for a while. It can feel like we are a house of cards—personalities emerge and die, real but not real—challenging assumptions that we are solid and separate like a woodcut. Then there is the impact of the movements themselves—dancers train to feel at ease falling through space and spilling into momentum, hurling our spines and heads upside down. Stubborn energies and views are not well sustained in this wildly shifting world.

People have danced throughout history, often for spiritual purposes. I relate to this impulse, even as someone in a contemporary urban setting, making dances for the proscenium stage. American modern dance was forged by women like Isadora Duncan, who expressed a spiritual urge by turning inward, toward her dancing body, as a means toward liberation. She took inspiration from the forces of nature around her, and recognized those same forces emanating from her solar plexus. Martha Graham built a technique around archetypal tensions of human experience with her contraction and release of the gut. Eric Hawkins wanted to lift dance above the fray as a means to embody, and in a sense practice, ease and freedom as opposed to neurosis. Hawkins said, "If you want to arrive at quality ... in the art of dance, you have to look at real quality in existence."[1] Balance and effortlessness, grounded in the sensuous body, was an aim of his dance technique. In his 1965 essay "The Body Is a Clear Place," he wrote:

> Sensuousness is living in the now, in immediacy; therefore there is no alienation. Here the body
> is a clear place. Sheer living is immediately experienced through one's own physical being in the

very tasting of the total feast of the world around. One cannot do this through the intellect, which is always mediate.[2]

The Four Foundations of Mindfulness

Meditation and dance practice have been connected for me since the beginning. The Buddha described four distinct ways of paying attention to experience which he called the Four Foundations of Mindfulness: mindfulness of the body, mindfulness of pleasant and unpleasant feeling, mindfulness of mind states, and mindfulness of how we create or dismantle suffering in our lives. I found the discipline of dance a fertile ground for investigating these ways of knowing. For example, dancers train to shape their body into sensitive, expressive instruments by knowing the body—the Buddha's first foundation of mindfulness. A dancer becomes aware of the pleasantness that attends a great performance, and the unpleasantness that accompanies humiliation—the Buddha's second foundation of mindfulness. Knowing her mind is what connects a dancer to her sense of power and the intention behind her movements—the Buddha's third foundation of mindfulness. And in the suffering of ego-identification, an artist has two options: to work from a defended and controlling place, or to get closer to the roots of stress and discover how to let go—this is the path that the Buddha articulated, and the fourth foundation of mindfulness. It is the way of great art-making and the way to the liberation we seek through Buddhist practice.

Training: Mindfulness of the Body

Technique class is the daily training ground of a professional dancer. Deliberate physical action—whether repetitive footwork at the ballet barre, or slow rolling along the floor—cultivates a visceral knowing of the body. Attention is directed away from thinking toward sensory experience. This is the training of knowing the body *in and of itself*. In order for technique to develop, the attention must be clear, sustained, and comprehending. A dancer develops a *felt* knowledge of the nuts and bolts of her physical system. She knows her breath, how it supports balance, and how to manipulate it to express tension. She feels her central axis, which is dynamic by nature, and critical to the execution of turns. At times, she touches on the physical bliss that arises through complete absorption in a task. On a broader level, she observes her body's response to foods, sleeping habits, and the use of caffeine. With injuries and strains, she learns the anatomy of knees, hips, ankles, and toes. She knows about calloused heels, foot fungus, and painful skin cracks. When facing audiences and critics, she is acutely aware of her nervous system. The body, in its luminosity and gritty materiality, is her daily business. By cultivating bodily knowledge, she creates the foundation for insight: feeling the body on its own terms, and becoming acquainted with its lawful nature.

The rigor of training in the modern dance studio can be like the rigor (and fruits) of *vipassana* meditation in a retreat setting. Intensive retreats, which might be ten days or longer, consist of silent sitting and walking meditation throughout the day. The meditator may attend to the breath for days, becoming absorbed into sensations at the tip of the nose, or her awareness may follow the whole of her bodily experience, tracking sensations of pressure, contraction, heat, cold, and vibration, in a wild chorus of coming and going. This is direct knowing of the body, whatever her posture, without added complication or interpretation. Thoughts are quieted; concentration deepens. There may arise a profound spaciousness of mind, absorbed in an ephemeral world of sensation. This experience radically challenges concepts of body and self. This is territory a dancer hovers around in the heightened wakefulness of embodied performance and in the burrowed concentration of dance-making.

Performing: Mindfulness of Feelings

Patterns of self-consciousness were obstacles in my training as a dancer and choreographer. Their presence in performance was especially disabling. On one occasion early in my career, I was en route from Jersey City to the theater in Manhattan where I was performing. The train broke down. The doors would not open and there was no indication as to when this might end. I got to the theater just in time to get on stage, but my mind was rattled beyond my ability to hold it. In one section of the choreography, I got lost. Fear set in, and then full-blown panic. I started flailing randomly among my fellow dancers, who were precisely synchronized and assembled. In that dramatic moment there was a crack of insight: these powerful patterns of fear and self-consciousness had a life of their own. My self-talk and tepid attempts to battle these patterns were not going to bear fruit. This was clear. These forces in the mind were impersonal with seemingly ancient causes.

In the aftermath of this event I had the good instinct to sit still with no agenda and see what was going on. I began studying meditation at the Integral Yoga Institute (IYI) in Greenwich Village, New York. The instructions at the IYI were simple: Follow the breath in the belly. When the mind wanders, come back. I was not asked to repeat a mantra or use the imagination in any way. The point was to settle the mind and to see what was there. This I could trust. From the first moments of practice, there was a discovery of refuge; a distinct flavor of safety. The simplicity of the room, the silence, the darkness, and the scattering of people with their cushions and shawls allowed me to do the internal work: quieting the mind to anything but the rise and fall of the breath. When anxiety arose, I could observe it with kindness and stability instead of hatred. I could make room for the unpleasantness of anxiety and self-doubt. I was learning the freedom of nonresistance.

For a while I lived and breathed these tools of practice. They became a lifeline, and a way out of a narrow and fearful mind that emerged most vehemently in performance and in the dance studio. With the insights from my practice, I gave full space (again and again and again), in thought and in body, to the fear that arose. I'm reminded of the story of the Tibetan saint Milarepa who, in an act of surrender, placed his head into the mouth of his most ferocious inner demon. In that demon, Milarepa was "encountering his shadow—all that he had suppressed and rejected in himself," describes Aura Glaser, a Dharma teacher and clinical psychologist.[3]

> Often when a painful feeling arises, we short-circuit that experience; we don't listen to it. We're afraid to touch it.… Instead of being accepted into consciousness, the feeling goes underground and enters the cells of our body. It doesn't go away; it goes in. Anyone who has had deep body work, has done intensive meditation practice, or has engaged in somatic practices on their own

has likely experienced how the body reveals our history in surprising—and sometimes unsettling—ways.... We may imagine that spiritual awakening is something separate from our physical embodiment, but awakening and embodiment go together.[4]

When Milarepa placed his head in the mouth of the demon, the demon dissolved. When I was willing to embrace and *embody* the discomfort of fear, without resistance, the mind relaxed. Identification relaxed. I could see the clinging that lay beneath the fear. If I could give words to it, the clinging might look like this: *I want to be a beautiful dancer; admired and loved. I don't want to be a mess. Ordinary. Hungry for everything.* In the pain of clinging, I began to loosen my grip on desires rooted in self-centeredness. I could see the delusion of it. In the still mind of meditation, an alternative to *becoming* began to reveal itself. This was ease. This was abiding in compassion and clear-seeing as opposed to a restless mind driven to make myself a more perfect person.

Choreography: Mindfulness of Mind

The body is moved by emotion, intention, and imagination. This is a natural process. Dancers and choreographers learn how the activity of mind is *felt* while using the body as an instrument of expression. As dancers perform, they become familiar with the terrain of the mind. They draw on the imagination and emotions for technical and expressive power. Through trial and error, they learn the pitfalls of either indulgence in or disconnection from what arises in the mind. Part of their craft is to train the mind to be in service of what they are trying to express. This requires an understanding of intention, a mental factor crucial to communication. Performers need to see the intention behind any gesture. They need to ask themselves, "Am I showing off, stuck in old approaches, or am I keeping front and center the intention of the movement?" This takes discernment of one's own habits and motivations.

As a 21st-century choreographer working in modern dance, it is my task to find a movement language to illuminate mental phenomena—the images, emotions, or concepts that inspire a new work. Whether that dance expresses a thing of beauty or something foul, we unwrap the seed at the heart of it, and let it grow. We give it voice in the body. This requires attunement to the flow of mental forces and its translation into a physical language. Mary Wigman, mother of German Expressionist dance, described this effort as the pressure between two poles:

Whatever the dancer has to say and wants to express, he has to make it visible.... You are nearly torn to pieces, the pressure between two poles, your own artistic idea and the artistic deed you want to achieve.[5]

Just as mindfulness of the body is required to develop strong physical technique, awareness of the mind, and the intention in the mind, is the basis for a strong creative process and expressive power.

Teaching: Mindfulness of Grasping and Its Release

Some of my first introductions to Buddhist concepts came through my dance teachers, Mary Anthony and Alwin Nikolais, who helped shape the evolution of modern dance in the United States. In my years as a student at the Nikolais-Louis Dance Lab in New

York City, Nikolais talked endlessly about the *guile* of the dancer, by which he meant the ego that gets in the way of the dancer's ability to express a choreographic intention. The Nikolais technique articulated how, as performers, we might *grain* (or focus) the mind and body's energy away from one's sense of personal presence toward the choreographic idea at hand. This was done, in part, through intention and the focus of the eyes toward an extended limb or twist of the spine. Just as wood reveals underlying forces of nature through its grain, the physical *grain* of the body reveals forces of the mind. Dancers were not "people" but forces of nature. We trained to relax the ego to make the mind-body available as a conduit for the intentions of the choreographer.

These instructions parallel the Buddha's basic approach to cultivating insight. The development of concentration, or *samadhi,* became a conscious practice for me in Mary Anthony's small dance studio on West Broadway. It was both nest and battleground. Anthony spoke about the "Big C," meaning concentration. "You don't SEE!" she told me once from behind her desk, in response to my inability to focus and follow movement correctly. "You do what you want, and not what's being asked for!" She held up her fierce hand, shaped like the letter C. Under her gaze, I began to live the questions: *What is a distracted mind? What is a gathered mind and how do I get there?*

Nikolais and Anthony skillfully directed attention to afflictive mind-states in a way that felt essential to my growth as a dancer, and indeed to my happiness generally. They offered a new means to look at the self-consciousness, agitation, and anxiety that were so present in my experience. What is self? What is fear? My dancing body was the place to investigate directly.

Observing this sense of self in its relationship to afflictive mind states continues to give rise to a deepening humility. The opposite of humility is conceit, which has a broad meaning in a Buddhist context. It is the basis for our sense of self and may appear in three ways: when we think ourselves as better, equal, or less than someone else. Christina Feldman, a Dharma teacher, writes:

> Within these three dimensions of conceit are held the whole tormented world of comparing, evaluating, and judging that afflicts our hearts. Jealousy, resentment, fear, and low self-esteem spring from this deeply embedded pattern. Conceit perpetuates the dualities of "self" and "other"—the schisms that are the root of the enormous alienation and suffering in our world.[6]

I recall a Dharma talk given in the mid–1990s by Corrado Pensa, a *vipassana* teacher, who talked about humility. *Humus,* he explained, means earth and is the root word of humility. When we abide in humility, we are connected to earth, we are "down to earth," as the saying goes. As long as we can construct a sense of self, up and away from earth, we can be humiliated—we can come crashing down. When I experience the pain of humiliation as a choreographer or performer, I ask myself, what kind of conceit is happening? What has been built up, and is it feeding on greed, anger, or delusion (the *three roots of unwholesome mental states* in Buddhism)? Even in asking those questions, a self-centered orientation begins to shift to a Dharma-centered orientation.

Starting Where We Are as Artists

Buddhist training shapes my creative process, the kind of work I create, and who I am in the studio. There is an active inquiry: Am I abiding in kindness and compassion as I interact with dancers, or do I approach my choreography with greed and expectation?

Is the mind narrow or spacious? Distracted or gathered? Fearful or trusting? Whatever energies show up, I know them and stay relaxed. I have learned the value of a light touch. In the college classroom, I try to be aware of how I observe my students. Do I judge them and compare them, or is there a radical interest in and acceptance of who they are, on their own terms? By modeling ease with my own afflictions and theirs, an atmosphere of trust and kindness is likely to arise. There becomes room for failure and risk. This is the fertile ground for powerful art-making, where student-artists can safely move closer to their own experience of body and mind. The Buddha's path and the artist's path begin when we can touch our pain, self-doubt, and vulnerability with wisdom. We become interested. The intimate act of dance-making and performing depends on this openness and inquiry. This is what I try to convey to my students.

As dancers we examine human tension—greed, hatred, delusion. We give form to our *dukkha*—grief, confusion, and restlessness—in the grit of our bodies. This practice is a means of release. By looking inward toward our stress and understanding ourselves through our dancing bodies, we invite the possibility of quite literally moving beyond what binds us.

Notes

1. Renata Celichowska, *Erick Hawkins (1908–1994)* (Dance Heritage Coalition, 2012), 3. Accessed March 21, 2015. http://www.danceheritage.org/treasures/hawkins_essay_celichowska.pdf.

2. Erick Hawkins, *The Body Is a Clear Place: And Other Statements on Dance* (Princeton: Princeton Book Company, 1992), 70–71.

3. Aura Glaser, "Into the Demon's Mouth," *Tricycle Magazine*, Spring 2012.

4. Glaser.

5. Joan Woodbury, "Mary Wigman at 70," *Dance Observer* 23.8 (October 1956): 117–118, in *Bearnstow Journal*. Accessed May 31, 2015. http://bearnstowjournal.org/wigman-woodbury-70.htm.

6. Christina Feldman, "Long Journey to a Bow," *Tricycle Magazine*, Fall 2008.

Sangha in the Spotlight
Performance and Community-Building in a Small Prairie City

Fran Gilboy

When I first began dancing it was a selfish act. I found a joy in performing, and was motivated to be the best. Classical ballet was my practice. It was rigorous and competitive, and I loved and succeeded at it from a young age. I liked it when I was singled out for my talents, and was much more interested in my solo career than performing with an ensemble. There was a lot of "I" in my world.

That seems a million lifetimes ago, and in some way I suppose it was, since we experience many mini deaths within this lifetime. Ironically, now my entire career as a dancer is lived as a shared experience, cocreating with dear friends. My work has become entirely about the *ensemble*, a dance term for a group that translates from French to English as "together." Together we build, share, and exchange within the troupe, and further still with the general public through performance. Selflessness has replaced the "I."

Deepening in Dance and Dharma

I separated from the world of ballet in my early teens, when I became much more interested in cultivating my social life and less interested in honing my abilities in the dance studio. Dance and I parted ways, for a time. I loved and lived dance again in the late 1990s when doses of LSD and electronic music took hold of my bones. My body was unlocked and introduced to a new form of expression. I loved being on the dance floor, moving freely, and mirroring the activity of a plethora of bodies around me, which I had never truly done before. Ballet had trained my body to respond to strict direction. In this new setting I found my dance transformed, and sensed a deep, forgotten longing for interconnectedness.

Alongside this new relationship with dance was a budding relationship with community and curiosity. I observed groups come together for a short period of time, deeply connect—often without talking (interconnection)—and then dissolve. In many instances, the people gathered would never cross paths again (impermanence). These electronic dance parties were the first of many experiences I'd have of groups arising out of common interest and then dispersing, having their natural end like all things. Meditation retreats, workshops I am teaching or taking, festivals, and audiences at performances—these gatherings have been essential in integrating my internal experiences of Dharma, of impermanence and interconnection, into the relational and external realms. Clinging to these groups, no matter how much I may enjoy the people and the experiences, only brings me suffering. Equally, if I don't engage fully and authentically, I suffer because of my unwillingness to connect in a meaningful way. I've thus had to find my own middle way between craving and detaching from these experiences.

Paralleling this radical time of transformation in my dance and social life, I met a woman who to this day remains my primary Buddhist teacher and beloved mentor, Sharda Rogell. Sharda is a teacher with the well-known Spirit Rock Meditation Center in Woodacre, California. She was beginning to put down roots as our guiding teacher in Regina, Saskatchewan, and it was with her that I sat my first retreat in 1997. Fortunately for me, she has come to our small prairie city twice a year for the last twenty years, and thus, ours is a strong relationship that has only deepened with time and experience. Gossamer threads bind our hearts.

Sharda has always been able to see clearly what I have not. I could share a list of countless experiences she has guided me through, but for the sake of this essay, I'll share just this: I'd always wrestled with loving kindness meditation, finding it forced and inauthentic. Loving kindness, or *metta* in Pali, is a practice in which we orient our attention toward the heart and send friendly wishes out to loved ones, to ourselves, to people with whom we have neutral relations, and even to the difficult people in our lives. It is meant to be the companion training for mindfulness, a practice to help broaden our scope and understanding of love and compassion. I personally found the repetition of the phrases to be difficult to stay with and corny in their expression. I had written it off as a practice I didn't really connect with, until she strongly urged me to attend a weeklong loving kindness retreat.

It was through Sharda's teachings during this retreat that I discovered a deep love and reverence for this practice I had previously struggled to trust. I stayed with the phrases and the difficult feelings that arose over the retreat. I gave space and quiet for my heart, as it broke a thousand times over at being forgiven and released from scrutiny. My entire practice shifted gears, and I dropped from my busy and judgmental mind down into my heart. I began to practice *metta* everywhere after that retreat—in coffee shops, the library, more coffee shops, and, somewhat to my surprise, while performing dance. The phrases became embedded in my mind, and the feelings they evoked were embossed on my heart.

Creating a Dance School

Amidst this deepening in my dance and spiritual practice, I helped a dear friend, who at the time was studying dance education, begin a dance class for adults who wanted to dance in a studio setting. Together we took the roots of creative freedom we had found on late-night party dance floors and transferred them into a dance class.

The class was a success, and with this small adult following and two classes of children, a school began: FadaDance. We modeled the school after our ideal—a safe and inclusive school for dancers of all ages, gender identifications, and abilities, where competition is not encouraged; offering a myriad of rich experiences remains our focus.

We define this genre of dance as "we get to make up whatever we want." While we do teach contemporary dance technique, our focus is on improvisation and personal expression. We facilitate dance, urging dancers to find their authentic movement. Whatever we discover through our own process as professional dancers, we share freely with our students.

With Misty Wensel at the helm and me on board to support her, FadaDance School became a reality. A year later our dear friend Heather Cameron came home from studying dance in Montreal, and the three of us became an inseparable dance force to be reckoned with, deeply committed to each other and our community.

In addition to our ideals shared above, mindfulness practice has fed our action and growth. Because of the diversity within even our small group, we approach mindfulness through different practices. For instance, I've brought with me seventeen years of committed Buddhist practice in the tradition of Theravada Insight Meditation, whereas Misty has a long sustained practice in classical Kathak dance, and Heather, a strong yoga practice. If mindfulness is described simply as paying attention without judgment to what is happening in our bodies and our minds, then we all approach our experiences of teaching, performing, and interacting with audiences from this place.

Years of somatic dance practices have also assisted our becoming intimate with our bodies, hearts, and minds. In fact, it is through "Open Source Dance" with a beloved dance teacher of mine, Bee Pallomina, that I have had some of the most profound experiences of those three centers coming together wholly without judgment. Our process is additionally informed by, and occurs within, Buddhist notions of selflessness, interconnection, and impermanence. Working artistically and administratively as a trio absolutely necessitates that one becomes selfless. The work involved in balancing three young families' schedules, each other's wishes, voices, concerns, ideas, and ideals requires us to be generous, lovingly aware of each other's needs, and untethered from expectation. Creating intentional community begins *within* the group. Without the strong connections we have created and committed to as a group, we would not be able to hold a larger community in any stable way whatsoever. Our hearts are inexplicably bound, interconnected. Our homes all reside on the same city block, we each have one son, we spend holidays together. Our love for each other expands beyond the threshold of the studio doors. We are family, and as family, we have witnessed impermanence in the ebbs and flows of our own and each other's lives.

Our Home

The FadaDance studio is located in the heart of Regina, the Canadian prairie city we call home. Specifically, we are housed in the Heritage Area, often referred to as "the core area." It's the inner city, and as such has many of the labels that inner city neighborhoods carry: gang activity, prostitution, used needles, and rundown buildings, to name a few. Outsiders, to some extent fueled by the media, project a sense of crime, poverty, and danger onto this space. To those who live and work in the neighborhood, though, it is viewed through a different lens. Once known as Pierogi Flats, it has housed many Eastern European immigrants, and to this day is dense with people of Ukrainian, Polish, Hungarian, and German descent, as well as indigenous peoples, new immigrants, and young artists.

The studio is housed in what was once a Jewish funeral home. When the small building was under renovation to become the dance studio it is today, somebody paid us a visit from the Regina Heritage Association. They asked us if we were aware of the Hebrew text etched into cement on the building front. Of course, we were. We assumed it said "Jewish Funeral Home" as that is what was written in English above the Hebrew writing.

We were informed that it actually read "The House of Truth and Loving Kindness." My heart beat a little faster and it was then and there that I knew this studio was destined to be a hub of community and love, a refuge for all who enter its doors. I, for one, felt immediately at home, and called to follow through on the message inscribed in the façade of the building.

To this day, there isn't a sign outside of the studio saying "FadaDance." Instead, we installed a wooden frame outlining the beautiful Hebrew text (and with our savvy business sense covered up "Jewish Funeral Home"). We are simply "The House of Truth and Loving Kindness," destined from the beginning to be guided by the four *Brahma Viharas*.

Dancing with the Brahma Viharas

The Buddha's four *Brahma Viharas* (divine emotions to live by, listed below) have played a central part in creating a safe and caring dance community within our city limits and beyond.

The *Brahma Viharas* provide a context, and prayer practice, to maintain and deepen our intentions as a dance company and in relation to the people we are serving, in the following ways:

Metta (loving kindness)

The space we create is one of safety. *May all beings be safe.* We want our audiences and dancers to be mentally happy and peaceful, without judging themselves or others. *May all beings be happy and peaceful.* We want our audiences and dancers to feel the life force flowing through their bodies, however those bodies may appear on the outside, and whatever their ability. *May all beings be healthy and strong and accept their physical limitations with grace.* We want all of our audiences and dancers to feel free from constraint. *May all beings be free.*

Karuna (compassion)

We build a community where there is space to hold difficult experiences. *May we hold each other's experiences with a heart of compassion.*

Mudita (sympathetic joy)

We build a community where we are able to share in each other's joys. *May a thousand more successes fall upon you.*

Upekkha (equanimity)

We create a space where the thousand joys and sorrows can move freely through the heart and body, and the arising and passing of all things are held with equanimity. *May we move with grace through all our moments, whatever they may bring.*

These four heart abodes continue to play an integral role in building trust between communities, their individual members, and the dance troupe. Whether the words are uttered aloud or not does not matter, for this practice of the heart is all about extending these wishes. I wholeheartedly believe that when we move with these intentions as educators and performers within the community, or are partaking in community events as participants, it is the intention that matters. Since the four abodes of the heart are natural states of the heart, I believe when we move out of our heads and into our bodies, these wishes emanate naturally.

Moments

I lie on the stage waiting for the show to begin. In a sense it already has. I am lying still on the floor with my cohorts as the audience enters the theater to take their seats. I sense into my breath. I feel my body pressing into the floor and space around me. My attention turns to listening. I can hear conversations alluding to love, separation, one who's been the recipient of a kind deed, and another, of an unpleasant experience. My heart opens to the myriad of feelings and experiences that are filling the space, and all the while, to the audience, we are seemingly asleep. My heart is awake. My heart is doing what the heart naturally does when left to be its beautiful self. I am filled with gratitude for the opportunity to perform in such a way, a way that allows space and time for me to become present with my inner and outer experience, and for this very quiet process of connecting deeply with our community. The practice of loving awareness is ever-present in the process of performance.

* * *

I'm at a music festival, dancing with children in a park where our trio is leading a workshop. An excited group of children wants to share what they have created together, based on the performance we have just presented for them. I crouch down so that I am eye to eye with the youngsters as they chat away about their ideas. I share their joy. One child feels that his ideas were dismissed in the group, and my heart quivers with compassion for him. The heart responds naturally to this engaging act of sharing, an opportunity for a different kind of teaching and learning to arise. I'm reminded again of the opportunity performance gives for sharing in each other's successes and practicing compassion. It can be such an engaging art if we open to what happens before and after the show. There is such beauty to be shared in the pre- and post-show connections.

* * *

We are rehearsing for an outdoor festival, at a park just down the street from the dance studio. It is early evening and the play structure has kids crawling all over it. Our studio and this park are located in a part of the city known for being a melting pot of cultural diversity. As we begin to set up our portable sound system, curious bodies start to hover around our makeshift stage, and eyes appear in the windows of surrounding houses. The slow realization occurs that what was intended as a rehearsal is about to become a park performance for its residents. At first everybody seems a little bit shy to interact, and so we go about our rehearsal as planned. As the dancing continues, people begin to gather and sit in the grass in front of us or on the stoops of their homes. My heart warms as this impromptu performance creates a spontaneous community, though I'm aware of its fleeting impermanence. We will part ways and perhaps never see each other again, but for now we are sharing space and an experience.

After the performance, the questions come. We sit and talk with the people, mostly children, who have gathered. They play with our props and dance around with them. We explain who we are and what we do. A couple of our own children who had joined us for rehearsal go and play on the monkey bars with neighborhood children. For a brief period in time, the event creates something close, connected, and safe, and it dissolves just as quickly.

Creating Community through Unconventional Performance

How our community is defined blurs conventional lines of us and them, dancers and audience, giving and receiving. We have been known to include audience members in our professional theater shows by creating intimate pre-show experiences such as feeding our audiences strawberries, creating games of hide and seek in the theater space, creating photo booths on stage with our costume pieces and props, and inviting our audience to stand and take pre-show oaths. This type of community engagement encourages others to dance, and we feel called to continue creating in unconventional ways, because our community both asks it of us and inspires us to do so. We aim to build community wherever we perform as a troupe. Most fascinating to me is how a loving, intentional community can be created within a very short time if we are generous and open to what is available to us.

For eleven years now, we have traveled nationally and internationally, creating, for the most part, dance in and for alternative spaces. These have included the Canadian Folk Festival circuit (which includes community workshops in green space), international dance conferences (where we share our creative processes and pedagogy with other dancers and movement educators from around the globe), electronic music festivals, and professional theater and gallery installations.

When we are hired to perform and give workshops, we rarely know who our audience will be, details about where we will be performing, or what will be birthed out of these unknown conditions. We have performed on top of picnic tables, on the beach, and in parking lots. I truly believe that these unknowns are a part of what keeps us authentically present, connected, and filled with that life-giving desire to continue doing what we do.

Perhaps more important than even our most informal of professional performance gigs are the community dance events that we throw. FadaDance loves a good party! As mentioned earlier, the whole evolution of the school and company was inspired by parties, and we have become known in our city for our dynamic and inclusive community events.

(Front, left to right) FadaDance members Fran Gilboy, Heather Cameron and Misty Wensel followed by their youth company, performing in "The Moveable Feast," a tribute parade for Michele Sereda in Regina, Saskatchewan, May 2015. Photograph by Shawn Fulton.

Some of these events have become annual because of the demand for them to continue. They are steeped in *mudita*!

One such event is our annual Christmas party, each year with its own theme and each year sold out. People have come to refer to it as a "family reunion that you *actually* get excited to go to!" Our professional troupe hosts the event and may do a short dance piece, but the focus—amidst the all-night dance party—is on our adult students of the dance school, who are the real stars of the show.

Our studio includes a large number of adult students between the ages of nineteen and fifty. For two months prior to the holiday party every year, we are working on dance pieces for them to present to the masses. While some members of this adult contingent danced in their youth, most have never danced until they were adults. Many of these grownups first registered for a class with us after watching their peers perform at our parties. The idea of what a dancer is—thin, athletic, inexplicably graceful and exquisite—is totally dismantled when perfectly ordinary people perform dance. Anybody can be a dancer. We have never rejected a student. Many come to their first classes proclaiming they will never perform, only to find themselves blind with the joy of a post-performance high three months later.

A second annual event we hold is called Combat Dance, a night of good spirited dance competition. We invite people to submit a team of one to four players to compete in a night of dance improvisation and challenges put forth by our troupe and invited artists. This again sees adults who might not otherwise consider themselves "dancers" playfully making up dances on the spot to sold-out audiences of their peers. Participants have included: teams of men who dance at the studio by night but have other jobs by day; a dance professor who entered a solo team; husband and wife teams; contact improvisors; sisters; mothers; even a team who had never met before they hit the stage. They aptly named their team "Blind Date."

Each team has to perform four challenges. They arrive with a team name and a two- to three-minute-long prepared piece set to the music of their choice. The other three tasks remain unknown until they hit the stage, where they are presented with challenges, have twenty seconds to confer, and two minutes to perform. We have a riot creating these dance tasks. My personal favorite was a round called "*Koans* to Cohen." We would present each group with a Zen *koan*, and the music we offered was, of course, a Leonard Cohen song. "What is the sound of one hand clapping?" performed to "Who by Fire," to this day remains one of my favorite dance pieces I've ever seen come alive before my eyes.

This event is the grownup version of the days when we kids would make up dances in our basements and then go upstairs to perform them for parents and their visiting friends. The audience participates with their enthusiasm, nervous excitement, disbelief, and raucous support. Being a part of people's spontaneous creative process is an intimate and unusual thing to witness. To put yourself on stage is an invitation to face one's own fears and dubious self-talk. To be the performer is making oneself vulnerable. To watch it is to offer support through the act of witnessing. To provide the space and opportunity for this to flourish is our great love. Together, this builds meaningful community, or *sangha*.

We take time to reflect on the impact of every event we produce or play a part in. This is a crucial part of the process, as it keeps us accountable and creative, fresh and excited. We are aware that our process is ever-changing and evolving. We dialogue about what worked and what didn't, not only among ourselves, but in discussion with people who took part in or witnessed the events. Part of the beauty is knowing that we don't know. We don't know how people will be affected, or how audiences will respond, but a blend of our wisdom and creativity persists in our pushing limits and discovering new ways to involve the community through movement. I, for one, love that much of what we do is an experiment led by our guts, and that always falling short of knowing keeps us curious and creatively inclined to keep experimenting.

Our troupe's commitment to finding creative ways to build meaningful community through an inclusive approach to performance, and the practices of the four *Brahma Viharas,* has left a lasting legacy on the prairie's arts and mindfulness communities. They have begun to entwine and intermingle. Students who dance with us have taken a keen interest in meditation and mindfulness. Fortunately, there is a mature, rooted Insight Meditation community in our city that offers a myriad of classes and sitting opportunities.

In turn, the Insight community has become interested in what we are doing as a dance community, supporting our events and performances and even beginning to take dance classes!

Mindfulness practice, through performance, has filtered into the greater community in profound ways. By exploring the essence of *sangha* beyond the existing communities of dance and Insight, and by performing in nontraditional public spaces, we have experienced firsthand what happens when we invite the general public to be a part of something intimate. What we've found is an understanding of *sangha* as the cultivation of spirited gatherings that unify otherwise scattered groups of like-minded individuals, and as the fostering of kindness, care, and sharing in each other's joys.

Commit, Amplify, Inquire
Dark Work and Remix as Contemplative Rehearsal Practices

SEAN FEIT

Spontaneous Breakthrough in Theater and Buddhism

One of the founding texts of modern theater, Constantin Stanislavski's manual An Actor Prepares, follows a hapless young actor as he stumbles through basic training with a stern but kind teacher, maturing both artistically and psychologically. Stanislavski was influenced by French psychologist Théodule-Armand Ribot's theories of subconscious drives, and by early popularizations of Buddhist and Hindu yogas. The manual frames its instruction as a spiritual narrative, in which a hero must learn authenticity through concentration and self-inquiry.[1] The text opens with the struggle of the narrator, Kostya, to prepare for a first performance, which begins poorly but then opens into a powerful cathartic moment:

> I was ready to turn myself inside out, to give them everything I had; yet inside of me I had never felt so empty.... I was making a failure, and in my helplessness I was suddenly seized with rage.... I flung out the famous line "Blood, Iago, blood!" I felt in these words all the injury to the soul of a trusting man ... [and] through the audience there ran a murmur. The moment I felt this approval a sort of energy boiled up in me. I cannot remember how I finished the scene, because the footlights and the black hole disappeared from my consciousness, and I was free of all fear.[2]

Though the passage describes a first opening, not the product of long training, it dramatizes a spontaneous shift from doubt and fear to disinhibition, confidence, and freedom. The sequence is structurally similar to accounts of spiritual breakthrough from many contemplative traditions: wholehearted preparation leading to a moment of heightened presence, then sudden shift. Kostya's moment is presented as a glimpse of the expressive power possible when emotional naturalness is attained, and is validated through the aesthetic lens of theatrical naturalism, in which fruition is the appearance of "real life" on stage. Stanislavski's system drew on the Indian concept of *prāna* (life energy), using breath cultivation, concentration, and yoga-inspired visualizations to effect purification of the actor's attention and motives, upon which "all the rest will be brought about subconsciously, miraculously, by nature ... real people and real life all around him on the stage, and living art which has been purified from all debasing elements."[3] The passage reads like a description of enlightenment, in which purification leads to an experience of "real life" brought about "by nature." Echoes of Indian concepts of dharma as "natural law" and the impersonal nature of the self or doer may be read in his appeal to the subconscious and the externalization of agency to an essential "nature."

Performers in many artistic traditions describe moments of spontaneous clarity while engaged in their art, both in rehearsal and performance, and may understand the moment either as aesthetic or personal attainment, often both. Such moments may be heightened versions of flow states or phenomenologically distinct states unto themselves. Since flow is often described as a state that persists for some time once entered, a possible distinction arises between flow states and moments of breakthrough, which may have a sharper peak and be somewhat more rare.[4] Further exploration is needed to clarify the relationship between flow states and moments of breakthrough, which will perhaps confirm a Buddhist distinction between states of meditative absorption (*jhāna, samadhi*) and insight or realization, which in most forms of Buddhism are considered to differ from absorption through a difference in conditionality.

This essay explores some implications of the special conditionality of realization in artistic performance, especially the relationship between methodical training and unpredictable fruition. To discuss the relationship between practice and fruition in theatrical performance, two separate dialectics are proposed: the material sequence of rehearsal and public showing, or "performance," and the inner process of training and realization. (I use the common contemplative term "realization" here as a synonym for breakthrough for its resonance of "to make/become real," and in the Buddhist sense of arriving at insight or fruition.) Rehearsal-performance describes a fixed dyad of recognized social activities governed by the material conditions of theatrical presentation, and thus can (and generally must) be planned and somewhat predictable. Training-realization on the other hand is open-ended, describing the ever-unfolding process of personal practice and the unpredictable nature of realization. Some nights you're "on" and some nights you're not, as all performers know!

If experiences like Kostya's are seen as comparable to spiritual breakthrough or "realization," and become a primary goal of practice, a practitioner's aesthetic orientation might shift from the material event of public showing to the inner experience of realization. This shift, emphasizing the subjective experience of the performer, decentralizes public performance since realization can, and often does, happen in rehearsal or elsewhere in daily life. Artists who understand live performance as a spiritual process may thus learn from contemplative traditions how to create conditions that prepare practitioners well for spontaneous realization, but may also find their relationship to public performance changing.

Buddhist and Hindu contemplative development consists of training in concentration and inquiry, peaking in transformative moments through which the practitioner understands themselves and their actions in the context of a lawful universe of cause and effect. A beautiful Buddhist description of such a moment, Patacara's poem from the Pali Therigatha, narrates a moment of realization arising unexpectedly in the course of long training, following upon doubt, self-reflection, and concentration, culminating in the enigmatic and powerful image of a lamp going out.

> When they plow their fields and sow seeds in the earth, when they care for their wives and children, young brahmans find riches. But I've done everything right and followed the rule of my teacher. I'm not lazy or proud. Why haven't I found peace? Bathing my feet I watched the

bathwater spill down the slope. I concentrated my mind the way you train a good horse. Then I took a lamp and went into my cell, checked the bed, and sat down on it. I took a needle and pushed the wick down. When the lamp went out my mind was freed.[5]

Patacara was one of the most revered early Buddhist nuns, and the commentary to the poem describes her family and children all killed in a series of natural disasters, her going mad with grief, meeting the Buddha, and dedicating herself to practice.[6] Like Kostya, Patacara has applied herself to her training, and like him experiences doubt upon considering that her training has not come to fruition. Both concentrate themselves intently on their task in the moment, and both experience an unexpected opening they describe as a liberation (Kostya: "I was free of all fear," Patacara: "My mind was freed"). Both narratives use the disappearance of light (footlights, lamp) as an important element in the moment of realization. It is impossible to say what the subjective experience of each person was, of course, especially since at least one of them is fictional, but the similarities can orient us toward some revealing parallels between the disciplines. Kostya's doubt leads to helplessness and rage, his own natural emotions, which become the pathway to feeling the pain of his character, Othello. He then "[flings] out" the famous line, and a murmur of approval either confirms, or helps trigger, his realization, his realness. Like Kostya, Patacara expresses frustration at the seeming lack of progress in her practice, then recovers, concentrating her mind "the way you train a good horse," which we might read as firmly but kindly, as she performs the simple tasks of bedtime. Concentration in action precedes and conditions her realization.

Both stories hinge on the unselfconscious performance of tasks (saying the line, preparing for bed), plus an absorbing mind state (emotion or concentration), and realization comes after the disappearance of doubt and full commitment to the moment. Both are examples of spontaneous and unexpected state-shift arising in the course of an oft-repeated task. Based in this, I will discuss a model of contemplative training centering on the cultivation of mind states and the unselfconscious performance of tasks, through which necessary conditions are established for spontaneous realization. The rest of this essay will use my own performance work to discuss the relationship between training and realization in a contemplative movement-based performance process. I describe two primary training forms, and a set of guidelines for improvisation inspired by Buddhist practice, considering the possibility of a contemplative performativity that invites realization, and how a shift of intention toward inner process affects public performance.

Dark Work and Devotional Remix as Contemplative Performance

In 2012, I assembled a group of eight University of California, Davis students and town residents with varying levels of performance training to devise "The Midnight Club" (TMC), a series of "late-night performance rituals" based in contemplative training and group process. We began with the discipline of Authentic Movement as a training in following movement impulse, subject-centered witnessing, and clear communication of personal experience. Using this basic skill set, we expanded into group practices that emphasized state shift and immersive environments. One primary rehearsal form was what I call Dark Work, which I have used in several recent projects. Consisting of group improvisation in a pitch-dark room, Dark Work decenters visual orientation and disrupts habitual pathways of perception, critical self-consciousness, and interaction. In TMC, Dark Work was primarily a training technique, though we did perform sections of the final events in very dim light. In "Luminous Is This Mind," a performance installation consisting of a dark space in which I encounter audience members individually, it was the primary frame for the piece. When used in rehearsal, Dark Work highlights a dissonance in the core dialectic of theatrical performance, as the internality of studio training contrasts vividly with the ritual exposure of public showing. When performed as an installation, it creates conditions for a state shift on the part of audience members, who in the absence of visual information may perceive themselves as foreground content more than when observing a lit theatrical event.

In a windowless rehearsal studio we begin by cleaning and organizing the space for Dark Work. Especially in the often dirty rehearsal spaces of a busy department, cleaning was the opening ritual of most rehearsals. Mopping the floor, I remembered the cleaning that punctuated my early Zen training, pushing a damp cloth across the smooth wood floors of the *zendo*. I learned from both Zen and dancing the palpable joy of a clean, inviting floor, and the simple clarity I felt while engaged in the task of cleaning. When the room was tidy and the door light-sealed as best we could, we would sit together and discuss the score for the practice. The score could consist of frameworks for improvisation or tasks to undertake, but most often we left it wide open, inviting responsive exploration as our state shifted with changing conditions. The beginning of group Dark Work is often internal, as participants tune proprioception, spatial listening, and social bodies to the new environment. As the group begins to move and make sound, improvising together, a group field quickly coalesces, with constellations of activity forming and dispersing, discernible primarily through soundscape, sometimes through touch.

Group Dark Work tends toward three types of activity: physical contact, sonic landscape, and solo movement exploration. The intimacy of touch is heightened, as each point of contact can feel sheltered in the privacy of invisibility, while sound becomes the primary medium of communal activity and witness. Highlighting the contemplative nature of the practice, silent movement in darkness becomes a solitary performance, witnessed only by the one engaging in it. This porous communal solitude approximates a powerful aspect of group meditation practice such as that found on a silent *vipassana* retreat, in which practitioners often report feeling supported by group presence even in the absence of visual or substantial aural contact. The simultaneous resonance of individual and group awareness itself can be a valuable site of psychological insight around self-image and group membership, and as theatrical training cultivates the skill of tracking personal and communal activity simultaneously. TMC participants reported heightened awareness of their senses in Dark Work sessions, feelings of safety and freedom from judgment, and feelings of being alone and together at the same time. They loved the practice and would ask for it. I consider the sense of safety to be imperative in immersive environments like Dark Work, in which emotional or nervous system activation may arise, sometimes in intensities that the participant's emotional regulation is insufficient to track without overwhelm. With sufficient physical, emotional, and social safety established, the immersive environment can then support dramatic shifts in both individual and communal states, guided by the skills of each practitioner to witness themselves clearly and shape their inner experience.

In all of our practices, including Dark Work, we used three guidelines inspired by Buddhist practice as a training in performative choice-making:

Commit—Whatever's happening, stay with it.
Amplify—Whatever you're doing, turn it up.
Inquire—As a situation unfolds, dig deeper.

Commitment trains attention away from habitual restlessness, boredom, and distraction by disciplining it to stay with one activity. It is a version of the Buddhist training in one-pointedness (*ekagatta*), supporting *samadhi*, or "unification of mind." Amplification, like the powerful qualities of heroic energy (*viriya*) and ardency (*atapi*) in meditation practice, undercuts hesitation, cultivates confidence, and trains discernment of what is most vital about a given activity. It is commitment combined with energy, and doesn't mean increasing force as much as wholeheartedness. Inquiry is the practice of not-knowing, in which the practitioner remains curious about her experience, neither judging nor seeking to understand it too quickly. Inquiry is the turn from training, which implies "in the known," toward realization of "the as yet unknown." It is the most contemplative of the instructions, leading the practitioner into a kind of improvisational *vipassana* or koan practice in which they engage with an unpredictable situation as a way to know themselves and their process more intimately. At times during our process, these three words were the only verbal instruction or shaping I would give during a practice. "Commit" might arise in response to a performer who seemed to be flitting from one impulse to another, not settling on any for very long. "Amplify" would be suggested to someone who was staying with an activity but not reaching potency of expression. And "Inquire" often arose as a response to seeing an activity that was engaging and wholehearted but didn't seem to be bearing fruit. These instructions originated in my personal meditation and yoga practice, where I use them as a concise version of more technical Buddhist terminology, coaching myself toward greater stability, energy, and depth. As the group work developed through training, I would remind us of the three guidelines as we entered an improvisation, but not intervene verbally after that, allowing individuals to assess and guide their own activity. This led to some choices that I would not have predicted (or wanted), but which I celebrate as evidence of participants finding their own voice and path.

After each practice we would circle and debrief, and it was common to hear reports of personally valuable psychological or spiritual insights. The realizations that arose during Dark Work specifically were more profound in rehearsal than in the eventual public showings, perhaps related to the more extreme conditions (we couldn't create pitch darkness in our final performance space), but more likely to the feeling of safety and unself-consciousness cultivated in the group field, which is often lost when strangers enter the room.[7] Group Dark Work may acquire its power by being the antithesis of public performance, since external observation is virtually impossible, and it creates a situation in which all present are participants.

The elevation of audience to participant manifested literally in "Luminous is this Mind" (solo installation, 2014), performed in a comfortable 6' × 8' light-sealed box with a low ceiling and padded floor, into which audience members would crawl, either alone or in pairs. The piece was inspired in part by the "Dark Retreat" practices used in Tibetan Bön and Tantric Buddhism,[8] and by Julie Tolentino's one-audience-member-at-a-time slow dance installation "A True Story of Two People."[9] Tibetan Buddhist Dark Retreat is an intense practice in which a practitioner may live in a small retreat cabin for days or weeks at a time in pitch darkness, with supporters bringing food and removing waste through a light-sealed enclosure. Immersion in darkness can give rise to insight into the nature of thought and identity, as the activity of the mind becomes vivid, clearly self-arising, and independent of the external senses. Because my installation would invite people in for a much shorter time, I intensified the space by making it small and womb-like.

For the duration of the daylong installation I was inside the box, and alone for the first several hours. The beginning of the performance was planned as solitary practice, and I spent the time resting and inviting my eyes and body to explore the darkness. In the second half, as audience members came in for ten minutes at a time (oriented by a friend who introduced the piece from outside), I would talk just enough to introduce them to the space and suggest that we could inhabit it together any way they wanted. Some talked, some asked for touch, some sat in silence. I made gentle suggestions if I felt like they were not at ease, or asked a leading question, "What do you long for?" Mostly I just let them be there. Two people spoke to experiencing fear of the dark, and I encouraged them to orient to the physical space in a gentle exploration of the sensations and affect that were arising. Both reported the fear decreasing, and in their written responses each described their experience transforming toward ease. One described a significant shift in perception after a childhood fear unexpectedly arose, triggered by the dark, small space.

> Sean helped me to stay with it and to explore space with open eyes and movement, exploring possibilities of what is constructed only by one's mind. It was liberating.... Time became time-less and space to a degree spaceless but full.[10]

In several responses, people wrote about timelessness, space, or an absence of boundaries. If conditions for insight include the unselfconscious performance of tasks plus an absorbing mind state, Dark Work provides a space for both via a simplification of activity, shifted sensory perception, decrease in habitual visual self-consciousness, and heightened awareness due to the unfamiliar environment.

A second primary training we used in "The Midnight Club," Devotional Remix, focuses on task performance and the affective state of ancestor reverence. Both Kostya and Patacara trained through repetition of tasks handed down to them by their respective lineages. Patacara's foot-washing, bed-checking, and use of her lamp are primary tasks in a renunciate monastic lifestyle, and she may have performed both every day at the same time. Kostya, of course, is performing Shakespeare, and so repeating text that count-less actors have spoken. The affect of devotion to lineage and the largely nonimprovisa-tional nature of their tasks both support mind states of concentration and mindfulness.

To bring a lineage of ancestors into our training, I showed TMC participants doc-umentation of body-based performance art pieces, my primary theatrical inspiration. We then created performance scores based on them, some similar enough to the original as to be recognizable, and some which used the original as a springboard but ended up somewhere else. We included several of these "remixes" in our final performances, accom-panying each one with a museum-style wall placard crediting the original artist. Partic-ipants chose to remix pieces by Julie Tolentino ("Honey" and "A True Story..."), Marina Abramovic ("Rhythm 10" and "Rhythm 0"), Matthew Barney ("Drawing Restraint"), Steve Paxton ("Goldberg Variations"), and remembering a bit further back, Stravinsky/ Diaghilev ("Le Sacre du Printemps") via Jérôme Bel ("Jérôme Bel"). The task-oriented scores, "I will slow dance blindfolded with anyone who joins me," "I will let the audience use any of these objects to manipulate my body," "I will try to draw on a distant surface while tied to this huge thing," "I will try to dance as much of Diaghilev's choreography as I can remember while listening to the whole Rite of Spring on my phone," served as movement inspiration, invitations to embodied memory, and devotional offerings to our ancestors. We imagined that in the specificity of the tasks is embedded the embodied knowledge of the lineage, and we know that we create the lineage ourselves by choosing and venerating the pieces.

Devotional Remix as a contemplative training emphasizes states of reverence and humility, and provides tasks that practitioners can engage in that are vetted for their usefulness by the originating artists. In many contemplative traditions, novices train by imitating their teachers' actions to the point of mimetic ritualization of what may have been initially idiosyncratic gestures. The commentary to Patacara's poem reveals that after her realization, which led to her becoming a venerated teacher, her students formalized the ordinary actions that led to her liberation, such as her foot-washing, and practiced them like a specific *sadhana* (contemplative ritual).[11] Taking into our own bodies the gestures and possibly states practiced by our performance art ancestors, we place ourselves in the lineage, an important declaration of faith in the process, and the antidote to the doubt that both Patacara and Kostya, like so many of us, experienced. The task-nature of the Remix scores also offers the possibility of surrendering into an activity free from the demon of unlimited choice, a subtle but chilling ghost that haunts postmodern improvisers. We don't have to know what to do. And not knowing is what makes realization possible, as we open to experience free from thinking we already understand it.

Realization Means the End of Performance

The movement scores created through the remix process seemed to serve mind states of concentration and wholeheartedness through the combination of task repetition and immersion in a specific somatic environment. Dark Work and Devotional Remix may be seen as forms of contemplative performance training through their focus on embodied states conditioned by a specific physical task and environment rather than rehearsal's traditional focus on eventual aesthetic product. Like other forms of contemplative practice, they subvert the material dialectic of rehearsal-performance by foregrounding the performer's subjective experience and the possibility of transformative realization, which may come at any time, public or private.

Hypothesizing a parallel between Buddhism and contemplative performance thus reveals similarities in praxis but a discontinuity in framing narrative, since performance is still commonly understood only through the material structure of rehearsal and public showing rather than through the process orientation of training-realization. The conventional sequence of rehearsal-performance in live art also creates a dialectic of absence and presence as the intimate experiences of private rehearsal tend to disappear in the bright footlights of public showing. Turning toward training-realization and away from rehearsal-performance respects the intimacy of private experience and undercuts neoliberal obsession with marketable aesthetic product, recognizing that the fruition sought can arise at any time when conditions are ripe.

The implications of this shift are apparent particularly in recent performance art and post–Judson experimental dance in which public showing has receded from prominence or disappeared altogether. Movement lineages such as Contact Improvisation, Ruth Zaporah's Action Theater, and Authentic Movement, as well as styles of improvised narrative theater that often integrate artistic and inner process rhetorics, thrive largely removed from the mainstream theater economy. All of these lineages not only emphasize a shift toward training and inner process but feature proponents who speak openly about spirituality in the practice. Overlapping with these lineages, contemplative performance artists like Anna Halprin, Deborah Hay, Marina Abramović, and Linda Montano have all created performance trainings that weave between aesthetic and spiritual orientations.[12] In many of these forms the combination of task repetition and absorbing mind state underlies the exercises through which the conditions for realization are cultivated, and the work manifests a training-realization model more than that of rehearsal-performance.

In my own performance work, immersion in darkness and devotional imitation of a chosen repertory both have served as training forms through which to cultivate clarity of attention and the conditions for realization, as well as amplified conditions for social interaction. To the extent that a given artistic process focuses on the intimate experience of the participants, its focus on public showing may dim, change, or disappear, and this has been true in my own work. As contemplative performers, like religious contemplatives, we train to engage fully with the situations we find ourselves in, cultivating skillful mind states and embodied action in both theatrical performance and daily life. Performers who deepen in this type of work may find the realizations that arise just as relevant to personal and existential concerns as to our craft as performing artists, or more so. "Performance" may recede from prominence as our own self-consciousness and doubts recede. The footlights disappear from consciousness. But the disappearance of the lights means also the disappearance of artist and audience as roles that constitute the experience of theater. Who is "performing" anymore, who observing? When conditions are ripe, and the lamp goes out, the show is over.

Notes

1. On Stanislavski and yoga, see William H. Wegner, "The Creative Circle: Stanislavski and Yoga," *Educational Theatre Journal* 28.1 (1976). R. Andrew White, "Stanislavsky and Ramacharaka: The Influence of Yoga and Turn-of-the-Century Occultism on the System," *Theatre Survey* 1 (2006). On Stanislavski and Ribot, see Natalie Crohn Schmitt, "Stanislavski, Creativity, and the Unconscious," *New Theatre Quarterly* 2.8 (1986).

2. Constantin Stanislavski, *An Actor Prepares*, trans. Elizabeth Hapgood (New York: Routledge, 2003), 10.

3. Stanislavski, 313.

4. For discussions of flow in performance, see Marc Silberschatz, "Creative State / Flow State: Flow Theory in Stanislavsky's Practice," *New Theatre Quarterly* 29.1 (2013). Also Kate M. Hefferon and Stewart Ollis, "'Just Clicks': An Interpretive Phenomenological Analysis of Professional Dancers' Experience of Flow," *Research in Dance Education* 7.2 (2007).

5. Susan Murcott, *First Buddhist Women: Poems and Stories of Awakening* (Berkeley: Parallax Press, 1991), 45 (line breaks omitted).

6. Murcott, 18.

7. Stanislavski's "circle of attention," his most well-known yogic visualization, in which the actor visualizes a large circular boundary around herself, was designed to prevent a similar loss of focus in the presence of the audience. See Wegner, "The Creative Circle: Stanislavski and Yoga."

8. Martin Lowenthal and Tenzin Wangyal Rinpoche, *Dawning of Clear Light: A Western Approach to Tibetan Dark Retreat Meditation* (Charlottesville: Hampton Roads, 2003).

9. See "A True Story About Two People." Accessed May 31, 2015. http://www.julietolentino.com/TOLENTINOPROJECTS/Performance/Entries/2005/1/1_A_TRUE_STORY_ABOUT_TWO_PEOPLE.

html, and "A True Story." Accessed May 31, 2015. http://hemi.nyu.edu/journal/4_1/artist_presenta
tion/jt_eng/truestory.html
    10. Personal communication.
    11. Murcott, 18.
    12. Anna Halprin, *Moving Toward Life: Five Decades of Transformational Dance* (Hanover: Wes-
leyan, 1995). Libby Worth and Helen Poynor, *Anna Halprin* (New York: Routledge, 2004). Deborah
Hay, *Lamb at the Altar: The Story of a Dance* (Durham: Duke University Press, 1996). Deborah Hay
and Susan Foster, *My Body, the Buddhist* (Middletown: Wesleyan, 2000). Linda Mary Montano,
"Another 21 Years of Living Art." Accessed May 31, 2015. http://www.lindamontano.com/another-21-
years-of-living-art-1998–2019/.

The Whole World Is a Symbol
Performing the Embodied
Landscape as a Buddhist Practice

ANNA TZAKOU

For the past five years, I have been practicing and performing in the landscape. This decision was not totally my own. It grew out of the historical time presented in Greece, my place of origin, and as necessity led me to seek meanings of home and belongingness which still mattered. Living in a society suffering from intensive processes of disintegration, I was compelled to rediscover my "own roots [and] routes" centered in the body and connected with the heart.[1] Since then, I have been exploring the ways through which the body relates with rural and urban environments to perform narratives of the landscape's "nowness"; to reconnect "the wisdom of the past with the present" and reaffirm the belief that "where you are and what you are, on the spot is very important."[2] Based on the Buddhist principle of *mandala* and the practice of *samatha vipassana*, which I will further explain, I have been investigating the body-landscape interrelationship to seek patterns of connectivity perceived as home and experienced as belongingness.

As a theater artist I am affiliated with postmodern performance practices of American and European lineages as well as with Buddhist meditation. Having being trained at Naropa University, this work orientation is not accidental. Through my vigorous years of study in the Naropa community, my performance training was enriched and structured by methods of somatic movement, psychophysical acting training, dance improvisation, and meditation practices.[3] These disciplines enhanced my creative process to work with not knowing, explore the hidden as well as the impulsive, and perform from a place of responding rather than doing. Returning to Greece, I was interested in creating scores of physicality and emotional edginess—investigating place as performance site and testing the performance act as social and political event. I soon realized that I had to integrate my training with the cultural contexts of my homeland, engaging myself with questions of translocation and translation. However, before I could enact this realization, the lived reality punched me in the stomach.

The Call

It is spring, May of 2011 in Athens. The phenomenon of the Greek debt crisis is already on display. The Greek government waits for the International Monetary Fund's verdict on new financial aid packages and pushes for austerity measures which affect all aspects of economic and social life. In Syntagma Square, the city's central space situated in front of the country's parliament, the Greek Indignant Citizens Movement emerges.[4] People occupy the area to protest and express their anger over the degradation of their lives. For more than a month, the movement endures peacefully. The night before the ballot of the Medium Term Fiscal Plan, the government passed further austerity measures, and people fight back. For days, demonstrations and riots constitute the everyday reality of the city. The center of Athens is being transformed into a battlefield. Everything breathes inside a zone of hostility and aggressiveness.

At that time I was doing training in the studio by myself. The gap between my work and the city's reality became paramount. How could I stay open to my creative process within the studio space when everything around me was forcing me to either shut down or react? How do the inner and the outer negotiate; where do my creative "I" and the place's reality meet? I decided to do a practice session outdoors. I went to the nearest mountain, located east of the city. From there, I looked at the city and it felt as if I was looking inside of me. *The outer space became me.* I could witness my urban body in the spatial structure of the city. I could perceive my urban armor in the silence of the mountain. For the first time, the outer environment was supporting me to open and be exposed to the reality around me.

Through the urgency of the present historical moment, I was called to relocate my practice as a performer. I was pushed to question big narratives: what constitutes "we," home, and this place which we claim as ours? Amidst all this mess, the landscape became an ally: a genuine and open resource that I could engage with my body; an investigational arena; a studio space to explore stories of connectivity and "placeness."[5] As the cultural geographer Mitch Rose claims, the embodiment of the landscape narrates the current cultural event like a "dream of presence."[6] Embedded in the landscape and resonating within the body, each physical activity onsite manifests "the body-landscape co-emergence" as an experienced reality.[7] By "attaching materialities to affectivities, and perceptions to places," the onsite somatic event unfolds the body's "movement[s] of care" and discloses its "effort to dream the world as a whole."[8]

The Heart (or, Experiencing the Landscape as a Buddhist Practice)

Motivated by my urge to make sense of the political, perceptual, and emotional present, I became engaged in practicing and creating work in the landscape. I soon understood that my inquiry into intellectual and cultural issues could jeopardize my performance process. I could easily disorientate myself among convictions, biases, and clichés, while at the same time shrinking or shutting down the onsite body and heart experience. Amidst these risks, there was a major dualism that I needed to overcome: my subjective experience within the outer world. To examine the body-mind correlation in space, I was already using Barbara Dilley's Contemplative Dance Practice (CDP) as my core discipline. However, I needed a way to integrate my practice's insights into the quest of embodying the landscape. It was from this place that I turned to and found support in Buddhist philosophy.

The Mahayana Buddhist doctrine of *shunyata* claims that all phenomena are "empty

Anna Tzakou improvising with the landscape on Imittos mountain, Attiki, Greece, May 2011. Photograph by Sofia Simaki.

of an independent existence, for [they are] co-dependently originated."[9] They exist in relation to each other and therefore they have no absolute foundation to stand on; they are "groundless."[10] When I see things as co-dependently existing, I perceive their emptiness; and if I experience them as devoid of an inherent meaning, I see their true nature. This "as they are" quality of things (their *tathata,* or "suchness" in Buddhist thought) is their emptiness and vice versa. This is the ultimate truth of seeing phenomena as they really are. To experience the world as *shunyata* is to cultivate with compassion and awakened heart the awareness of a nonsegregated existence between the world and the I who perceives it. Like a bird flying through an open sky, the I experiences its open beingness of *shunyata* and witnesses the world in its "primordial intrinsic awareness," in its wisdom.[11] This never-ending and centerless experience of space initiated by the body and mind, according to the Vajrayana Buddhist tradition, metamorphoses the world into a vast symbol. The revealed potentiality of this space is called the *mandala* principle and the act of its symbolic conversion, the practice of *mahamudra.*[12]

Integrating the notion of *shunyata* in the quest of embodying the landscape, reality becomes a creation of the I as it experiences the world; landscape is recognized as the manifestation, the consciousness of that reality; and the body-landscape interrelationship is spatially manifested as one great *mandala.* Everything is now. The inner and outer become one. The landscape is transformed into a centerless circle, a meditative space in which the moving body functions *both* as its seed and expressive means. Experiencing "no difference between form and space," the beingness of the body is attuned to the "secret experience" of the world, the direct experience of *mahamudra.*[13] Physicality (outer) and vulnerability (inner) are interwoven into a revealed secret territory within which the somatic event stands as the narrative of the landscape's becoming. The moving body is evolved into the expressive medium of the space's embedded life-stories-wisdom and the world manifests itself as a symbol. As Chögyam Trungpa states: "The whole world is a symbol—not symbol in the sense of a sign representing something other than itself but a symbol in the sense of the highlights of the vivid qualities of things as they are."[14]

Within this context, embodying the landscape becomes the examination of the ways the I makes sense of its world *while* perceiving it. The practice of *samatha vipassana* constitutes the fundamental means for this approach. The word *samatha* signifies "inner stillness" and *vipassana* "'insight' into the nature of things."[15] They are complementary qualities practiced through the same technique: sitting still in an upright posture with an object of concentration, usually the breath; each time the mind wanders, acknowledging it and returning back to the point of attention. *Samatha* facilitates a bare witnessing of the present moment and creates a platform of concentration whereupon *vipassana* arises and is cultivated.

Grounding the embodied landscape as a *samatha vipassana* practice, the performance training was organized accordingly into a discipline of attunement and actualization. *Samatha* is the practice which attunes and listens to the way consciousness is embedded in the landscape's experience; this is the center, the seed of *mandala*.[16] The practice of *vipassana* expands the listening into the space and hence actualizes the experience of the place; this is the circumference of *mandala*.[17] The discipline of attunement, which is the first phase of the practice, focuses on opening up the body, deconstructing the social self, and establishing the exploration of the inner and outer landscapes. It builds and grounds the mindfulness practice on site. The discipline disintegrates the living experience of the environment by discriminating and identifying mental and physical patterns, sensations, feelings, and impulses. It establishes mindfulness in and of the landscape based on practices informed by the First and the Second Foundations of Mindfulness in the *Satipatthana Sutta*; the contemplations of breathing, walking, the four bodily postures, and everyday activities and feelings as pleasant, unpleasant, and neutral.

The Embodied Landscape as a "Living Myth"

The mindfulness developed by these Buddhist practices is extended into the landscape by the performance disciplines of Somatics, Grotowski-based actor training, and Dilley's "dance.art.lab" disciplines.[18] I chose these practices based on the following common points: They consider movement as perception, hence the moving body as a perceptual investigational tool. They acknowledge the differentiation between the inner and outer space, initiating either from the experience of the I or from the body's positioning in the environment. They train the "inner eye" to be materialized as movement and the outer view as a physical presence on site; or they set a zone of practicing their negotiation in between sensing and acting. They respectively explore feelings, associations, and memories arising in and from the body as kinesthetic mappings of the inner and outer landscapes. They elaborate physical instructions based on nonstylized movement to explore noncognitive action as impulse and improvisation as its living register.

From the Somatics tradition, I have been exploring the developmental movement patterns of Body-Mind Centering® to investigate beingness on-site. From Grotowksibased actor training, I have been focusing on the *plastique* exercises to elaborate the landscape's emotional scripting. From Dilley's dance.art.lab work, I have been working on the Red Square practice for sensory as well as spatial awareness and CDP for devising performance material with and in the landscape.[19] These practices create the passage from the sitting meditation posture to the psychophysical exploration of the landscape's materiality. They are the base ground for the practitioner to *perceive landscape experientially* as a mandala. They become the excavators to uncover kinesthetic motifs of care, relatedness, and meaning mutually being actualized and actualizing the space. The practice now moves to its second phase. The found patterns of connectivity, the bodily catalysts of affect and effect in the landscape, are identified as material that worked and are transcribed into a task, an instruction set, a choreography formulating an ordered and layered sequence.[20]

From this point on, the training becomes a creative process of structuring the material into the score of a performance narrative. Meaning still is indeterminate and obscure. I am not interested in identifying an intellectual thread, a story line implanted into the performance material. I seek to recognize a subject matter or a question derived from the found on-site performance activity. I allow the material to arrive into a structure, a container to hold the endless event of the body-landscape interconnection; to reenact the experiences that have already connected me with the landscape's presence. This "narrative pattern giving significance to our existence, whether we invent or discover the meaning" is regarded by Anna Halprin, a pioneer of the American postmodern dance, as a "living myth."[21] Ongoing and at the same time genuine to the present moment, a "living myth" is my effort to examine questions of "individual and group identity combined ... with the environment."[22] Perceived as a living myth, the devised onsite material becomes a mythology of what still matters and formulates the narrative of the body-landscape performance event.

Site-Specific Performance: A Contemplative Participatory Event

Anna Halprin claims that performance is an instruction set, a "score" to be accomplished: "It does not mean you are required to exhibit a professional stage presence.... A performance can be a ritual, an exercise, a massage, a meal, a sensitivity walk and many acts of communal creativity."[23] To enable these events as mythologies of present, Halprin argues that they need to encounter their spectators as witnesses.[24] She states that the performer-witness relationship formulates a larger field physically and emotionally activated by executing the score. Creating a movement format accessible to everyone (i.e., walking), performers and spectators are met as "a single body ... and moved by a group body-mind spirit."[25] Their togetherness generates awareness of their distinctive collectivity and like a shared experience reveals "a sense of their own community."[26] Hence and according to Halprin, to function as a living myth, a performance must be organized as "an audience participation event."[27]

During the Bridge Project, a body-landscape performance residency, I undertook the creation of a site-specific living myth as a participatory performance event. The performance took place on Aegina Island in March of 2012, and it was the outcome of a two-week group residency comprised of performers, musicians, and filmmakers. I organized and facilitated the training based on the Buddhist-inspired landscape performance practice elaborated above. The twenty-five spectators were either natives of the island, invited by the residency community, or guests of the project (relatives, friends, and collaborators). The performance started at noon and was based on a tour around the residency site, including a nearby beach. It began by introducing a group practice to the audience: walking in silence, gazing softly at the horizon, moving individually yet with a sense of the whole group. This practice transformed the spectators into participants and expanded their perception in time and space: "My body posture started to change…. I started being an observer of myself as a spectator, of the others and the occurring actions, silence was essential; it moved us away from our everyday patterns."[28] Within this frame, the first text was performed. It was a poem of someone's inner dialogue expressing his alienation from his homeland, naming himself an "interior immigrant."[29] The text gave the emotional and communal context of the landscape's narrative, providing a theme: "The poem enlivened the landscape within me and the route on it."[30]

At one of our stops throughout our course, the performance group enacted a movement improvisation based on the "Open Space" stage of Dilley's CDP. I gave the audience instruction to walk freely among us and observe from different directions, as if in a gallery. Performers and watchers thus moved amidst each other, interacting and meeting one another in a mutual creativity: "The landscape became us and I sense a quality of quietness among us, [the improvisation] revealed to us more space…. It was a ritual…. I felt a participant and at the same time responsible as a spectator."[31] Finishing the walk, the performers started to sing a familiar Greek song.[32] The combined activity more powerfully integrated the landscape with the performance narrative: "Reality's every little detail took enormous dimensions like our return to the residence from the pathway full of thorns, the nasty dogs and the long concrete wall with the fence along us … after passing this 'dark' experience, the sweet familiar song and the affection of the residence's garden followed."[33] Completing the presentation, we all sat together for a small feast. The silence was broken and we shared our inner story lines: Ulysses' myth, immigrants' journeys, a returning route to the Self, a story of the land's history, and a therapeutic collective performance were some of the titles participants articulated.[34]

The example above does not illustrate the whole event, but rather shares a window into a landscape narrative developed by movement, text, song, and site. This narrative induced performers and witnesses to feel part of the site as if they were off-key instruments being tuned to it. Their bodies became projections of the landscape while the landscape was projecting on them. Communing with space, they communed with time (past and present), relocating themselves within cultural and sociopolitical story lines. The performance required detachment from expected ways of seeing and signifying; openness to nonlinear structures of meaning-making; and the availability to connect with the self, the other, and the here and now.

To devise and perform on-site, one needs to experience place as landscape and landscape as the open, direct experience of *shunyata*. The practices of *samatha vipassana* and performance enable the body to be attuned and engaged with the environment. The embodied landscape becomes the seed of the site-specific performance act inviting spectators to participate in the ceaseless encounters of the inner and outer, body and landscape, we/me and world. Shaped as mythologies of the present, these experiential meetings encourage us to relocate our relation with the world's "newness."[35] It is not about understanding and interpreting the existing time; it is rooted in the present and at the same time wider than that. As Chögyam Trungpa shares, it is about connecting with "the inconceivable vision and wisdom of the cosmic mirror on the spot."[36]

NOTES

1. Paul Willis and Mats Trondman, "Manifesto for Ethnography," *Cultural Studies—Critical Methodologies* 2.3 (August 2002), 397.

2. Chögyam Trungpa, *Shambhala: The Sacred path of the Warrior* (Boston: Shambhala Publications, 2007), 99–100.

3. I studied the Six Viewpoints technique with Wendell Beavers, Contemplative Dance Practice with Barbara Dilley, and a Grotowski-based psychophysical actor training as taught by Steve Wangh.

4. Syntagma in Greek means "constitution." The Indignant Citizens Movement was formulated in May 2011. It was influenced by the square occupations the same year in Spain, from which it took its name "indignados," and it was organized by the social media as a call to react to the government's austerity measures.

5. The notion of "placeness" is a human geography term first introduced by Edward Relf. It has been used to describe the "physical or symbolic qualities" given by a community to an outdoors space. See E. Relph, *Place and Placelessness* (London: Pion Limited, 1976) 35.

6. Mitch Rose, "Gathering 'Dreams of Presence': A Project for the Cultural Landscape," *Environment and Planning D: Society and Space* 24 (2006), 538.

7. Rose, 538.

8. Rose, 549, 544.

9. Francisco J. Varela, Evan T. Thompson, and Eleanor Rosch, *The Embodied Mind: Cognitive Science and Human Experience* (Cambridge: MIT Press, 1993), 224.

10. Varela et al., 224.

11. Herbert V. Guenther and Chögyam Trungpa, *The Dawn of Tantra* (Boston: Shambhala Publications, 1975) 17.

12. Guenther and Trungpa, 17, 37.

13. Guenther and Trungpa, 25.

14. Chögyam Trungpa, *The Myth of Freedom and the Way of Meditation* (Boston: Shambhala Publications, 1976), 156.

15. Walpola Rahula, *What the Buddha Taught* (Oxford: One World Publications, 1974), 68.

16. Guenther and Trungpa, 37.

17. Guenther and Trungpa, 37.

18. The "dance.art.lab" is a body of movement and composition practices. Generated by Barbara Dilley, it integrates contemplative awareness and movement improvisational disciplines. The laboratory includes CDP as well as other exercises such as the Corridors, Red Square, and Aunts/Menus.

19. For more details on these exercises and the ways they are integrated onsite see my chapter in the Guided Practices section of this book.

20. In this stage, the process may be enriched by other performance material beyond movement (e.g., objects, texts, songs, music). This material could be originated on site, inspired by the place's context, or could be brought to interact with the found material and the landscape.

21. Libby Worth and Helen Poynor, *Anna Halprin* (London: Routledge, 2004), 107.

22. Worth and Poynor, 110.

23. Anna Halprin, *Moving Toward Life: Five Decades of Transformational Dance*, ed. Rachel Kaplan (Hannover: University Press of New England, 1995) 50.

24. Halprin, 249.

25. Halprin, 229.

26. Halprin, 55.

27. Halprin, 50.

28. Audience Writing Feedback, March 3, 2012.

29. Nanos Valaoritis, "Meta-Etymology," in *Exiled in our Skin,* ed. Rigopoulou Calliope (Athens: Topos Publications, 2010). The chosen poem was brought by one of the participants.

30. Audience Writing Feedback, March 3, 2012.

31. Audience Writing Feedback, March 3, 2012.

32. Written by Manos Hatzidakis for Elia Kazan's film *America America* (1963). During the project this song occurred in the group as a practice song and hence afterwards the group decided to

use it in the performance event. The song is about a young man saying goodbye to his country as he becomes an immigrant.

33. Audience Writing Feedback, March 3, 2012.
34. Audience Writing Feedback, March 3, 2012.
35. Trungpa, *Path of Warrior*, 125.
36. Trungpa, *Path of Warrior*, 125.

Ritual

Dharma Jam
A Modern Buddhist Dance Liturgy

Harrison Blum

"If one perceives the Dharma with one's own body ... then one is indeed an upholder of the Dharma"—The Buddha[1]

Thirteenth-century Zen poet Wu-Men Kuan wrote, "The Gateless Barrier is the Dharma entry. There is no gate from the beginning, so how do you pass through it?"[2] With the brevity of two words, he encapsulates the interplay between ultimate and relative truth. "Gateless" suggests an absence of obstacles, with nothing to unlock or attain. We have arrived. This is it. Ultimately, our world is gateless. Meanwhile, "barrier" speaks to our clouded perception and the need for practices, transformation, and realization. Relatively, our world has barriers. Ultimately, there is no problem with our existence. Relatively, we experience ignorance, and the suffering ignorance causes.

Dance floors are manifestations of the Gateless Barrier. They are by nature ritual spaces, clearings dedicated to celebration and expression through movement. They offer a unique space in society to move freely, inviting the possibility of transcendence. Dance floors are also often social spaces, susceptible to the hopes and fears of our social worlds. Dancing amidst the Gateless Barrier may thus host both communion and competition, realization and reaction.

Since the late '90s, dance, along with sitting meditation, has been a primary form of Dharma practice for me. I fell in love with both during my first year of college, and my skateboard trips from West Philly to downtown were most often either to meditate at the Shambhala Center or to get down to live music. It was an empowering time. At Shambhala, I first began to put into practice the concepts and techniques from Buddhism that had previously just been highlighted in my religious studies textbooks or favorite Alan Watts volumes. At the Trocadero Theatre, I found a new form of embodied delight dancing freely in the pockets of space at the back of the crowds.

I'd often carry a journal in the cargo pocket of my patchwork pants, stealing away time from the dance to inscribe some fresh insight or sense of wonder. Seventeen years later, I've traded a skateboard for a bicycle, and now sit at my local Insight Meditation center rather than Shambhala, but it's still meditation and dance that occupy many of my evening outings.

Dharma Jam: Structure and Ritual

Choreographer-philosopher Sandra Horton Fraleigh writes "the present-centered moment ... [is] the vital moment of both art and religion."[3] Dancing with Dharma inhabits that vitality shared by spirituality and expression in the present moment. Since 2006, I've sought to host that experience for others in Dharma Jam—a format that integrates mindful movement and sacred dance as Dharma practice.[4]

Jams are divided into three phases of Tune In, Get Down, and Join Up, corresponding with the Three Gems of Buddha, Dharma, and Sangha. Tune In affords time and space for personal arrival. We begin in seated meditation, followed by a standing meditation, and then slow movement. Spacious music invites us to let go of the busyness of the day and show up in our bodies. We observe our impulses to move, and then allow our movement to have momentum. We begin to dance with our partners of breath and balance, as we honor our human potential, our Buddha nature.

Get Down welcomes a greater range of motion and speed. The music gains intensity, and we blur the line between movement and dance, holding dance as being playful and curious about movement. We focus on how we feel more than how we look. We continue to breathe and know that we are breathing. We follow our joy and authenticity, welcoming the ways in which truth, the Dharma, enters our lives.

Join Up expands the focus from me to we. We enter the collective ritual by paying more attention to how others are moving around us. Small similarities in dance gestures and styles act as bridges, connecting our individual dances into a group creation. Music remains mid- to high-tempo and opens into a more playful tone as we celebrate our shared practice, our Sangha. These three phases close with a dancing dedication and a seated reflection circle.

Undergirding this choreographic progression is a Dharmic process infused with what the Buddha called the Three Marks of Existence. These are impermanence, non-self, and the suffering that arises when we live in resistance to these first two. *Anicca, anatta,* and *dukkha* in Pali.

We live as mortal beings in a changing world. Change is a constant, from the vibrations of molecules to the slow erosion of mountains. As the world changes, we change with it, down to our bones. Every seven years even our skeletons are made up of completely different cells.[5] While we may feel and act as separate beings, apart from the rest of the world, truly we are more interconnected than separate. This built-in interconnection is what Buddhism calls non-self. Much of the suffering that Buddhism is so well known for talking about arises when we push against these natural laws of change and interconnection. The word *dukkha* originally referred to an axle that didn't fit well— quite literally a square peg in a round hole. We experience *dukkha* when we try to live in an unchanging world as separate beings, when we do not surrender to what is.

Dharma Jam offers a format for this surrender. By tuning in with awareness to our body's impulses to move, we contact the impermanence of sensation (*anicca*). A few moments observing our physical sensations show us that our body itself is a constantly changing landscape. In receiving more than creating our movement, we release concepts of "me" or "mine" (*anatta*). Our dance is happening without our needing to drive it— dances without a dancer. As we align with change and selflessness in this way, we also align with the natural order of things. We ease that square peg away from the round hole (*dukkha*). We become like the bees the Buddha mentions in the *Dhammapada*, drinking the nectar without harming the flower.[6] We are present without needing to attain or defend anything. Our dance thus becomes a ritual offering. We offer two of our most precious possessions—time and ourselves—back to the universe. We offer these as we realize they are not ours to begin with. We offer the universe back to itself.

In holding Dharma Jam as a ritual practice, I resonate with anthropologist Edmund Leach, who located ritual in a continuum. Writing in the 1950s, he stated:

> At one extreme we have actions which are entirely profane, entirely functional…[and] at the other we have actions which are entirely sacred, strictly aesthetic…. Between these two extremes we have the great majority of social actions which partake partly of the one sphere and partly of the other. From this point of view technique and ritual, profane and sacred, do not denote *types* of action but *aspects* of almost any kind of action.[7]

In this statement we can hear Leach naming the Gateless Barrier as present in "almost any kind of action." In a world with sacred potential in every moment, every action carries the potential to be ritual. Dharma Jam is neither inherently functional nor sacred. It simply names the sacred as possible and invites a doorway into the gateless. It is upon each participant to take the invitation, to surrender to our fluid interconnection.

Writing more recently, religious studies scholar Catherine Bell coins the term *ritualization,* pointing to how the qualities of action assign meaning to the acts, as opposed to actions possessing inherent meaning. Bell speaks of the "ritualized body [as] a body invested with a 'sense' of ritual," and holds that with practice one may attain "'ritual mastery': '[whereby] schemes of ritualization' come to be embedded in the very perceptions and dispositions of the body."[8] Dharma Jam invites practitioners to re-pattern their perceptions and dispositions, shifting away from desire, aversion, and delusion into a direct embodiment of clear awareness.

When I tell people about doing work with Buddhism and dance, a question I often get is "What does Buddhist dance look like?" My answer points to each mover's experience on the inside. The Buddhist part of the dance happens internally, in how we perceive and respond to experience. At any given moment in a Dharma Jam, different participants dance quickly and slowly, gracefully and spastically, with others and alone. There's also usually at least one person in stillness or stretching. Amidst this eclectic dance floor, it is each mover's experience that makes it Buddhist, or spiritual, or transformative. Northeastern University student Katy Davis shared her thoughts after a Dharma Jam I held for the campus Buddhist Group. "Dharma Jam was the first time my mind and body felt completely in sync. Even being a dancer for my whole life, I had never moved so freely and spiritually as I did there. There was no disconnect between what I felt and how I moved."[9]

Creating the Ritual: Inspiration and Process

In creating the Dharma Jam format, I was inspired by Dance New England's Contact Improvisation jams, barefoot boogies, and summer dance camp. While employing elements of technique and instruction, these free-form venues accept and explore the moving body in largely improvisational terms. Over almost two decades and countless dance floors, they have deepened my connection to dance as a spiritual practice. From the ecstatic, high energy invited by DJed boogies to the trust and intimacy offered in a Contact Improv jam, I learned to receive the moving body as a vehicle for awareness and expression.

Amidst an element of spirituality in these dances, I was hungry to have that quality more directly named and fostered. I was engaging in the dance as a transformational practice, and wanted to share in that intentionality. Seeing that there were already a handful of local dance jams in the Boston area, but not finding one overtly named as a space for spiritual practice, I resolved to offer a new jam. While I had personally been nurtured by my Buddhist practice for several years at that point, I thought it best to present the jam's spiritual identity in open, non-denominational terms. I didn't want to turn anyone away who might not identify as Buddhist, or "Buddhist enough."

I called the new event Dance Path, and in December of 2006 made arrangements to hold its first iteration at the Beacon Hill Friends Meeting, a Quaker group in downtown Boston. With minimal publicity, a crowd of fifteen people showed up. For an hour and a half we danced to an arcing playlist off my iPod and small speakers, book-ended by intention and reflection circles. Seeing potential, I moved Dance Path to a community center and ran it as a monthly event for the next six months. It felt significant to hold the dance with a sacred and contemplative purpose, and to open and close in that spirit.

A year later, I was living in Northern India, working as a study-abroad co-director. As I was immersed in Buddhist culture and imagery, a question arose for me: why *not* make it about Buddhism? Buddhism was my practice and I was the facilitator. Why not draw more directly from the wisdom of my home tradition and be up front about doing so? I saw that in trying to cast the widest possible net of inclusion, I had shied away from the specific strengths I could best offer. I resolved to change my approach. I decided to get down with the Dharma.

Dance Path became Dharma Jam, and I embarked on an action-reflection cycle for the next several years to refine the format and my role. At the first Dharma Jam, I sequestered myself into a corner and spent the two-hour Jam fiddling with an audio mixer while playing mainly high-energy dance music. I was told later that the music was too fast paced, and that my facilitation was missed on the dance floor. I overcompensated in response, front-loading the next Jam with a long Dharma talk only to be told that if people wanted a Dharma talk they'd go to a Dharma center. People wanted an *experience* of Dharma. They wanted their Dharma blended with their Jam.

Through trial and error, I made changes. I added an opening refuge prayer, lengthened the opening sitting meditation and closing reflection circle, gave a more gradual rise and fall to the music playlists, and spread the Dharma talk component throughout the movement and dance periods.

Along with being the facilitator of Dharma Jam, I've also had to figure out how to produce and promote it. Was it a dance event with a Dharmic twist, or a Dharma practice that incorporated movement? Would it draw more dancers or meditators? Should I host it in a dance studio or a Dharma center, and how often should I offer it?

As I developed Dharma Jam over the years, it's shifted from being a monthly event in a community center, and then a dance studio, to a seasonal offering in the spectacular Andover Chapel of my alma mater, Harvard Divinity School. Jams generally draw between a dozen and three dozen people (depending on the venue), with both repeat attendees and first-timers showing up. Especially satisfying has been the smaller, but steady participation of meditators wanting to try something new, those who have seen Dharma Jam fliers posted in local meditation centers and decided to take the leap. I've been pleased, but not surprised, when members of the local improv dance scene showed up. To be told, however, "I was waiting in line for the bathroom at the Cambridge Insight

Meditation Center and I saw your flier," has been wonderful to hear. These people were coming from a place of Buddhist practice, curious to find out how movement and dance could complement their work on the cushion and in life.

Parallel to offering and refining Dharma Jam, I made efforts to create and share other movement and dance practices in explicitly Buddhist contexts. Suspecting that programming with children and teens would be an easier sell than with adults, I first got my foot into Buddhist venues by volunteering to lead movement and dance activities for Spirit Rock Meditation Center's Kids Dharma Class during January of 2008. While adults went to the Dharma Hall to hear Monday night talks, I guided mindfulness-based hip-hop and creative movement exercises. I've since offered half-day retreats grounded in mindfulness-based movement and dance for adults in Buddhist centers, as well as programming for groups of other religions, college courses, conferences, and mental health inpatients and outpatients. A Muslim woman who attended one of my workshops commented that it helped her "realize that there is a common interfaith point of mindfulness that has its roots in different religions and spiritual beliefs."[10]

More recently, I've blended the elements of what I offer into Breakin' with Buddha—a one hour workshop that includes standing and walking meditation, hip-hop instruction, set choreography, and a mini-Dharma Jam. In February of 2015 I led this workshop at Coming Together 7—an international gathering of interfaith college leaders hosted at Yale University. Across many different religious affiliations, ethnicities, and backgrounds, we shared embodied presence, existential inquiry, and joy.

Harrison Blum (directly in front of piano) leading a series of symbolic postures at a Breakin' with Buddha workshop for Coming Together 7, Yale University, February 2015. Photograph by Christian T. Maxwell.

As I've started to offer this workshop format more than full Dharma Jams, my efforts of late have also shifted toward another improv jam structure. Since December 2013, my fiancée and dance/movement therapist, Amorn O'Connor, and I have created and produced Nectar: A Conscious Dance Gathering, at the Dance Complex in Cambridge, Massachusetts. Nectar is a talk-free event inspired by conscious and ecstatic dance, and is sustained with the help of a rotating crew of Facilitator-DJs (FDJ). FDJs lead an opening circle with some invitation to help participants deepen embodiment and set intentions, followed by a progressive music set that begins and ends mellow while peaking with high energy music in the middle. Amidst both similarities and differences between Dharma Jam and Nectar, I feel it's a way of following through on requests I used to get to hold Dharma Jams more frequently—a request I was not able to accommodate as one person. Together, the Nectar crew is able to hold space twice a month for dozens of people to explore and celebrate their embodied existence. Our closing circles invite participants to share about their experience in the dance, and most comments speak to the healing, insight, and bliss fostered by moving freely.

Especially beautiful has been the three different women who—over the two years we've been holding Nectar—have danced while pregnant, given birth, and then returned to the dance floor with their infants, now toddlers. The Nectar community has witnessed these three youngsters begin to grow up as movers and dancers before any of them could walk or talk.

While not an explicitly Buddhist event, Nectar aligns with the Dharma in a way somewhat akin to the relationship between secular mindfulness (when taught well) and the Buddha's teachings. When I teach mindfulness meditation to adolescents on the acute psychiatric unit where I work as a chaplain, I guide them to be aware of pleasant, neutral, and unpleasant elements of their present moment experience, while lessening their instinct to grasp the pleasant and fight off the unpleasant. This approach is both secular and consistent with much of the meditation technique presented in the *Satipatthana Sutta*. Similarly, while Nectar FDJs rarely draw directly from Buddhism in leading the opening circles, the facilitation and structure does foster a safe space to be present with and compassionate toward the details and totality of one's experience, to be and breathe and move with the Dharma.

Expanding the Benefit

"One heel up, one heel down. Only move the flat foot." These are the two basic instructions I use to teach the moonwalk. I've found that teaching the moonwalk works well to break the ice toward the beginning of a meditation workshop. It also serves as an embodied metaphor for mindfulness practice. Both have two simple instructions. The moonwalk requires that (1) one heel be lifted and the other flat on the ground, while (2) the flat foot is slid backward along the ground. Switch the lifted heel, and repeat. Mindfulness invites the two aspects of (1) present moment awareness (2) without resistance or judgment. Both are easy to describe and harder to do. Both are possible with practice. Both can lead to joy.

I opened with the moonwalk in the first class of a mindfulness series I taught in the spring of 2012 at the Margaret Fuller Neighborhood House (MFNH), which serves low-income residents of Cambridge, Massachusetts. As this group of new peers practiced the moonwalk, with the accompaniment of Michael Jackson's "Billy Jean," they got into their bodies, loosened up, smiled, and laughed.

I offered this series as a response to a question I'd been asking myself—How can Dharma Jam be an ally to those with fewer resources? Participation in Dharma Jams thus far has been reflective of the demographics of Western Buddhism more broadly. The majority are white, well educated, financially stable, and privileged.[11] There are indications Western Buddhism is evolving. People of color practice groups and retreats are on the rise. Practitioners of color are also showing up in greater numbers in racially mixed venues. In 2013 the Insight Meditation Society, for the first time, had over 30 percent registration from people of color for their annual three-month retreat.[12] This is exciting news, and still we have much work to do toward making *sanghas* more inclusive.

A question thus began emerging for me—If Buddhism is about relieving suffering, whose suffering does Dharma Jam relieve? My solution thus far has largely been to use *dana*, or donations, from Dharma Jams, workshops, and related presentations to fund the Mindfulness Allies Project (MAP). With the goal of increasing mindfulness equity—access to mindfulness training regardless of identity factors such as race and class—MAP offers a model to forge partnerships in offering free mindfulness classes to under-resourced populations.[13]

The class at MFNH was the kick off to the first MAP mindfulness series. More than half of the participants were people of color and more than half earned less than $15,000 a year. I was told by several participants that my offering the classes free of charge, along with providing free childcare during and free dinners after each class, were significant enablers of their attendance. Feedback was tremendously positive, with self-reported well-being improvements in relation to one's self, family and friends, and even chronic pain. In the words of one participant, "I believe I learned to be more aware of different situations and have more acceptance and to be less judgmental. I learned that pain is inevitable. I knew it, but I accepted it more as a part of life, not as a punishment."[14]

In addition to the moonwalk, I incorporated mindful movement activities, walking meditation, and qigong into these classes. Amidst the benefits of seated meditations and discussions, the movement-based practices were cited as highlights of the course.

From college students seeking relaxation to adolescents trying not to self-harm, and from yuppies aiming for enlightenment to single mothers struggling to pay their rent, I've seen dances with Dharma bring ease of heart and clarity of mind. May it continue to be so.

NOTES

1. Gil Fronsdal, trans., *The Dhammapada: A New Translation of the Buddhist Classic with Annotations* (Boston: Shambhala Publications, 2005), 68.

2. Wu-Men Kuan, *The Gateless Barrier: The Wu-Men Kuan*, trans. Robert Aitken (San Francisco: North Point Press, 1993), 3.

3. Sondra H. Fraleigh, *Dance and the Lived Body: A Descriptive Aesthetics* (Pittsburgh: University of Pittsburgh Press, 1987), 157.

4. Please see my essay in the Guided Practices section of this book for a guide to running a Dharma Jam yourself.

5. "Research," Institute for Stem Cell Biology and Regenerative Medicine, Stanford School of Medicine. Accessed August 13, 2013. http://stemcell.stanford.edu/research/.

6. Fronsdal, *The Dhammapada: A New Translation*, 13.

7. Edmund R. Leach, in *Anthropology in Theory: Issues in Epistemology*, ed. Henrietta L. Moore and Todd Sanders (Malden, MA: John Wiley & Sons, 2014), 74.

8. Catherine Bell, *Ritual Theory Ritual Practice* (Oxford: Oxford University Press, 1992) 98, 107.

9. Personal communication, December 2013.

10. Personal communication, June 2015.

11. Harrison Blum, "The Mindfulness Allies Project: Partnering Insight Meditation Centers with Marginalized Communities," MDiv thesis, Harvard Divinity School, 2012. Available for free download at http://www.movingdharma.org/writings-resources/.

12. "Sangha News," Insight Meditation Society, February 2013.

13. For more information see Harrison Blum, "Mindfulness Equity and Western Buddhism: Reaching People of Low Socioeconomic Status and People of Color," *International Journal of Dharma Studies* 2.10 (2014). Available for free download at http://www.internationaljournaldharmastudies.com/content/2/1/10.

14. Participant feedback on post-course questionnaire. For more participant feedback please see Blum article cited above in *Dharma Studies*.

Charya Nritya
Nepalese Ritual Dance of Deity Yoga

HELEN FOX APPELL

At the beginning of an introductory dance class, my teacher tells the story of Buddha's enlightenment. When the historical Buddha, Siddhartha Gautama, sat meditating for years in extreme austerities and yet could not reach his aim of liberation, he finally nourished his emaciated body. Refreshed, mind cleared, he again sat, hands forming the *dhyana mudra* of the meditation posture. Still not fully confident in his enlightened nature, he sat firm. Then, spontaneously with a gesture from the heart, an inner *mudra*, he wholeheartedly moved a hand to touch the earth, acknowledging that it is necessary to be grounded in this body, and in this world, while the mind rests in transcendence. With the earth as his witness, he gained impenetrable confidence. In this way, moving from inner stillness into engaged gesture, the Buddha overcame all afflictions and suffering and fully realized his enlightenment.

What initially shifted my hands from *dhyana mudra*, the meditation gesture, into the *mudras* of sacred dance was a wish to integrate the spiritual and physical in my practice. The dance that changed my world is a Buddhist ritual dance from Nepal called Charya Nritya. Charya Nritya is part of the rich, Sanskrit-based Newar Vajrayana tradition of Buddhism that practices deity yoga, embodying our Buddha nature, through dancing the section of a *sadhana* that describes the attributes of a deity.

Following the Mahayana Buddhist goal of attaining Buddhahood to benefit all sentient beings, the deities of both the Mahayana and Vajrayana pantheon are expressions of various facets of enlightenment, each exhibiting transcendent wisdom and universal compassion. These Buddhas and *bodhisattvas*, or altruistic beings, subtly manifest throughout the universe to liberate sentient beings from suffering and guide them toward enlightenment. They manifest in many forms as skillful means to meet the varying needs of practitioners. A deity can be invoked by a practitioner through a meditation practice called a *sadhana*. A *sadhana* encompasses recitation, visualization, reflection, and mindful lifestyle, with practitioners devotedly connecting to a particular deity's qualities. Experientially, these divine presences are the spiritual aspect of our human realm—something other than our usual worldly ways—that draw us to reach beyond our limited views and behavior, realizing, even if for a moment, the deity within.

Charya Nritya includes the traditional elements of Newar Vajrayana ritual and reflects a *sadhana's* components: Sanskrit chanting, meditation, visualization, *mudras*,

155

and movement, as well as ritual implements. These share the purpose of enacting one's highest aspirations and of discovering and imprinting the significance of the ritual in one's sensory body and mind through mindful attention. These ritual elements in Charya Nritya point to the divine nature in everyone, on the principle that all are worthy to be empowered with the indestructible confidence of a Buddha. The words of the chants and songs are terse descriptions of the deity being danced and embodied. The *mudras* follow the deep iconographic significance of a deity as well as expressing the deity's qualities described in the songs. These gestures are to be performed with wholeheartedness in body, mind, and outward expression.

The ritual implements of the dance are the ornaments and colors that are worn, which appear similar to the deity's, and connect us to a new physical paradigm within our own body. Heightened attention to perform the ritual is also an integral element, letting go of both concepts and desired results, and instead simply and mindfully performing the movements. The imprint of the ritual experience is then stronger and can be received more deeply and carried naturally into daily life.

The world of Tantra, of which Charya Nritya is a part, is a particularly elaborate path of devotion, faith, and individual exploration. It emphasizes using any tool toward enlightenment that can heighten and transmute one's practice, no matter how challenging and unspiritual that tool may appear, as long as the appropriate motivation and understanding are there. In this chapter I describe my own path and exploration, how I met the dance, and my own understanding of it.

Two Streams Converge: Ancient Tradition and Modern Practitioner

The Kathmandu Valley in Nepal lies at the crossroads of the ancient civilizations of Asia. Legend holds that the area was once covered by a lake. Nepal Mandala, as the Kathmandu Valley was known, was created by the divine intervention of the altruistic deity Manjushri. Using his flaming sword that cuts through ignorance, this lord of wisdom sliced a gorge that drained the lake and created a lush valley suitable for human habitation. The Newars are the earliest known and by all evidence the original inhabitants of the valley.

As Manjushri's divine land, Nepal Mandala gave rise to a profoundly rich culture of spiritual wisdom and sacred arts. These arts serve as ritual offerings to the vast pantheon of Buddhist divinities and provide soteriological methods to awaken the deity within both artist and appreciator. Charya Nritya, one of the ritual arts that arose in this "Land of the Gods," is a dance to invoke, embody, and realize internally the deities in form and spirit.

It was a Newar painting of this origin story of Manjushri cutting the gorge that first sparked my interest in the Newar sacred arts. Although I had long taken a keen interest in Buddhist deities and iconography through years of intensive Tibetan and Zen practice, this portrayal of Manjushri was not a form I had ever seen. In images I had studied, Manjushri was sitting, his sword used internally to cut ignorance from the mind, his left hand holding a lotus with a scripture of wisdom.

My initial interest in Buddhism came through meditation in karate classes. At that time I was not attracted to, nor did I embrace, the sacred arts. With deepening interest in following a Buddhist path, my mind strongly aspired to the ideal of renunciation on every level. "Leaving home" for me meant also leaving the body behind, including my karate practice, in pursuit of stillness and inner purity. I couldn't make sense of the material world in relation to the spiritual realm, and so I immersed myself in Buddhist practices with an approach of mind over matter, imposing my will with fierce determination.

Although I renounced the body, and ritual along with it, ignoring their importance, I gradually recognized that something significant can be transmitted through a bodily gesture. While immersed in study in India, I was deeply affected by the handshake of a Tibetan *lama*, feeling more profoundly what was transmitted through the full engagement of energy of his hands than through his words of wisdom.

Around that time, a younger *lama*, still engaged in his monastic education, told me of his love for movement as he used his hands and body in the traditional debate form. Because he could move with intellectual and verbal expression, he found his mind more energetic and accessible and enjoyed the body and mind working fully together. His experience was that body, speech, and mind became united as one.

Eventually, after fifteen years of having the good fortune to dedicate myself to study and sitting practice in India with Tibetans and in Zen monasteries in the West, it became clear to me that I needed to move and express. I wanted to integrate all yogic arts into my Buddhist practice, feeling compelled by my love of *sadhana*, the deities, and the historical basis of that lushly artful spiritual world of ancient India and Nepal. I felt drawn to live my life as a *sadhana*, as a mindful ritual. I started learning Bharatanatyam, a classical Indian dance available to me in the Bay Area, and Iyengar yoga. I studied Indian raga singing and classical Sanskrit.

When I began dancing and singing after so many years of sitting, I first noticed a general mood-altering effect. I was impressed that I could walk into a class feeling resistant and tired and leave feeling buoyant, present, and joyful in the whole body, not just the mind. Grounded and uplifted, some balance in energy restored, I could learn about the challenges that my body and mind face in an environment of heightened joy!

It was my love for the Buddhist pantheon of innumerable deities that then brought me to the practice of Charya Nritya. My Indian dance teacher had spoken highly of this dance form and its principal teacher from Nepal, who was now living in the U.S. I sought him out and found in this ancient Newar ritual tradition all the yogic disciplines and branches of knowledge I was pursuing: dance, singing, Sanskrit songs, meditation, Buddhist deities, and iconography. Charya Nritya was for me a wish-fulfilling jewel. While exploring this dance, I saw the embodiment of the deities in the practice of my teacher, Prajwal Ratna Vajracharya. Having begun Charya dance in his early childhood and been taught within the household by his father, a scholar-priest, Prajwal was formed both in body and in mind by dancing the deities.

On first introduction to Prajwal, I closely studied his form and his movements, both in dancing and in daily life. When Prajwal speaks, his whole body speaks, the reverberation of a spoken syllable subtly rippling through his body, the expression of a fully engaged being. It was clear to me that it was a rare turn of remarkable good fortune to have such a skilled teacher of this unique sacred art form in the U.S. Prajwal is the only priest, dance master, and teacher of the lineage sharing his tradition in the West, for he realizes the value of this practice for serious practitioners everywhere, not only in Nepal.

For the first few years, I traveled regularly to study the dance from the Bay Area to Portland, Oregon, where Prajwal and his foundation, Dance Mandal, are based. Eventually, to commit myself more fully and study more intensively, I moved to Portland. Dance became one of my main Buddhist practices in the form of Charya Nritya. Through it I studied both my mind and the movement of my body, gradually working to open the blockages and transform habits I experienced from life-long patterns. With a master as my role model, I watched two videos on two screens—one of Prajwal dancing and one of me performing the same dances simultaneously to the same recorded Charya song. I noted the differences and tried to model my movements after his. In contrast to Prajwal's continuous flow of movement, I recognized my tendency to relate to positions as separate goals, to quickly complete a movement and then wait for the next move, in stillness like a statue, without any feeling for the process and the time between postures. At times the rhythm of my feet lagged behind the rest of my speeding body. My movement quality was sometimes wildly erratic and unclear, and at other times tightly constricted by a habit to hold back.

The clear difference in our movement pointed to a difference in our minds. His dancing was not about reaching a position as if it was an intellectualized future goal, but rather about spaciously and joyfully experiencing the present through his active expression. He lived a fluid world of continuous subtle movement, precision, and inward focus. My mind's long-standing tendencies towards impatience, towards quick attainment so I could move on to the next thing, and of being pulled outside myself by the senses, became clearer with further understanding the energetic tendencies in my body, providing more focus for transformation. Deep inward attention and mental stillness had been part of my sitting practice, but the dance now provided a means to learn this quality of mind in movement.

This in turn sparked a deepening interest in the iconography and details of the deity images as I started to make connections between how these images, along with the movement and songs, relate to how our own bodies and minds work.

Dance and Deity Yoga

The images of divine forms give us clues about their minds—enlightened minds beyond anger, desire, and ignorance—through their display of perfect form, expression, gestures, implements, and ornaments. Just as my teacher was a role model for understanding my mind and seeing my potential, and biographies or stories of realized practitioners provide examples that inspire our practice, deities can serve as role models, worthy of true refuge. Their ethereal form, made up of the glow of their spiritual attainment, looks similar to my human form, which conveys that I can manifest such a presence as well. Each detail of a deity's image in sacred art displays a blessed reality of inner beauty, bringing to the world the spiritual teachings of the Buddha in visual form that we can relate to kinesthetically, rather than through conceptual language. In this way, images of deities convey a subtle energetic body that is a bridge between transcendence and earth, body and mind, form and formlessness. The deities are our own spiritual nature expressed in artistically graphic form.

Studying ourselves in movement, and in relation to these role models, we can see the ways we tightly restrict or discursively move our bodies at the psycho-physical energetic level, as well as how we can enhance their potential. Practicing deity yoga through the dance affirms this body as a vessel, as a tool, and enhances its capabilities and capacity, going beyond assumed limitations—physical, emotional, and spiritual—in order to be of highest service. The deities' natures appear either compassionately peaceful or wrathful, protective of practice and of truth, male or female, at times for healing, and all to aid others on their path to complete realization. These aspects of Buddha nature can be tapped into if their essence, iconography, and movement are studied and understood. No matter who you are, the deity can be revealed within you through your very own vessel.

It is common to experience the impact of color in daily life, and in deity dance practice it becomes clear how the color of a deity is significant. Wearing a green costume of the serene female deity Green Tara—green as the growth of nature toward full potential—feels quite different from donning the fiery red costume of a *dakini*, a semi-wrathful female of intuitive wisdom. When putting the colors on, those energies can begin to arise in me, whether Tara or the *dakini*. The movement for each dance also reflects these energetic differences: soft and all-embracing or sharp and definitive, both stemming from great wisdom and universal compassion.

In Charya, a dancer can begin to understand experientially in the body many points of Buddhist thought. The Six *Paramitas*, or Perfections, of generosity, wholesome conduct, patience, and so forth, manifest as divine ornaments in specific places of a deity's form as seen in statues and *thangkas*, or religious scroll paintings. These ornaments are worn by the dancers and can be perceived not only mentally and visually as symbolizing the Six *Paramitas*, but also kinesthetically as recognizable, subtle accumulating energies in specific areas of our body for particular spiritual purposes.

The power of deep intention through the altruistic vow of *bodhicitta*, to be of benefit to all sentient beings, propels those who adhere to this vow to express it to the world around them. Coming from each purely balanced internal energy center, or *chakra*, it is then delivered by a corresponding *vayu*, the vital wind forces responsible for all levels of motion of the mind and body, both coarse and subtle. Each ornament a dancer wears, if worn with awareness, can then be experienced, with intentional movement, as the outward offering from one of these *chakras*, serviced by one of the five *vayus*.

As an example, the deity's necklace at the heart center, the Dharma *chakra*, is the place of the first *paramita* of generosity. Through the *bodhisattva* vow, the psycho-physical energy from this heart of generosity is released and directed through the arms to give appropriately, only for the welfare of others, while being contained by

Sitting atop a lotus and a double vajra, the sign of indestructibility, Golden Tara Vasundhara (danced by Helen Fox Appell), Goddess of Abundance, gives infinite blessings. Observers surround her mandala in the sacred space of Nritya Mandala Temple in Portland, Oregon, September 2010. Photograph by Ishan Shakya, Dance Mandal.

morality, the second *paramita*. The arms' subtle energy shimmers with the ornaments of perfection, the bracelets that manifest from the pulse of this virtue expressed to the world. The wholesome energy is directed through the center of the palm, an outpouring that is of full benefit through this focused engagement. In the process of the dance movement, through knowledge of such a deity's qualities, visualization, attention to the ornaments worn, *mudra*, and supportive breathing, the *chakras* and *vayus* become felt experiences. When the dancer, with the breath, brings mindfulness of the body to the ornament at the heart center, the heart naturally begins to open confidently to infinite giving.

Through these practices of dancing deity yoga a practitioner is aided in experiencing the potential to go beyond limited views and bodily imprints. Dancers can develop wisdom by seeing in their own form the contrast between the comportment of divine confidence and the difficulty of their particular human existence. Our humanness is both the foundation and the fuel for transformation, and therefore not to be hidden or judged, but discovered and understood, and digested patiently layer by layer. Only through disciplined and honest self-awareness can the deity within be realized.

The Dance Ritual

In the dressing room, a dancer mindfully puts on the necklace of the perfection of generosity, feeling the energy opening, while visualizing and reciting the mantra of the deity to be danced. Now and then a thought arises, almost spoken ... "this belt has never fit right, need a...," but the thought dissolves ... composure continues undisturbed. The mind returns to the physical connection, dissolving the emphasis on self and its preferences, and enjoying the upper necklace that encircles and contains the light energy at the throat center, the gift of appropriate speech and silence. This is the ultimate aspiration of the dance ritual: to make every movement of the body and mind and every sound with the consciousness and awareness of a deity, until you and the deity are one and the same.

Handling the crown with care, tying it at the back, the base at the hairline and its five points directed up, it draws one's energy upwards to the center. There, all phenomena, five elements, five wisdoms, and so forth, splay outward in each direction and return, merging as one unit, to the center. Feeling the uplift, head meeting crown, focusing inward, the dancer's energy becomes heightened.

From another room, the warm silence is broken. "This crown is so painful! Can I wear something else?" Suddenly other dancers have something to complain about, the dissatisfaction of human existence reverberates with full force. I am reminded of something I heard that Suzuki Roshi once said during a Zen *sesshin*: "You all look so enlightened ... and then you talk!" Back to ordinary reality and the world of comparison and dissatisfaction. The dance ritual accentuates those contrasts of divine pride and human insecurities. Going back and forth between our sense of ordinariness and the divine, becoming more familiar with, confident in, and empowered by our deepest nature, this is the practice of deity yoga embodied.

After the dancers are fully dressed, we sit meditating on a particular deity that will be danced. In the sacred space of a temple or center that has been prepared for ritual performance, the dance ritual begins. Surrounded by observers who partake in the *rasa*, or essence of the ritual, the dancers set their motivation through the Refuge and *Bodhicitta* Prayer Dance. This is followed by making offerings in the Five Buddha Mandala formation through the dance of Sixteen Offering Goddesses. Dancers embody each of these Five Buddhas in a still meditation posture while the goddesses dance, offering gifts portrayed through *mudras*. These offerings, visualized and imagined, are to heighten the senses and are made with pure motivation, dropping judgments such as "not good enough" and "better than." This prepares the dancer's mind for the purity and elevated intention of the deity to soon be danced.

Following these preliminaries, the different deities from Charya Nritya's Buddhist pantheon can then arise. As the preliminary dancers spin off to the sides to observe, another dancer enters in full deity attire, dancing prescribed movements to a devotional song of a *bodhisattva* who works to benefit all. *Bodhisattvas* are active and the dancers embody this—a stark contrast to the straight, still shape and meditative lowered gaze of the Buddhas. Now, from this inner stillness, they are fully engaged in movement, in service, as seen in the *tribhanga*, a three-part side bend with the hips, torso, and neck, following a sliver moon curve of the spine. This form is characteristic of the statues and *thangkas* that portray these subtle bodies. In movement, and in the dance, *tribhanga* becomes a smooth undulation from side to side while the embodied deities display their altruistic activity. With this movement the dancers peer out gently, eyes no longer lowered but now in the universal gaze, open fully, not fixed on or attached to any one thing. With this gaze altruistic beings are open to everything that arises, and spontaneously move to offer nurturing protection whenever invoked. With kind faces, enchanting ornaments, and colored silks, these beings are breathtaking forms of conventional beauty. Their peaceful, serene movement nourishes us, giving us what is needed so that we can practice earnestly with our fears allayed. The dancer experiences this energy of the *bodhisattva* being danced, this fluidity of movement and grace, of openness and benevolent activity.

Then enters the fiery red *dakini*. Energy intensifies as the beautiful golden crown has turned to a headdress of skulls, an insight into the "bare bones" reality, no embellishments. This semi-wrathful wisdom female displays the power of fearlessness. She prods practitioners with the "not so easy to accept" truth commanding them to go beyond conventional responses and needs into an experience of the simultaneity of dualities, of attraction and repulsion. When things are going well and we are getting comfortable in our practice aided by the *bodhisattva*, the universal *dakini* energy yanks at our attachments and exposes our aversions without compromise.

The boundaries between deity and dancer blur. The *dakini* dances with fervor, blissfully, the sharpness of her gestures conveys that sharp quality of her mind that can remain centered and clear in the most horrific of circumstances. The open stare of her eyes from an inward focus on emptiness creates a spacious intensity and depth to every precise move. The *dakini's* heart intention is directed through the right hand of skillful means to an envisioned *vajra* chopper, her blade of discriminating wisdom, and with it she decisively swipes through all attachments as they arise. She raises her skull cup to drink and digest the life essence of the remains, generating the fuel to respond beyond limited conventions. Dancing and stomping on any negative force that takes us away from our deepest aspiration, the ankle bells of firm discipline ring out loudly, claiming her place in the world, demanding the observers' attention, no complacency possible.

The *dakini* then disappears, the room quiets, and for the finale, suddenly with great ferocity, the *dharmapala*, or Dharma protector, storms in. Dark, wrathful, and masked, the dancer shakes and stomps with precision, snake adornments dangling and spinning off from his body. The *dharmapala* appears in order to protect the practitioner from taking a worldly response to the harsh challenges of the *dakini's* wisdom. His movement and *mudras* are fiercely powerful, exact and yet wild, shaking the mind up from its superficial wish to take the old familiar road.

In the wake of his fury, from a quiet awe and openness that settles in the room, all dancers join to dance a dedication. Recognizing our humanness, our hands perform the *mudras* while chanting to purify any faults in the ritual or in embodying the deity. We seal in what we have learned—as well as the deities' energies and power—circulating it throughout our bodies and minds, and connect it to all, praying that the benefits of this ritual may reverberate out to every living being, none excluded.

Concluding Reflections

An observer recently commented after a performance, "When I stop judging or analyzing or thinking about what I'm seeing and what it means, I can tune in to a thread of movement expression. That is when I understand something beyond words and thought. That's when the magic happens."

Dance ritual is a universal language pointing towards non-conceptuality. As a Charya dancer, it is not thought that moves us in these wholesome ways but the strong, deep intention to be of benefit. This is a gate to the mind of enlightenment, the mind of a deity, which ultimately leads to spontaneous action.

Because of the profound significance, the rarity, and the beauty of Charya Nritya, Prajwal and Dance Mandal are invited to perform throughout the world, in museums, universities, Dharma centers, temples, churches, schools, and performing arts centers. To appropriately share this dance practice in its traditional sacred environment, we built a Newar Buddhist temple in Portland, the first and only one in the West. The temple serves as a space for Newar ritual of all kinds and particularly for the dance classes and offerings of Dance Mandal. Those who study there learn to appreciate the practice value of performance ritual, of the costumes, and of the consecrated surroundings.

Charya Nritya provides a Buddhist practice for those who have spent their lives as dancers, but most folks have little or no dance background. Many view themselves as having two left feet, or as incapable of memorizing step sequences. These limited views change as they practice and perform, shifting from a fixed idea of themselves to a feeling of empowerment.

One of the beauties of Charya Nritya is that a class brings together practitioners from many forms and sects of Buddhism, and from other traditions as well. Some students come to learn Charya Nritya not knowing anything about Buddhism, and therefore learn through dance.

People become interested in studying the dance for different reasons—for the sheer buoyancy and the expression of different dynamic energies within them, for enhancing deity yoga practice, or for understanding their bodies through movement. Often why they come changes as they dive deeper.

The meanings of this dance can touch on every aspect of the Buddhist tradition[1] and, as a yogic practice, boundaries can dissolve and the truth of inseparability becomes palpable. In general and over time, dancing the numerous deities of Charya Nritya directs the mind toward wholesome views, aligning both body and mind with Dharma, leaving positive imprints for this life and beyond. If all bodies are appropriate vessels to reveal the deity within, and all minds have enlightened Buddha essence, then anyone can dance the deities and meet the challenges of transformation through Charya dance.

NOTE

1. More on Charya Nritya can be found in a researched exploration by Buddhist scholar Miranda Shaw, author of *Passionate Enlightenment* and *Buddhist Goddesses of India,* in her forthcoming book on Charya Nritya, tentatively titled *Dancing Enlightenment.*

The Mandala Dance of the 21 Praises of Tara

PREMA DASARA

Dancing Tara

The dancer walks out of the pulsing mandala. She is looking directly at the audience. She imagines her sources of refuge arrayed in the sky before her. She is radiating her compassion to the world, embodying the wisdom of interconnectedness, embodying the feminine commitment to awakening. She is Tara, the Tantric Buddhist deity who vowed to remain in the body of a woman until every being is free.

The dancer has been well prepared for this moment. Every gesture, every word of the songs, every meditation taught with so much love supports her ability to engage in this way with the world. The pulsing women around her, chanting, "faith, surrender, send out light" are her inspiration and support. She knows that should her concentration falter, they are there to support her. The line of protectors she dances within are chanting and gesturing the quality she represents.

The music of the praise she dances is slow and evocative. She dances the essence of Tara, her dancing body emanating her gift to the world, the dance itself modeled after one of the traditional four-line praises of Tara. Perhaps she has not been trained as a dancer from childhood, as previous cultures prepared their sacred dancers. This may have been a challenge. But it is her dance, her expression. It reflects the journey this practice has taken her on and she is prepared. She has also been prepared to accept that at any moment she could forget, or her body may move in a way she had not anticipated. She is not worried about this. Because it is Her dance, only she knows what it should look like, feel like. There is only one concentration that she must maintain. She is Tara. She is the embodiment of Wisdom and Compassion. How she moves is how the moment will move her.

Twenty-two times the mandala turns and a Tara is born, each represented by a woman dancing to the ancient prayer, the 21 Praises of Tara. The leader of the dance represents the Central Tara, Tara Zero, and she dances the meaning of the mantra. She is the fullness of all the Taras. They emanate from Her: Tara Number One, the Red Tara of Swift Protection; Tara Number Two, the White Tara of Creative Wisdom; Tara Number Three, the Green-Gold Tara of Impeccable Virtue. The mandala continues to turn and so it goes until every praise, every quality of Tara, has been expressed.

164

Linda Lopez being born out of the mandala as the Tara of Irresistible Truth at a formal offering of the Mandala Dance of the 21 Praises of Tara, Maui, November 11, 2011. Photograph courtesy Tara Dhatu.

To the audience, it is magic, watching the mandala open, the Tara being born, each one unique. All ages, sizes, colors, each woman willing to step into her power, to manifest wisdom and compassion.

The audience has been instructed to keep an open heart and an open mind. These are not professional dancers trying to impress. These are sincere spiritual aspirants engaged in a practice that provides inner awakenings. In that relaxed state the audience lets go of their burden, and according to the Venerable Bokar Rinpoche, they are able to experience the relief, even if it is just momentary, of a release from self-obsession.

Throughout the dance, the mantra is chanted, and the dancers focus on profound meditational practices. His Holiness the Dalai Lama assured the dancers, when a group of them danced for him in Dharamsala in 1998, if you enter Tara's mandala with a sincere heart you will surely have deep experiences of your spiritual possibilities. And for the audience, because you are chanting Tara's mantra, they will be touched with the blessing of Her Power, Her Wisdom, Her Compassion. She is like the wind, they do not need to know anything about Her to feel Her touch.

Shortly after their creation, I shared these dances with the old Kalu Rinopche as well as Chökyi Nyima Rinpoche, and they both encouraged me to continue the work. We have since had audiences with many great Lamas and meditation masters of the Tibetan Buddhist tradition. His Holiness the Dalai Lama. The 17th Karmapa. His Eminence Tai Situ Rinoche. His Eminence Jamgon Kongtrul. The Venerable Bokar Rinpoche. The Venerable Kunga Rinpoche. Sogyal Rinpoche. Lama Tarchin Rinpoche. Tara Rinpoche. Dagmola Kushog. Jetsun Kushog. Khenpo Khatar. Bardor Tulku. Each one, with hands pressed respectfully before them, bowed to the wonder and blessing of Tara appearing in our world in this powerful way. Each one made prayers that I be able to continue this work.

Origins

I am often asked where the dances came from and how I got into this work. I am not the standard issue for presenting Buddhist practice. I am a rough and tumble Western woman. I do not consider myself a Buddhist. Too limiting. Shakyamuni was not a Buddhist. He was a Buddha. I have engaged seriously in several religious traditions. I am more interested in showing where the mystical worlds connect.

Throughout my life I have followed the thread of the Divine Feminine. My devotions led me to Catholic Mary, Mother of Jesus; Artemis, Essence of Nature's Wisdom; and the triune expression of Hindu's Saraswati, Lakshmi, and Kali/Durga/Parvati. When I encountered the Tibetan Tara it was like an old friend, just a different name.

At the time I was an Indian temple dancer, living in India. I was secure in my spiritual expression, and though I dropped in on Tibetan Buddhist classes I was not at all attracted to the intellectual nature of the transmission. Meditation was torture, sitting still not my style.

The Lamas, though, were engaging and magnetic. Beginning in the early 1980s, I enjoyed a friendship with Lama Sonam Tenzin, who had been sent from North East India to Maui to start a Dharma center by the esteemed Kalu Rinpoche. Some time later, His Eminence Tai Situ Rinpoche visited the center and gave teachings and empowerments, and I was impressed with his style, his humor, and his deep compassion.

I had been dancing all my life, and was professionally trained in ballet and modern dance. Rejecting the dance world as superficial and unsatisfying, I danced on my own in nature, until I found my dancing aspirations fulfilled in India where I studied Odissi, the Temple Dance of Orissa. My relationship to the dance and my teacher was of reverence. I danced as an expression of the sacred. I was trained to personify the deity.

As I assimilated into the culture of the Hawaiian Islands, people were curious about the dance work that I was engaged in, so I created a temple atmosphere and offered the dance in a sacred way. I invited Lama Tenzin. He saw the sacredness of my approach and asked me to dance in his Dharma center during certain festivals he celebrated.

In 1985 Lama Tenzin asked me to take the traditional *sadhana*, or ritual practice, of the 21 Praises of Tara and re-write it so that it could be sung. This was a sweet task, and though I knew little about the meaning, power, meditations, or teachings imbedded in the practice he had given me, I did know something about devotional music.

I enjoyed working with the prayers, shaping the words so that they were poetic and evocative. I worked on this in my remote mountain home on Maui with my neighbor, Jeff Munoz. He had brought me the melody, his beautiful voice full of devotion. He played a do-tar he had made, a simple Indian instrument of two strings, and a sruti box. My husband played open tuning accompaniment on the guitar.

As I walked in the mountains I would sing the praises, and of course, being a dancer, I would dance. Influenced by my classical Indian dance training, I would embody and dance as Tara. As I danced, I also could see Tara dancing before me. It was quite an ecstatic experience, and I had no idea that I was engaging in methods of Tantric practice. I offered to create a dance of Tara for Lama using this text, and he embraced the idea.

The text of the 21 Praises of Tara certainly lends itself to dance. The praises were similar to the *sutras* that I had studied as an Indian dancer. I invited two of my dancer friends to join me in creating the dance. One of them insisted on inviting our other friends, none of them trained dancers. I was skeptical, but then the visions started and I was able to see the choreography of the golden spiral. I felt drawn to create the dance in a symbolic and sacred circle, a mandala of devotional movement.

Because we were offering the dance to Lama Tenzin I wanted to place it in context for him. I developed simple movements to open the ritual offering with a gesture of refuge and *Bodhicitta*, the intent to manifest our wisdom and compassion to benefit the world. These were traditional prayers taken from the ritual texts that Lama had shared with his students at the center. Tibetan Buddhist texts are methods combining prayers of supplication, intricate visualizations requiring the power of the imagination, and precise meditation techniques.

The fulfillment of the text requires the activity of body, speech, and mind. Developed over several thousand years, they are designed to stimulate a practitioner into certain specific realizations, opening deeper possibilities of the mind. Over the millennia, these texts have developed to suit the needs of a teacher's transmission. They are not fixed entities.

I kept the entire structure of the text of the 21 Praises of Tara that was used in the Dharma center. It was a condensed version of a much longer practice, a mind treasure revealed to a yogi named Chokjur Lingpa. I condensed it further as I sought to keep it easily understandable, rhythmic, and relevant, while maintaining its integrity in preserving the essential meditational elements. Usually, such Tibetan practices are done sitting down. I simply added the dance.

When I started working with this material I had no idea exactly what I was getting into. As a text it was evocative enough for me to see a dance. Even when I was burdened with the idea of having untrained dancers work with me, the choreography revealed itself.

Because of the enthusiasm of the dancers and the Lama requesting that I continue to lead the dance, I realized I needed to know more about just what we were dancing to. I entered into a period of study and traditional Tibetan Buddhist retreat. I was fortunate to be granted the use of a friend's isolated cabin, filled with excellent Dharma books. Engaged in a practice of Tara from four a.m. to ten p.m., during my breaks I read. And I was astounded at what I discovered. The text was a map to awakening.

Each part of the text stimulates a very specific part of the brain. Even without any scholarly training, the dancers were having experiences that were clearly meditative, powerful, and deep.

Audiences were also a revelation. When we danced it was common for people in the audience to weep. I knew that most of the audience really did not understand what we were doing, despite my attempts to give a clear introduction.

The first time the Mandala Dance of the 21 Praises of Tara was offered as a performance the fourteen dancers cried, the full room audience cried, and Lama Tenzin was beaming like the sun itself. Everyone asked me to offer it again.

I couldn't see what was getting them so excited. As a trained dancer, I was not able to recognize any one element that was especially compelling aesthetically. Of course, as the choreographer, lead dancer, and director, my mind was totally occupied by the logistics of pulling it off. There was no time for me to get into any kind of devotional or meditative state.

It was fortunate that throughout this work I have had the ear and the eye of some of the greatest Tibetan meditation masters of our time. Through their guidance I was able to understand the power of what we were doing, the meaning behind the prayers, how to meditate, what we were seeking to connect with internally, and how the focus of using our dancing bodies was opening our experience in ways that were extraordinary.

The practice itself was informing us. Over the years I modified some of the words and movements as I saw more clearly what it was we were trying to accomplish. I found colloquial modes of expression so that the words we used in the practice would stimulate the appropriate awakening. And always, leading us deeper was the power of the mantra and the meditations married to the movement.

Sharing Tara with the World

I have traveled and taught this practice since 1986. I often have women in a community approach me, declaring that they had danced with me fifteen, twenty years ago. They still play the cassette of the music of the dance of Tara and consider the experience of Dancing Tara to be one of the most powerful things they have ever done in their life. They often declare that their connection with Tara, the mantra and the practice, has helped them through the many challenges of their lives.

For twenty years I traveled the world giving weekend workshops. I would start the training on a Friday night, inviting anyone to join as an introduction to the dance. A typical evening would open with lightly guided free movement. Using playful, evocative music I would instruct everyone to feel into their bodies, relaxing, working out a few kinks, bringing their attention into the room and into their bodies. I would then direct them to dance with each other. Next I would gather them in a circle and open centers of the body through gentle, guided movement. This was all very playful.

While we were gathered in a circle I would explain that there is one purpose to this work and that is to help them to manifest their human potential. According to these teachings the highest achievement of a human being is to be "enlightened," to embody wisdom and compassion. We already have everything within us. We do not need to get anything from anywhere else.

The Prayer of Motivation makes this really clear. I have everyone follow the very simple movements. The music is rhythmic and seductive. I give a brief explanation before we dance but do not get too intellectual. The words are like a catalyst. The more we reflect on them the deeper they stimulate realization.

> I am here to manifest the wisdom that rests within.
> I am here to radiate my loving compassion into the world.
> I am here to gather the skill and the power to bless and empower all.

I then explain that this is not an easy task. We need sources of inspiration and support. I introduce the movement meditation of refuge inviting them to repeat the English words after me as the prayer is being sung.

Then I give a brief explanation of *Bodhicitta*. Because of our interconnected nature, whatever we do affects everyone else. We make a commitment (even if it is only for the evening) to engage in these practices, to be the best that we can be, because it is the greatest gift that we can give the world—to manifest the fullness of wisdom and compassion within our own body/minds. We dance through the movement meditation of *Bodhicitta*.

Next I sit them down and I elaborate a bit on the relevance of the practice to their daily life. I introduce the practice of Tara, Her origins, Her vow, Her Mantra. I guide them through a series of brief meditations, visualizing Tara in front and then themselves as Tara.

Then we dance. I have created a simple, condensed version of the mandala, working with invocation, purification, and dancing the qualities of the Central Tara and the 21 Taras—as Tara. We seal that energy with a brief and simple practice of dissolution, imagining that the world and all the beings in it dissolve into open space that contains everything. We let the mind rest in open awareness for a few moments. The leader intones a prayer of benefit and the dancers arise from open awareness into the meditational dances of the mantra.

Om Tare Tutare Ture Soha.
Connecting with the power of our sources of refuge we bless and balance the elements within and without.
Offering our enjoyments to our sources of refuge we receive their blessings and empower each other.
Taking the power, the joy, the awakening from our heart we send it into the world, removing the suffering and consuming it in the flames of our wisdom and compassion.

We end, as I will end here, with this sincere prayer,

> May All Beings Be Happy.
> May All Beings Be Free.

Moving in Grace
A Buddhist-Inspired Ritual Dance Practice

Hilary Lake

A Moving Journey

Moving in Grace was developed out of my need to connect with myself and others in a safe, vastly creative, open space. I was at the end of my second year at Harvard Divinity School (HDS) in the Masters of Divinity (MDiv) Program. I had just shifted my focus from the ambitious plan to become a Unitarian Universalist minister (with a Buddhist practice) in two years to diving fully into the Buddhist ministry track. This pursuit had less clear outcomes. Who would I be as Buddhist minister? What does Buddhist ministry look like, feel like, or even mean? I was, and am often still, asked such questions. I frequently ask them of myself even now, and yet I knew that this more open, creative, unstructured path was the right one for me.

I was twenty-six years old, feeling more like a five-year-old much of the time. I had recently unearthed a great deal of childhood trauma and hurt while working in social services and living in a cooperative community, shortly before going to graduate school. Daily yoga and meditation practices were a part of my life, as was dancing Contact Improvisation and African dance as much as possible. I had also studied Buddhism and Eastern philosophy and religion since I was 14 years old, having completed a BA in these areas at a liberal arts school. This education included living in Thailand for a year studying sustainable development and Theravada Buddhism all around the country, from urban to indigenous contexts. During part of this time, I lived in a Thai Forest temple, which dramatically shifted my personal values and purpose. I was still integrating this experience while at Harvard, learning much more about the social, cultural, and religious contexts in and around Southeast Asia.

I had a number of highly influential teachers at Harvard, including Roshi Bernie Glassman, a Zen Buddhist teacher and visionary. Roshi Glassman taught us his Zen Buddhist Peacemaker's ministry, which emphasizes the practices of bearing witness, not knowing, and allowing loving kindness to arise out of the space of relationship. John Makransky, a Tibetan Buddhist lama and professor at Boston College, taught us meditations to cultivate devotion to our ministry and social work in the traditional form of guru-yoga. In this practice one visualizes the teacher in front of oneself to receive love and support, and then dissolves the visualization into oneself, becoming the teacher who is then able to give love and support to others. I also took a class in the dance department on the Rite of Spring, a turn of the 20th-century ballet that was a radical departure from the traditional form, displaying an imagined indigenous ritual from ancient Russia. We examined the Rite as it has been recreated across the decades through anthropological, religious, and artistic frames, and then created our own version collectively through improvisation. These are just a few examples of the wealth of resources that were enriching the soil of deep exploration into which I was attempting to plant my own seeds.

While enrolled in a full load of classes, from Buddhist philosophy to pastoral counseling, I worked with a dedicated, consensus-based group to organize and raise the funds needed to buy and create a Unitarian Universalist cooperative house. I was also in weekly psychotherapy and receiving regular shamanic healings, practicing Kundalini yoga daily, and dancing as often as possible, knowing that I needed to heal myself deeply before I was going to be able to be of true service to others.

Amidst all this I was considering taking a break or leaving graduate school, feeling that I was always failing and behind, needing to drag myself around and push myself to perform most days, finding little inspiration in intellectual pursuits or community. I needed to feel, to be, to create; to move and sing and nourish myself and others. Now I see that I was yearning to be with my feminine, receptive self while burning out my masculine, action-oriented self. I needed to have a space to allow my feminine, emotional, fluid self to show and share herself with me and others, and to simply be in feeling, joy, and bliss. Moving in Grace became this sacred holding space for her vulnerability to shine and her power to emerge. Because I also needed to complete a thesis for my MDiv within the next year, the question of how to make this sacred, creative space into an analytical project became my mission.

A Moving Ministry

During my first two years at HDS, a few friends, fellow students, and I had been holding a weekly movement space called Moving Ministry that became a laboratory for exploring how movement and dance could inform, or be, one's ministry. I had also collaborated with a small group of friends to co-create the Moving Dharma Dance Lab, a Buddhist dance company in which a practice evolved organically out of our weekly, two-hour sessions of sacred silence and embodiment. I knew that these, as well as other practices, were essential in my work as a minister. I wouldn't just use them as hobbies to nourish myself; they would be the very vehicles through which I helped others receive nourishment. Yet none of them felt complete in themselves. They needed to come together, just like the many parts of me needed to find integration. I needed a new model of minister, and ministry, to fit the experiences and growth I was going through, and I trusted that there were others who could use and benefit from such a practice as well.

Out of this trust a new model and definition of minister and ministry emerged as Moving in Grace, a form of "emergent ministry." I began to see ministry as a process of connection and reconnection to oneself and others, through bearing witness with presence and holding the space of not knowing. These qualities set the stage for performative action that inspires individuals to find themselves in their connectedness. This is a vehicle for integrating and expressing one's full mind, body, and speech, which can be accessed through improvisational dance and song when an individual's whole being is invited to

An improvisational performance of the Moving Dharma Dance Lab by (left to right) Julia Beauchamp, Sunny Hitt, Januar Ciel, Hilary Lake, and Harrison Blum, Arnold Arboretum, Boston, May 2009. Photograph by Morgan Blum.

show up and share. It is something new, something co-created, that emerges out of the connection between at least two beings and is the basis for emergent ministry.

The practices that most inform Moving in Grace—Buddhist meditation, Kundalini yoga, and improvisational dance and singing—offer ways to reconnect the body to the mind, self to other, as well as to the community, the natural environment, and the infinite. Buddhist philosophy is specifically relevant because it addresses the need for not knowing as a prerequisite for transformation. Within the Tibetan Buddhist tradition that I practice, not knowing can be likened to the cultivation of emptiness, where things, ideas, beings, etc., are empty of an inherent existence separate from other things and beings. They and we are all connected and related to each other in ways that we cannot necessarily know; holding this space of not knowing allows what is unknown to become present.

I experience and practice not knowing as holding this space of the unknown between me and another person, thing, or experience. I trust that what I don't understand has value and can teach me more about who I am and what is important to me. While I have experienced some transformation toward being a more present, compassionate, open-minded, and open-hearted person through my practices and studies of ministry and Buddhism, bringing these modalities and ways of knowing together through the creation of a unique spiritual practice has helped me to believe in myself and experience my self worth in a way that I've never known before. This knowing and feeling of my worth gives me more confidence to trust my inner guidance and to share what I believe and think with a greater diversity of people, while still remaining interested and curious about other perspectives.

The Moving Practice

The structure of Moving in Grace guides participants in moving through an imaginary day, and allows for the benefits of the practice to integrate into all of one's daily life. The practice itself starts with an opening circle and then moves into a meditation that is inspired by *samatha* (calm abiding) and *vipassana* (insight) meditations I learned from the Thai Forest tradition of Buddhism. I first invite the practitioners to find their own piece of ground or the floor to lie down on. We then bring our attention to how the floor is holding us up and to the connection that we feel with the ground. This calls us to be present to our bodies in relationship to the ground, feeling supported and held and noticing how our weight is spreading out across the floor. Practitioners are invited to focus their attention on the breath as it expands and contracts the body (*samatha* meditation), which helps calm us as we follow the breath. I then guide us to find a place in the body where the breath is the strongest and focus our attention there, calling this place "home," a place to return, to renew, to center. After a few silent minutes, I invite exploration of other parts of the body that may be calling for attention; we send attention with the breath from our "home" to one other part of the body. This exploration gives a taste of a *vipassana* style meditation that acknowledges the insight that can be gained by focusing attention on sensations in the body. This other part is likened to a seed of potential that has been stored within us and is now emerging to be explored and shared.

I then lead us into a visualization of deep sleep where we are as still and silent as possible, held in our inner darkness. After some time resting here, we awaken slowly from an imagined, emerging dream in the early hours of the morning. This dream can be a feeling, vision, or intention that emerges out of the unknown in the darkness of sleep in this visualization. A dream could be a faint vision of an ideal way of being, a way of feeling in the body, or even an intention of what one is creating in one's life. I invite participants to explore what feels true, relevant, and of interest to them. We each have different ways of processing our inner lives; some use images, some feel, others verbalize. We allow our body-minds to guide us towards awakening into this imagined day in whatever mode with which we most connect. We practice waking up to each day with more consciousness and gentleness. I then guide us to continue to awaken, sending awareness through the breath to the entire body and being, exploring the sense of wonder and mystery between waking and sleeping, expanding it into the day and the light.

We then continue our journey through the various stages of our imagined day. Just as a poem or an image can be carried with us through a day, I invite the practitioners to bring a felt sense, or visual sense, of their dream with them. I welcome them to expand the feeling or enlarge the vision to include their whole lives and beings, and to move and share it in dance and vocal expression. There are no prescribed movements or actions; instead, we are all invited to trust our own bodies to guide us into movement and vocalizing, however we are called. Sometimes this looks like wiggling and yawning on the ground, and sometimes it looks like everyone joyfully dancing and singing together in chaotic connection. The particular arisings within the group depend on the stage we are in during the imagined day, and the needs of the individuals for their own self-expression. What emerges within the practice is different each time I share it, depending on the context, community, comfort, experience levels, and relationships of the practitioners to each other and the space.

As we move through six different energies that correspond to six periods of a day, I call upon common daily situations that may arise for those who are present, based on both my personal knowledge of them and inferences that I make. I do this in order to invoke their mundane lives in this ritual context. I even call in moments of conflict that arise for us and challenge us to be creative about how we can relate to these awkward or painful circumstances with our full bodies in improvisational dialog. The intention is for the practitioners to recall both the mundane and more charged experiences of their daily lives, while being able to express themselves freely through movement and vocalization. They don't necessarily act out what they would do, but rather release the tensions stored around these situations and practice embodied creativity in a safe, neutral space.

At times I invite spontaneous or seasonally appropriate visualizations and metaphors. While many of my guiding comments are improvised, they align with a consistent structure (the six energies and parts of a day) that holds the larger vision and gives meaning to the practice as a transformative ritual. As the practitioners move through the phases of a day in the practice, I periodically remind them to return to their breath, their "home," and to notice how and where the dream is now, as a way to be present to the moment. Bringing consciousness to an imaginary day helps us to carry this level of awareness throughout our actual days.

As the day rounds out, the practitioners are guided to return home, both to their imagined home and to the home they found in their bodies earlier in the practice. I invite them to bring all of their imagined experiences of the day—joyful, awkward, painful, sad, etc.—back with them, to integrate and offer up to those with whom they want to share. The practice then ends with a diminuendo, ideally with a cultivated state of blissful reflection, gratitude, and intention planting, as the practitioners prepare to go back into sleep as the day ends. The participants use their breath to come into a place of stillness. The space of a circle is then offered for sharing personal reflections.

Moving Ritual

I believe ritual guides a transformative process that requires creativity, and that all creativity is play. Furthermore, it has been said that dance is the "purest form of play," making Moving in Grace a ritual of play.[1] This particular practice invites improvisational play, through movement, dance, and voice, into a ritual space that is both structured and creative. My intention has been to facilitate transformation through an embodied encounter with Buddhist philosophy, cosmology, and the practice of meditation. More specifically, I draw from Tibetan Buddhist practice and cosmology and a Nepalese Newari Tantric dance called Charya Nritya. I have also woven in relational and therapeutic tools I acquired from counseling and facilitation experience in community contexts. The integration of these practices and perspectives allows for tensions and held emotions to be released and transformed into self-expression, simple enjoyment, and physical pleasure.

Music, whether recorded, live, or improvised by the practitioners, accompanies the ritual and inspires the movement of participants. Over the music, I verbally drop images and open-ended questions to bring the participants back into the present moment. For example, I might ask, "What is your vision of wonder? What does it feel like?" "What are you opening to?" or "Where is your breath now?" These are laid over the basic visualization of the imaginary day, which holds the linear progression of the practice. The questions are intended as wake up calls to re-orient the participants, reminding them to consider what else is happening in the present beyond what they had otherwise perceived. These questions are inspired by Japanese Buddhism's *koans*: short, puzzle-like questions or statements that aid the practitioner in breaking through mental constructs and reaching greater mental awareness and freedom. It is this fine balance created between structure (form) and improvisation (no-form) that holds open a space of creative potential for both the participants and myself as the guide. In addition to music, spoken images, and questions, I also use my own movement to engage the bodies, speech, and minds of the participants.

The intention to cultivate connection to oneself, others, and the environment is supported by the practice's emphasis on mindfulness. Mindfulness, in this case as a syncretization of what I've learned from many different teachers, refers to a discipline of recognizing one's physical, mental, emotional, and spiritual experiences and their constantly shifting nature. Awareness of one's state, including motivation, can direct energy towards intentional (though not necessarily rational) action. This action could be performed alone in the expression of feeling and emotions through movement and sound, or in relationship with others, possibly including touch. Mindful release of feelings and emotions can allow for greater awareness and connection to self, others, and the environment without the confusion of the past blurring the present. Such release may also clarify how one can engage or express powerful emotions in healthier ways. Mindfulness supports the practitioners in waking up to each moment of the dance as an opportunity for release, expression, connection, and co-creation, which can then begin to integrate into one's life outside the practice.

Moving Through the Mandala

A primary source for the philosophical and theological structure of Moving in Grace is the Six Buddha Families from the Tibetan Kalachakra Mandala, which I connect to the stages of a day and their corresponding activities. The Kalachakra Mandala is the intellectual and visual representation of the Tibetan Buddhist cosmology and a model for harmonious relationship between the 722 deities represented. The word Kalachakra, meaning "the wheel of time," also refers to a union between bliss and emptiness, which is represented by the masculine and feminine.[2] The Kalachakra Mandala is practiced to cultivate the realization of *bodhicitta*: the motivation to enlighten oneself in order to help liberate all sentient beings. This intention, put into motion, creates harmony within oneself, others, and the whole community of life.

Through the traditional Buddhist practices of meditation, visualization, prayer, mantra recitation, and *mudras* (hand postures that represent relational actions), one aligns his or her being with the sacred structure of the Mandala and the deities within it. The dynamic diversity within the Kalachakra Mandala serves as a complex constellation of resources to help us creatively use all of life's experiences for awakening. Anything and everything that arises in life can aid in one's enlightenment if there is the presence to recognize its teaching.

The Six Buddha Families are a part of the basic structure of the Kalachakra Mandala, and each corresponds with an element, color, moral value, and virtuous behavior, among other things. Though these aspects are a part of the structure of Moving in Grace, I do not explain the Kalachakra during the practice; instead, I hold this layer internally as I facilitate. I trust that my presence and embodied knowledge of the Buddha Families can guide the energy in the space and how I relate to the practitioners. It informs the verbal directions and reflections that I offer, which are different each time based on who is present, my perception of their needs, the season, and my personal process, among many other influences.

The Six Buddha Families are particularly useful in this role because they are also guides to the various qualities of being in the human experience. They represent a range of qualities, from a calm, kind presence to a wrathful, fierce protector, all of which are necessary, each showing itself in each of us in unique ways in different circumstances. This approach of embodying archetypal qualities is also consistent with aspects of the deity yoga practiced in Charya Nritya. I offer guidance for embodying these attributes in relationship, so that we can have a more complete, well-rounded reality, internally with ourselves and externally with others. We can consciously cultivate these qualities to bring us back into our own personal balance, as is the intention of the Kalachakra practice. Moving in Grace utilizes movement, vocal expression, and contemplation as generative ways to unearth and integrate the buried parts of ourselves, so that they can come back together into a healthy, more harmonious inner family in each of us.

Without explicitly teaching Buddhism or the Kalachakra, Moving in Grace cultivates the same openness to connection and helps us receive the energies of transformation and the richness of life. I thus consider it to be within the historical lineage of my Buddhist tradition. Beyond the frame of Buddhism, the Kalachakra relates to the Western concept of unconditional love, teaching how to visualize, receive, and embody the energies personified in the Buddhas, *bodhisattvas*, and other deities. Those energies guide us to the unconditional source of love, and support us to align with what we truly want at our core. Our personal energy and effort are redirected from worldly attachments toward personal and collective enlightenment. Personally, I have found these practices, both the Kalachakra and Moving in Grace, essential in my own progression toward enlightenment.

Moving Through It All

Although Moving in Grace is held in a framework that includes contemplative Buddhist and improvisational dance elements, it is a conglomeration that only emerges fully in the moment, out of the spontaneity of movement and the relationships present. The creativity that surfaces from a diverse ocean of perspectives and experiences, from my life and those of the participants, inspires the practice as it continually finds its form in ritual space.

While I have been the holder and main shaper of Moving in Grace, it has become what it is because of everyone who has moved within it. It is a co-creative, emergent practice that is different each time it is shared in response to and as a result of the connection between the participants, as well as the place in which it is practiced. It is co-creative in that the participants, through their movements, sounds, and presences, collectively create the experience moment to moment. It is emergent in that its form grows through the relationships and experiences that I, as the guide and holder of the practice, continue to have within and outside of the practice itself. One's life affects the form and flow of the practice and the practice also informs the flow and form of one's life. Moving in Grace has been a microcosm of my life, helping me to focus the immensity of the unknown into a specific time with a clear intention. It has helped me to deepen, open, receive, release, create, share, and reflect.

Personally, Moving in Grace helps me to open to the vastness of what is possible when I maintain an embodied connection to the feeling of my dreams and the wonder within them. I can then expand this wonder into embodied relationship with others, loving them unconditionally. My practice is to return to the wisdom of my connected body again and again in my daily life. Moving in Grace is one vehicle through which this cultivation is possible. May you find whatever way inspires and suits you and your needs for connection. Graceful awakening to all!

NOTES

1. Johan Huizinga, "The Nature and Significance of Play as Cultural Phenomenon," in *The Performance Studies Reader*, ed.Henry Bial (London: Routledge, 2007), 118.

2. Andrew Wistreich, oral teaching during Kalachakra Retreat at the Tushita Meditation Centre, Dharamkot, India, July 2014.

Circles in Our World, Rituals for Our Time

Dances of Universal Peace

Anahātā Iradah

What I have noticed the most, over the course of nearly thirty years of teaching sacred dance, is how much we human beings long to move and merge with a reality more expanded than the one we occupy in our ordinary, every day lives. We have a thirst that longs to be quenched. We have a longing that must be met. We long to connect. We long for a chance for our goodness to come out and shine. We long to get enough distance from our problems and responsibilities that we can see them through an expanded lens of interconnectedness where the meaning of our life takes on a deeper purpose.

In my own life, one of the responses to this longing was answered in the form of the Dances of Universal Peace, dances experienced in a circle as participants chant a sacred phrase from one of the spiritual traditions of the earth. I have led the Dances of Universal Peace for much of my adult life. From one perspective, I no longer *need* the Dances. The initial purpose they played in my younger life no longer exists in the same way. When I was younger, I felt ecstasy as I encountered the teachings of each path as if I had known "the secrets" in my bones and now they were being spoken out loud. I also was thrilled to encounter a practice that used movement and music to connect at a soul level, without having the dance aspect being socialized (as at a dance club) or competitive (as in some dance classes). Now I swim in an ocean of spiritual teachings and I am used to this Dharmic way of connecting with other people. The Dances of Universal Peace became my way of life over time.

When invitations come my way to share my particular flavor of the transmission of the Dances I usually say "yes." A transformation of consciousness happens in almost every circle, a transformation that changes lives, one by one. If I am capable of facilitating such transformation, then it is part of my life's purpose and Dharma to do so. As my life was changed, it is my duty to open the way for others.

Imprints from the Past

I was raised to be a dancer. In fact, it was my mother whose heart was called to the dance, but she channeled her own desire through me. From the age of five through eleven

178

I did competitive dancing in England in the form of tap, ballet, and modern. In those days all the music was played live by a pianist. Though I had some success and talent in stage dancing, it was in watching the hands of our pianist that I went into ecstasy. I was engaged in the dance, but transformed through the music. I went on to become a professional musician and composer, playing many instruments and studying music from around the world.

In 1980 I moved from Bath, England, to Los Angeles, USA. I was twenty-five years old. After some time I started to study to be a healer at the Healing Light Center Church in Glendale, California. During this time I made a very strong prayer that the gifts I had been given (as a musician, healer, educator, meditator) all be used in one activity. I made the prayer on a Monday night. The following Sunday the prayer was answered.

I had written the theme music for a cable TV show called *Women to Women*, and as a thank you the producers invited me to have whoever I wanted as guests on one episode. I wanted my laying-on-of-hands healing teacher Rosalyn Bruyere (whose work had been scientifically documented at UCLA) and a medical doctor, to be decided, who was interested in natural healing. I was introduced to Dr. Susan Bennet as a possible second guest on the show. Her business card read "Dr. Susan Bennett Shakura." I asked about her unusual last name, and she responded. "I am a Sufi and I teach the Dances of Universal Peace. Would you like to come?" She gave me the time and the address, and on the following Sunday, less than a week after my prayer, I had my first encounter with the Dances of Universal Peace.

It was love at first sight. I was completely at home in my being. Everything about the Dances helped me to know more about myself, more about the needs of my soul that had not been awakened in this way before. It was clear to me that meditation was a key ingredient to the practice, as well as being present with each other in nonjudgmental and affirmative ways. It felt as if the agenda was love, but without the self-absorbed emotional and romantic agenda that had so often accompanied the use of that word. Something transformative and transcendental had happened, and I really wanted to know more. It was a spiritual awakening.

After this initial exposure, my early involvement with the Dances included teaching guitar at many of the national and international training camps. After some time I realized that I also wanted to teach from this tradition and I began leading locally in California. It quickly spread to out-of-state teaching engagements and eventually to international invitations. I found that in leading the Dances, I did indeed utilize all my gifts, including everything I learned in the domain of dance as a child.

Around the year 2000 I led a circle of the Dances of Universal Peace at the consecration of a Peace Stupa at a Tibetan Buddhist Center on the Coromandel Peninsula in New Zealand. Lama Zopa Rinpoche (head of the Kopan Monastery and co-founder of the Foundation for the Preservation of the Mahayana Tradition) and several Geshes were sitting in the center of the circle. Rinpoche was furiously spinning his prayer wheel and turning the beads of his mala as I led three Dances inspired by the Buddhist tradition. At the end, somewhat nervously, I asked him if he had anything to say to the group, not having any idea what he might be thinking. He said, "I have been sitting here making prayers that you never stop doing what you are doing. The airwaves of our world are polluted and these songs and dances help to purify them. You have no idea of the power of this practice so please keep doing what you are doing."

This was a very impactful moment for me, and I made a promise to myself that I would honor this request. As a practicing Buddhist and meditator, I have focused on creating Buddhist dances that share the teachings of that tradition. I have sought to share these dances, both in person and by publishing a volume of fifteen Buddhist dances with Prema Dasara called "Dancing the Heavenly Abodes," which celebrates the teaching of the Four Immeasurables through walking meditations and dances. Amidst my own grounding in Buddhism, I believe that expanded states of consciousness can arise from any dance, in any tradition, as the qualities that ennoble the human experience exist within all spiritual traditions in their essence.

The Dances and Their Origins

The Dances of Universal Peace originated in the late 1960s. They came to and through Murshid Samuel L. Lewis of San Francisco, California. His Sufi teacher, Pir-O-Murshid Hazrat Inayat Khan, had created the Universal Worship Service where candles were lit to honor all the sacred traditions of the earth, known and unknown. At the lighting of each candle a scripture from that tradition would be read. Hazrat Inayat Khan brought the message of the Unity of Religious Ideals from the East to the West in 1910. In his day it was almost unheard of to worship in such an ecumenical way. It was something of a spiritual revolution to recognize the unity of all paths.

Murshid Samuel Lewis, his loyal student, extended this practice from reading the scriptures to embodying them fully in the form of body prayer, walking meditations, and dances. In that time period in San Francisco, Lewis considered one of his missions to be teaching the hippies of the Haight-Ashbury district "joy without drugs." The young people were gathering and searching, and Lewis was right there in the thick of it, available to be a teacher to all who were drawn to him. When he passed away, some of his young students were experienced enough to carry on his work. It was with these direct disciples of Lewis that I trained.

Each Dance is a ritual. Each dancer is equal. The circle creates sacred space. When we employ the elements of movement, sacred phrase, holding hands, singing, breathing, setting intention, and consciously cultivating love and compassion within community, we touch the innate perfection in each other. In most Dances there usually isn't strenuous movement, but there is enough movement to feel energized, enough effort to keep us alert, enough melody for beauty to surround us, enough harmony for interconnectedness to sustain us, and enough rhythm to unify us.

Each Dance has a leader to model and embody the sacred phrase that is at the heart of the Dance s/he is leading. Each of the Dances of Universal Peace has at its heart a sacred phrase from one or more of the earth's spiritual traditions. Most of the Dances honor one tradition at a time, therefore a Dance honoring the Hindu tradition would have a text or phrase from the Hindu tradition. The sacred phrase is sung to a melody, which requires some mastery of the use of one's voice. Hazrat Inayat Khan said that "the voice is the barometer of the soul." He said that we can experience the weather of the soul when a person speaks. After learning the phrase and the music, the movements are then taught clearly, and succinctly. Once the Dance is going, the leader works with the musicians, especially the guitarist and drummer, to guide them in accompanying the Dance without the music dominating.

Outer Dance, Inner Transformation

When internal difficulties arise in the Dance (which they naturally do), one can process them within the form through meditative attention. For example, many people have been told at some time in their lives that they have a terrible voice and should never sing out loud. When they come to the Dances they are expected and encouraged to sing. When they hear the internal voice of judgment, they simply move through it. The sensations of shame, humiliation, and distress may arise, but they simply watch the sensations without judgment, a form of observation similar to (and supported by) Buddhist meditation practice. They can watch the sensations change and pass away, and even generate compassion for themselves and others in a similar circumstance. It is the same way for people who arrive with "two left feet." They are aware that they are moving out of sync with the circle, and judgments may arise about not having rhythm or the talent to dance, but when they pour acceptance and awareness into the sensations, everything relaxes. In the relaxation, subtle shifts start to take place.

This pattern of accepting and dissolving self-judgment can happen in many ways. We become aware of our judging and comparing mind, and let go. We become aware of tensions in the body and tightness in the mind and consciously soften, bringing our awareness back to the present moment. The circle is able to hold our emotional states, our bliss, our longing, our yearning, and our pain without analyzing or talking. By remaining present with just what is, without pushing and pulling on our emotions, we are able to see the play of the mind. We are able to live it all as we recite the names of God or chant a scripture, moving and singing in unison, being channels for the Divine to flow through us.

There are many things we learn about ourselves, both as dancers and leaders of the Dance. We not only learn about the spiritual traditions of the earth, but we learn about our impulses, our habitual tendencies, our reactivity, and that which clouds the purity of our heart. This can happen in a number of ways. For example, if we have the impulse as a dancer to constantly correct the leader or offer "helpful" suggestions, we learn that there is a protocol, a time and a place, to offer feedback and advice. As the urge to do so arises we can watch the impulse without having to act on it. It is the same with the sensation of boredom, or the wish for the Dance to unfold in another way than the leader is guiding it. The thought arises and passes away, and we can gently observe our reactions without having to do anything about them.

The Dharma of the Dances

As a Buddhist practitioner, I consider the Dances to be exactly half way between the cushion and everyday life. Everyday life moves at such a pace that it is difficult to maintain a meditative awareness at all times. The cushion provides a slowing down of impressions and experience, allowing us to track each sensation with precision and calm. In the Dances of Universal Peace, we can maintain a similar moment-by-moment awareness of just what is. When thoughts arise, we simply allow them to recede into the background and return our awareness to the movements, words, partners, leader, and exactly what we are being asked to do.

When I teach, I bring the teachings of the *Brahma Viharas* (Heavenly Abodes of

Anahātā Iradah leading Dances of Universal Peace at Sukha Wellness Center, Avila Beach, California, March 2014. The dance, The Big Sigh, is a healing process set within the Hawaiian tradition of Ho'oponopono. Photograph by Mary Sage Syverson Sennewald.

Consciousness) into many of the Dances. I talk about *metta*, loving kindness, the warmth of our human friendliness, and help people to generate *metta* not only for themselves, their partner, or the group, but for the benefit of all beings everywhere. I talk about *karuna*, compassion, the trembling of the heart when we allow ourselves to feel what another feels, when we are willing to breathe in the suffering of our world and digest it in the flames of our wisdom. I talk about *mudita*, sympathetic joy, when we practice generating happiness for another person's happiness, independent of our own circumstances. I talk about *upekkha*, the great way of equanimity, when we can stand in the center of our experiences without pushing anything away or craving anything. I talk about these Four Immeasurables because the Buddha said that if we want to bring heaven to earth we have to abide in the *Brahma Viharas*. The Dances are the perfect place to practice these teachings. Negative mind states such as "the comparing mind" can arise at any time, and instead of reacting in habitual ways we can apply meditative antidotes and purify consciousness. The Dances can become a meditation. Sometimes I even start or end a Dance with a seated meditation.

The Dances can also facilitate insight into the Buddhist concept of *anicca*, or change, through movement. In many traditions, especially in the West, people do not move their physical bodies. Often people worship in pews. Somebody talks at them, but there is little or no movement, and therefore little embodiment of the message. Murshid Wali Ali Meyer, who was an original disciple and secretary to Murshid Lewis, once said to me, "in the Dance you get off your position, you are in motion, you are in flow." This is a crucial point. Fixed positions, opinions, and beliefs help to reinforce the illusion that things are solid, but once everything is moving, changing, it reminds us of the impermanent nature of all things and we learn to take refuge in change instead of fearing it.

This awareness of change can help to cultivate a fluid sense of self. In Buddhism, we often say there is "no self," but rather a fluid relationship to experience that expands and contracts. As the Vietnamese Buddhist master Thich Nhat Hanh says, "'Emptiness' means empty of a separate self. It is full of everything, full of life."[1] There is nothing solid. We are activity, not a "thing," a verb not a noun. Sometimes a Dance is full of connectivity with partners or the whole group, and in another Dance we may be much more introverted, with little or no connectivity with others. We are not defined by any one experience, in the Dance or otherwise. Leading the Dances can appear deceptively easy from the outside, but it requires a very subtle blend of "self" and "no-self," as the personality is initially used to engage the group, and then the sense of self recedes so that (what the Sufis would call) "The Spirit of Guidance" can come through. As the leader, one must constantly refine and meditate on one's internal process.

For myself, as a long term *vipassana* meditator, I use many of my meditation techniques when I both dance and lead to deepen my experience of the Dance. I use my concentration power so that I can guide each Dance from beginning to end without distraction. I also use the practices of the *Brahma Viharas* to constantly develop auspicious mind states so that I not only benefit the group I am working with, but send the energy far and wide where ever it is needed.

Rituals for the New Age

Murshid Sam, as he was affectionately known, said, "The watcher is the prayerful devotee, but the dancer becomes divine." The Dances are not a spectator activity. They are participatory. I have led several international peace delegations and witnessed with great interest the power of the Dances when we offer them overseas as citizen diplomacy. I have led Hindu Dances in India, Muslim Dances in Jordan, Jewish Dances in Israel, and Buddhist Dances in Nepal. In all situations the local population unhesitatingly joins in the Dance. When they hear their names of God chanted with reverence, with simple movements accompanying the songs, it is like a magnet or a moth to the flame. Men, women, and children all join the Dance as if life itself is being affirmed.

In some cases we may practice a deity dance from the Tibetan Buddhist tradition, and we suspend our limited sense of self and dance as the deity. In doing so, we positively imprint the mind stream and accumulatively replace negative imprints and impulses from the past. It is not a miracle cure. It is a practice, and like any spiritual practice it takes time. I have witnessed people's voices change as a result of chanting such positive phrases. I have seen people with two left feet gradually move with grace and ease. Most importantly, I have witnessed a deepening appreciation for the abundance of blessings on the planet manifesting through the many sacred traditions.

In the early 1990s when I was exploring the work of Joanna Macy and Father Matthew Fox, they described the need for rituals for the new age. They said that we didn't have the rituals to accompany this age in which we have the power to permanently end life as we know it on this planet. It seemed clear to me then, and is still clear now, that the Dances of Universal Peace are part of the new rituals that are being called into being. They are a communal expression of our need to come together and say "no" to destruction and "yes" to life. They are part of the solution to the loneliness and isolation of our times. They are a way to come together as community where we show up for each other without an agenda. The Dances are a safe place for people to meet, greet, and go deep. Healing between the sexes can also take place as we practice simply being present for each other.

Amidst the abundant blessings the Dances bring forth, the most challenging aspect of the Dances of Universal Peace are sustaining the states of consciousness beyond the duration of the dance/practice/walking meditation and taking the atmosphere, attunement, and realization into everyday life. Everyday life is much more stimulating and overwhelming than a dance experience. The Dances of Universal Peace give us permission to slow down, yet still interact. We are longing for this. Our nervous system wants to settle. We want to drop the bravado, the need to perform. We long to come home and relax into our original pure nature. It is one thing to reach this state alone and in stillness on one's meditation cushion, but to reach this state with eyes open, in a room full of people interacting with each other, can provide a bridge to experiencing such a state in everyday life.

As the years go by, we witness our dancing deepen. We soften. We no longer need the experience for ourselves alone, but we continue to show up because we are part of a group, a community that raises the vibration of the planet, one Dance at a time. We are aware of the different states of being in the circle and we sing to give each other comfort, inspiration, joy, courage, support, love, recognition, and solace. Sometimes we are the sun radiating and sometimes we are the moon, reflective and receiving. There is no need to declare our states. We each have our place in the cosmos. In a circle there is the wisdom of equality. It is truly something extraordinary. Young, old, male, female, tall, short, round, and thin make up the Mandala, a circular form representing the universe. At the center of the Mandala of the Dances of Universal Peace is the Unity of Religious Ideals that suggests that all the spiritual paths point humanity to the essence of the truth.

The national mantra of India says it so beautifully. "Sarva Dharma Samma Bhav," which translates from Sanskrit into English as "All The Dharmas [Teachings/Paths] Have at Their Center the Same Essential Nectar." This sums up the experience of the Dances of Universal Peace. We honor the sacred traditions of the earth. We listen to the teachings of those traditions. We embody the meaning of the words and send a message to our deep mind that we can connect to the purity of our being, which is our birthright. We uncover our Buddha nature.

NOTE

1. Thich Nhat Hahn, *The Heart of Understanding* (Berkeley: Parallax Press, 1988), 16.

Theory

Somatic Meditation
Rediscovering the Body as the Ground of the Spiritual Path

REGINALD A. RAY

Meditation: From Top-Down to Bottom-Up

Among many modern people, meditation is approached as a kind of mental gymnastic, a way to fulfill yet another agenda or project—attempting to become more "spiritual," less stressed out, more focused, more effective in our lives, or even more conceptually adroit. Meditation becomes another means of managing and superseding nature, controlling *the other*, ourselves, our bodies, and our own experience. Ultimately, what we are trying to override in the attempt to fulfill our various ego aims through meditation is our own somatic experience of reality. Unfortunately for us, it is there, in the Soma, that the spiritual path, and life itself, are actually and truly found.

Within the Tibetan Buddhist tradition, we may distinguish two quite different ways of practicing meditation. The first method, by far the most common in the Tibetan Buddhism taught in the West, is based on the labeling, thinking, agenda-driven functioning of the left-brain. In this approach, the practitioner is given a set of instructions on how a particular practice is to be performed, where the practice is intended to lead, and what the goal is to be attained. He or she then sets out to perform and accomplish the practice as it has been explained to them, to fit their experience into the template that they have been given. Or, alternatively, they try to use meditation to meet their ego needs—to gain certain preconceived experiences or to feel the way they think they should.

In neuroscience, one way to talk about this is as a "top-down" process—the process of meditation is carried out under the watchful and judgmental eye of the executive function of the cerebral cortex. In top-down meditation practice, we are constantly attempting to approximate what we think we are supposed to be doing and what we think is supposed to be coming out of it. In short, we are bringing the managerial function of the left-brain to our practice, to control and manage our meditation in a top-down way. This approach is not without important benefits, helping us to calm down, reduce our stress, become less distracted and more focused, sleep better, and so on.

Another method of meditation within Buddhism—less well-known but characteristic of the yogic practices considered the most advanced in Tibetan Buddhism—is based on entering and identifying with the Soma. By *Soma* I mean not only our physical body, but also the entire neurological network within which it is embedded, including the right brain and the subcortical regions that include other parallel processing systems—for example, the intelligence centers of the limbic system, the reptilian brain or brain stem, the heart, the gut, and the neural pathways that exist throughout the entire body, each with their own kind of awareness. This somatically-based meditation could be characterized, in neuro-psychological terms, as a bottom-up approach.

What I have found in my more than forty years of teaching meditation is that when meditation is presented as a left-brain, top-down practice, it can be very difficult to sustain and frequently doesn't really lead to long term results; certain superficial benefits arise, but people often don't fundamentally change in the ways described as being possible in the tradition. However, when meditation is taught as a somatic, bottom-up, embodied practice, it works in a very natural, effortless, and beautiful way. By softening control and conscious agency, this approach allows the journey to unfold naturally, bringing often profound transformation and enabling us to experience the innate goodness, clarity, and compassion that meditation is all about. By drawing on the yogic practices of Tibetan Buddhism, which explore the body from within, we can learn to allow the experience of the Soma to communicate with our conscious mind and to become known to us in a direct—that is, nonconceptual—way. In the tradition I teach, this method of meditation is anchored in some twenty-five progressively-unfolding somatic meditation protocols that we refer to as *the bodywork*. Frequently begun in a lying down posture, these practices use a variety of techniques—such as the breath, visualization, and the simple direct physical experience of certain key gates in the body—to bring us into a new, intimate relationship with our body, the limitless awareness that resides in it, and the objective information it is constantly sending our way.[1]

These practices enable us to contact our body, or Soma, in a new way, beyond and outside of the conceptualized body or body image that we all habitually interpose between our conscious, ego selves and the direct, unmediated, naked, nonconceptual experience of our body. We gradually discover how our uncontrolled anxiety, ego reactivity, and endless discursive proliferation obscure the natural health and wisdom of our Soma, and end up creating physical and psychological distress and illness. As we move through this process of deepening somatic awareness, we can find intensity, meaning, fullness, and fulfillment in the most mundane details of our life.

Body as Revelation

Over time, these practices experientially demonstrate the essential and transformative role of embodiment in the path of meditation. The body becomes a revelation in of itself, outside of any thought of a spiritual journey or commitment. A much larger range of emotional and perceptual information becomes available, and we begin to sense the limitless terrain of our so-called "physical being"—the endless, open spaces we can enter through the body. Practicing in this way opens a context within which one can actually experience the energy of the body, and the tremendous inspiration that arises for life, without the mediation of the ego.

I have mentioned the left-brain, top-down approach to meditation; another set of terms I would like to introduce here is *endogenous control*—a left-brain oriented, top-down approach—and *exogenous stimuli*—a right-brain oriented, bottom-up somatic approach. Endogenous refers to ideas, concepts, assumptions, judgments, conclusions that already exist in our consciousness, based on past conceptualizing, and that we seek to impose on our experience in order to "know," manage, and control it. Exogenous refers to phenomena that arise naturally and spontaneously from the darkness and unknown (i.e., subcortical) regions of our Soma, feelings, sensations, intuitions, memories, arriving in our awareness in a direct, utterly fresh, immediate, and naked way.

The endogenous part of us is a relatively closed system, cycling and recycling abstracted concepts that are already existing within us. Not surprisingly, the left-brain, without our larger brain, is the most far removed from actual experience. In fact, the left-brain cannot feel, sense, or experience anything directly, because that is not its function.

The exogenous part of ourselves, or Soma, by contrast, is all about direct, unmediated, nonconceptual experience. It beholds things exactly as they are without any judgment, evaluation, without even any filtering whatsoever. It receives reality as it is in all its diversity, color, and multiplicity without comment. Moreover, it beholds things as wholes, not through the limiting eyes of preconception, hope and fear, or ambition and agenda. It sees people as they are, in all their uniqueness and individuality, and in all their fullness and their totality, with everything included. And what it sees, it loves. It feels the utter sacredness of the earth, of each person, animal, cloud, star in the sky. It loves and it appreciates. It also sees the connections and the communions that bind us all in one vast cosmic reality. For the Soma, strict and separationist personal boundaries do not exist; what is clear and compelling are our connections with each other, our links and bonds, the natural communion that our deepest self—our Soma—has with everything that is. The Soma's way of being, it seems, is to see the totality of what is and to love and appreciate it all, simply because it is.

So, the purpose of this somatic work is to connect us with the reality, goodness, health, and possibilities of our basic human situation. In modern culture, all of us live in a state of disembodied abstraction, and we chart our life journey according to a bunch of more or less random ideas and hopes and fears—and a huge amount of wishful thinking—rather than based on who we are as people and what our lives are actually like. When we address our disembodiment directly through these bodywork practices and invite the wisdom and vibrancy of the Soma back into our lives, a new constellation of embodied experiences, along with their intelligence, insight, and wisdom, begins to become available. These somatic learnings or accomplishments, listed below, arrive of their own accord and on their own schedule; while they may seem to be arranged in a progressive manner, the order they take is ultimately unique to each practitioner. Trusting the body's process is an integral part of this way of relating to meditation practice and to ourselves.

1. You develop the awareness that you have a body that is actually independent of your ego, and not purely a function of your conscious mind.

2. You begin to include this new awareness as part of your ongoing way of feeling and sensing yourself and of being at home in the world.

3. You become sensitive to the livingness of your body: it's dynamic, an ever-changing reality, almost an independent entity, filled with energy and life.

4. You see that what you *think about* and what you *experience in* your body are often not the same thing, and that your thoughts, when they take over, often simply disconnect you from your own experiential ground, which is your body.

5. You begin to see the impact on your body when you turn away from it through discursive thinking—you become numb, tense, feel that you've lost your ground. Because you've had the experience of the simplicity and directness of your body, purely conceptual and filtered experience doesn't feel right anymore.

6. You discover that you can actually best address a difficult or challenging situation by coming back to your body and listening deeply to it; you are learning how to heal yourself.

7. You begin to experience a state of being that is embodied, visceral, grounded, open, and always in process, and you begin to feel this is your home.

8. You realize that there's a much bigger range of emotional and perceptual information coming to you than you had ever been aware of before.

9. You begin to sense the limitless terrain of your physical being—the endless, open spaces we can enter through the body. Now you have a context within which you can actually experience the energy of your body, and the tremendous inspiration that arises for life, without the mediation of your ego.

Taking Refuge Through the Body

Working with the Soma restores to us the basis and ground of our human life. We become present to who we are and we discover resources of health, sanity, and well-being we didn't know existed. We begin to take who we are as the foundation of our human journey, rather than something to be shunned or transcended. This work also naturally creates an unbelievable ground from which to make the spiritual journey. From this perspective, you can see how difficult and limiting it could be to commit to a spiritual path—in Buddhist terms, *taking refuge*—in a completely disembodied state, where you really have no idea about your physical body or what's happening there. It would be something like your thinking mind trying to take refuge in *an idea* of taking refuge; meanwhile, the experience of the full spiritual journey, of showing up as who you are, would not be possible, because you wouldn't even fully know who you are.

As Pema Chödron says, "Start where you are." What the bodywork does, in a way that is very mind-blowing for all of us, is it actually shows us where we are. On the one hand, where we are is very grounded and real. It includes everything that we are. After some basic training in the bodywork, we have a pretty good idea of where we go off track. We have a pretty good idea of how neurotic we can be and of how open we can be. We can feel. We are bringing everything that we are to the table. If we don't have that, taking refuge is frequently an attempt to escape from one's pain and blockages, to escape from oneself, rather than taking the reality of what you are as the point of refuge. And that is the *point* of refuge—to take the person that you actually are as the ground of the journey.

With this genuineness as a person, you become very grounded, very open. There's a softening of the ego process as you come to understand experientially that the body is more fundamental than the ego. The ego is not so hard and rigid and arrogant any more. And that's the moment at which you can truly take refuge. You can commit to a spiritual journey because you know who's taking refuge; you're coming to it as a full person, an open person, and you can make the journey.

So, this work really becomes the ground not only of the journey but the ground of human life. Having a sane and healthy human life is really what this is about, in a certain way. In the traditional Buddhist cultures, they call it the *prtagjana yana*. "Prtag" means "ordinary" and "jana" means "person." So, it's the *yana*, or vehicle, of the ordinary person who is starting to have a healthy, dignified, wholesome life, and it's considered to be very important in Buddhism. It's the foundation of everything we do as humans.

But this is a very fundamental change for most of us; being an actually healthy person is extremely unusual in the modern world. "Healthy" means that there's a healthy relationship between your thinking, ego-mind and the wisdom, openness, and spontaneous healing of your body. The neuro-pathways linking the Soma and your thinking mind begin to open. As we've discussed, the more they open, the more we feel a very deep sense of connection with our self as a person, with the world we live in, and with other people.

This brings us to a point where we begin to get a sense of what we could do with our life. We begin to see that there are places within us that are tremendously open and unbounded, and that there are places within us that call us, communicating in many different ways. We begin to relinquish our obsessive and often maniacal control over our experience and see that we could commit ourselves to a life that is much vaster, and more inclusive of our actual experience, than the one we currently inhabit. It's very beautiful. It's very powerful. It's very transformative. With this experiential foundation, the spiritual journey becomes a constant, unfolding, embodied process that is inseparable from our lives. It transforms us and our lives as practitioners—our very experience of reality—in ways that the purely conceptual understanding of the left-brain never can.

NOTE

1. For an example of one of these protocols, see my essay in the Guided Practices section of this book.

Body as the Dharma Gate

WILLA B. MILLER

"Even if you understand the nature of mind as emptiness, and though your understanding may be profound, if you do not know the nature of the body, you will be in the dark as to how to actualize that truth."—Gyalwa Yangonpa[1]

There are times when we feel as if the body has betrayed us. This body, for all its benefits, easily falls ill and becomes injured. It is through the body that we feel physical pain, a common and sometimes daily experience. The Buddha's famous "four great rivers of suffering"—birth, aging, sickness and death—all relate to transitions of the body that deeply and profoundly affect us. These are not easy transitions; they are painful transitions, for the most part, and spiritual practice is often framed as a way to deal with these.

A few years ago, I remember lying on the couch in my living room. I was in the middle of a miscarriage. It had only been ten weeks, but, as many women will tell you, that can seem like a long time. Long enough to grow attached to the sense of a baby growing inside you. Long enough to write a letter to your unborn fetus. Long enough to imagine a future with a new member of your family. Long enough to say prayers and meditate for your unborn child.

It felt as if all four great rivers of suffering were cascading through my body. I was birthing something, but not at all what I had imagined. It was occurring—or so said my doctor—because of an aging body. And then there was the physical pain, intense and constant, with the sense that something had gone wrong. My body felt sick. But most intensely, here was death, with the same sense of grieving and loss that one would have for a child, yet somehow a kind of death un-grieved by the world at large. A private pain. An unspeakable pain.

No matter what sort of positive self-talk I tried, no matter how I attempted to meditate, my heart was heavy with grieving, sadness and even an irrational shame. Dharma practice was a refuge. But even so, my emotional self felt ashamed of my body, as if my body had failed. As if it had betrayed me. It was a window into a suffering I had never before understood. The suffering of having a body that betrays. That ages. That will someday die.

Yet, for all the raw truth of this body's sufferings, there are many times when I have felt blessed by bodies, my own body or that of others. In the two years that I had the good fortune of studying with Dilgo Khyentse Rinpoche, it was his body—rather than his words—that taught me the most. His movements, expressions, and demeanor were saturated with relaxation and compassion in a way that I had never witnessed in a human being before. It seemed as if the very teachings he was delivering had shaped his body and movements.

There was something about being in the presence of his awakened body that made *my* body—as ordinary as it might have been—feel different. When I was physically in the presence of Khyentse Rinpoche, my body began to feel more relaxed, less reactive to the environment, more at comfortable and at ease. Of course, we might say that this was his mind's wisdom and compassion. While that was doubtless true, his wisdom and compassion was expressing itself through his body. The Dharma seemed to have saturated his body. He was spontaneously giving those around him a body–to–body transmission of the dharma.

More Than a Horse-Drawn Cart

When I was in my teens, I began to compile my first books about Buddhism. As a high-schooler in Berkeley, I sampled such classics as *Zen Mind Beginner's Mind*, *Taking the Path of Zen*, and *The Tibetan Book of the Dead*. My red plastic milk-crate of a bookshelf, surviving the multiple moves of a twenty-something, slowly filled with others: *The Life of Milarepa*, the *Dhammapada*. At one point, the *Dhammapada* become especially beloved. I read and re-read its verses, slowly fingering the large, yellowish pages, turning over the meaning in my mind, trying to apply its lessons to my young life. I felt as if I was mining the wisdom of the ages—the Buddha's words, ancient, true.

One verse stuck with me like peanut butter. I could not shake it: "Mind is the chief and takes the lead. If the mind is negative, whatever you do or say will lead to suffering. It is like the cart which trails the horse."[2] The analogy offered in this verse was that the mind is like a horse ("the chief"), and the body and speech are subsidiary and passive, like a cart drawn behind. Wherever the horse goes, the verse implies, the cart will follow. The implication seemed to be that the mind was more powerful and influential than the body, its strength and ethics superior. The body, these verses seemed to say, follows the will of the mind. So the purpose of life must be to train and tame the mind, like one might train a horse.

The depth of this verse was surprising to me, given its simplicity, and its logic seemed infallible at the time. Yes, this must be it. The mind is the key. And indeed, everything I learned about Buddhism in the coming years seemed to validate this perspective. Meditation was a mental discipline, it seemed, and it had a power to free you. If this mind could just be controlled, everything would fall into place, the negative emotions would be tamed and inner peace would result.

As I moved forward in my practice of Buddhism, this verse from the *Dhammapada* became like a guiding light. I grabbed onto it in all its literality. The body, as I framed it, was a tool, a temporary home for consciousness. Subtly, I began to bow to this hierarchy of the human experience in my daily life. While I had previously loved my practices of yoga, running, and dance, these now took a back seat to this new endeavor of taming the mind. Previously reveling in long hikes in the mountains, I now found a home in a monastery and my main practice became visualization and meditation.

It was not until I was 27, in the middle of a three-year silent retreat, that my allegiance

Lama Willa B. Miller (facing, far right) leading lujong practices (Tibetan body training) at Wonderwell Mountain Refuge, Natural Dharma Annual Winter Retreat, January 2014.

to this hierarchy was shaken. We had spent over a year practicing primarily meditation, chanting, and ritual arts. The teachings continued to convey a message that the mind mattered most—to realize the nature of mind was everything, the key to our awakening. Then, one day, our teacher came into the retreat house carrying—of all things—rainbow-colored leotards. "It is time for *lujong*," he announced, tossing the leotards in our direction, and with that, everything changed.

Lujong means "training the body" and it refers to elaborate, vigorous, and rhythmic exercise routines traditionally taught in deep retreat. This form of hatha yoga has been practiced in the Tibet for over a thousand years, and holds a sacred place in the tradition, yet I had never heard of it. When we began this phase of the retreat, suddenly we were spending two hours daily stretching, leaping, and moving rhythmically together, practicing synchronized yoga. These sessions were integrated fully into the retreat, as fully valid as our meditation sessions, and every bit as likely to lead to awakening. I could not believe it. Where had this been all these years when I was struggling with the sedentary nature of Buddhist practice?

On the one hand, I felt a profound sense of relief. So my love of physical movement, yoga, and dance was not some kind of disease to be tamed by Buddhism's stillness. To see my own past in this new light was a relief. But on the other hand, I also felt some frustration. Why had we not learned such practices sooner? Why had we been taught that the mind alone was the key to our awakening? Where had the body been?

I have now had many years to contemplate these questions, and they are still open and alive for me. Here, it will suffice to say that my exposure to *lujong* helped me reclaim my own body as a safe harbor for practice. Even the practices I had previously believed to be about the mind emerged in a new light.

I now saw the rituals and hand gestures as an invitation to be fully present in the moving body. I felt the rhythm of the drum during evening prayers, which previously had seemed like a way to keep time, as a call to wake up the vibratory subtle body. I noticed that when I paid attention to the body and breath in sitting practice, I meditated with much more ease and wakefulness. Slowly I began to notice the body in the entire path I had traveled so far, as if it were subversively central, if such a thing is possible.

The Precious Human Body

On the Tibetan Buddhist path, the very first contemplation we learn is called "the contemplation on the precious human body." In this contemplation practice, we think about all the reasons that our body is precious and rare. Sometimes we also think about how our human life, in general, is precious and affords us many opportunities, but the phrase used is "precious human body," and I think there is reason for this.

The body is a blessing. If we did not have a body, we would have no home in which to live in the world. We would have no instrument to follow a spiritual path. We would not have the opportunity to find meaning in life, or to reach out to help others. We would have no arms to hug. We would have no hand to offer to another person in friendship and compassion. We would have no legs to walk. We would have no eyes to see beautiful sights. No ears to hear music. No tongue to taste delicious food. We would not even have a home of this mind and awareness. The more you think about it, the more the body's blessings are numberless.

The body is a door to enjoyment and beauty, but even more meaningfully, it is vessel that can be used skillfully to offer love, comfort, and service to others. It is the door of altruism and love, the deepest kinds of actions that actually make a better world. So we might say that body is root of enacting a meaningful life.

But, most of the time, we do not recognize this truth. Every day, we take these many blessings and gifts—offered to us by and through the body—for granted. When we take these for granted, it is like overlooking a precious treasure buried in our own back yard.

In the reflection on the precious human body, we work to counteract our tendency to take this body for granted. First, we pause to reflect deeply on the many ways the body serves as a blessing and a gift. In my own practice lately, I have been framing this reflection as a gratitude practice. We can take time, every single day, to be grateful for the body. It works best if we do not reflect generally, but rather, specifically. I once asked a group of students in weekend retreat to keep a gratitude journal during the retreat. One of the students came back on Sunday morning to report that she had written "I am grateful for my eyelids" in her journal, and then she proceeded to tell us all about how she had come to an insight that her eyelids work hard all day long, keeping her eyes moist, so that she can see. She never had felt grateful to them before. I thought this was an exceptional understanding of the practice—it was specific and therefore profound.

The body's "small" blessings are really not so small. The body is miracle in action. It sweats when we are hot, shivers when we are cold, digests our food so that we have energy to think and act, and carries us from place to place.

We can be grateful for every little part of the body, and every way it functions, no matter how "ordinary." We can be grateful for our kidney, our liver, our stomach, our intestines, our bones, our blood vessels, our heart. When you think of parts of the body in this way, savor the feeling of gratitude. Recognize and dwell in a state of deep appreciation. Be slow and leisurely when taking time for gratitude, not rushed. In this way, you begin to make a habit of loving and appreciating the body.

The Body as Temple

When I was in my teens and twenties, I remember treating my body as if it were dangerous. It was something to be controlled and disciplined. I think many of us are like this: we are afraid of our own body, and therefore are not very kind to it. In my own case, like many young women, I was determined to be thin. I was focused on controlling my calorie intake, my weight, and my waistline. When I think back on this time, even now, I feel a sense of shame about my mind-state back then. I was not anorexic, but I was on the continuum of unhealthy eating (and thinking) patterns. It took me several years, after the end of college, to break this way of thinking and behaving, to throw out my scale, and to stop adding up calories in my head every time I had a plate of food in front of me. Our habits around bodily control and abuse can be very pernicious and persistent.

At around that time, I encountered a meditation practice that helped me tremendously. It was a practice called deity yoga. In that practice, you imagine that your body is the body of a deity. In a sense, you receive permission to understand that your body is naturally divine and sacred. Not only that, but your speech is also divine and sacred. Not only that, your wild and unruly mind is naturally divine and sacred. You spend your entire meditation session working with this perception of your whole being as inherently divine.

This practice, over time, profoundly changed my relationship to my body. I started from a place in which my body was imperfect, dangerous, and ugly. But in this practice, my body—by my teacher's instruction—was naturally perfect, safe, and beautiful. To think otherwise would be to stray from the practice.

As I began to apply this new understanding, it clashed with my previous perceptions, and I experienced a cognitive dissonance. Many of these perceptions were barely conscious before I began to practice deity yoga. But once I was practicing it, it was as if the bottom of a muddy bucket were stirred. My previous conceptions of my body were gradually revealed in all their destructiveness. As these body-perceptions became more conscious, I began to question them. As I questioned, I started to realize how untrue they were, how they were mere perceptions. It would take time, but my sense of my body began to change.

The Organic Body

Anyone who owns a dog can tell you that dogs have feelings. They also communicate via touch, movement, and eye-contact in ways that are similar to speech. When I look into the eyes of my dog, we recognize each other in some way. That is because we, too, are animals.

We are also born of the elements of the earth. We are stardust. If we reflect on our animal nature and our organic body, we discover that to be with the body is to be close to nature. To be away from it is to be alienated from the natural world. If you are suffering from nature deficit disorder, you can find some solace by bringing attention down into the body. The body is a natural organism, an animal body. When we die, we will re-inhabit our home of the earth.

One of the reasons we feel so good when in a beautiful, natural place is that we feel a part of it. The reason we feel a part of it is that our body recognizes its true home. It recognizes its innate wildness.

This is also a reason that we love animals (or perhaps also that we dislike some animals). Animals remind us of our own wildness, our own animal nature, our instincts. When I bury my head in my dog's belly, I feel this kind of communing that is not only love of one being for another. It is a recognition of our shared animal-ness, our shared wish to be happy and to avoid suffering. In this, my dog and I are the same.

Mind Time versus Body Time

We spend a great deal of our time in our head. In this society, especially, many of us have been raised to believe that our mind is our greatest asset. We have been taught that intellectual prowess will land us in a good school, a good job, and implicitly in a happy life. However, there is little evidence that a sharp intellect correlates with happiness.

When we begin to meditate, we become gradually aware of how very full the mind really is: full of thoughts, memories, worries, plans, and stories. The mind is full of ideas. In meditation, we begin to notice all this mental activity. Most of this activity is rooted in memories and reflections about the past, and anticipations of the future. In fact, the mind is not very present.

This is a bit of an issue for us because the past and future are fictions. Memories and stories of the past exist, but there is no past. Ideas and predictions about the future are made, but there is no actual future. The past and future exist as ideas and as traces, but not as realities. We cannot, even if we tried mightily, visit the past or the future. Only the present is accessible as a real experience for any one of us. The present is as true as it gets. But the mind is not in this place of truth much of the time. It is engaged with fictional time.

The body, in contrast, is very present. The body is always in the moment. If you drop down from the thinking mind into the feeling body, you will notice this utter presence instantly. The body is feeling at this very moment. Our skin is feeling the breeze of passing air. Our arms and legs are feeling their presence in space. Our eyes are taking in the present surroundings. Our ears are hearing sounds. As soon as we pay attention to the feeling body, we enter the present moment. So one efficient way to redirect our attention from the past and future, which are really fictions, into the present is to drop down into the feeling body.

This can be done on the spot. Sometimes, when we are thinking, it literally feels as if we are inhabiting the head-space, rather than the body-space. When your mind is swirling with busy-ness and thoughts, you can pause and suddenly drop from the thinking mind into the feeling body. I do this as a visual dropping of my attention down from the head into the whole of the body below the neck. You can gradually cultivate an experience of your mind traveling down into the body, from thoughts of past or future into an embodied experience of the present moment.

The Body as Teacher

The body has a great deal to teach us about reality. Take one of the most ubiquitous facts about the body that we can find: its changeability. This body has not stayed static since the day we were born. After we were born, we grew fast, our body and our brain. We learned to speak and walk. We endured puberty. We eventually reached our full height, but even then our body was not static. Most of us have gained and lost weight, been fit and unfit, been ill sometimes, and continued to learn. As an adult, we might even have taken up new skills, such as playing an instrument, learning to dance, learning a new language.

And then, there is aging. Our body will not be around forever. Maybe already, we are experiencing arthritis and our memory is becoming less reliable. This body is one of the best teachers we have on one of the deepest spiritual truths: the truth of impermanence. When we notice this aging of the body, our usual reaction is to mourn the loss of our youth and vigor. I too experience this sadness with some frequency. But we do have an alternative avenue of reflection. We can rejoice for a moment in receiving a lesson from the body, a lesson in impermanence. This is not a bad thing to know that our body is aging. It is a truth, rather, that points us in the direction of recognizing the preciousness and frailty of our own life. This truth can and should lead us to embrace this life moment to moment, and to accept its changes, even welcoming our death.

Why would we welcome death? In Buddhist understanding, death is not a termination of all good things. Death rather is a profound opportunity. In fact, one of the reasons that we undertake spiritual practice is to be able to meet this opportunity with appreciation and grace, rather than fear. Recently, a friend of a friend was diagnosed with Alzheimer's, one of the most feared diseases in our society. Just a couple of weeks after I heard of his diagnosis, his wife sent out an email informing us all that he had decided to take his own life. In the context of our culture, her husband's decision was understandable. He feared losing his autonomy, and his clear mind. Who would not fear this? Yet, in one sense, it is also the action of a culture in which death is a negative, in which loss of control of the body and brain—even death itself—is somehow "unnatural." After all, we hide these truths away in hospitals and hospices, behind the walls of mortuaries.

Yet, the inevitability of this loss of control is universal. We will all face death in one way or another. We will all lose our autonomy as the body ages and dies, and this is completely natural. It is a part of life. From the point of view of the great masters, it is a profound opportunity to completely let go into the clear light of awakening.

Body as Sadhana

At this point in my life, the body is back, front, and center of my practice. I trust the body's dimensions of feeling and physicality as doors into momentariness and awakeness. The practices of dance, hiking, running, and hatha yoga that I left behind in my twenties are with me most every day, not as exercise but as *sadhana*, or spiritual practice. At Wonderwell, my Buddhist retreat center in the White Mountains of New Hampshire, I integrate hatha yoga and hiking into our meditation retreats. I have finally come to believe that exercise need not remain as just healthy movement. When we move, my teachers have said, we have full permission to access of the powers of subtle energy, presence, and awareness. We even have permission to let movement propel us into full awakening. This possibility lives in our body right now. So even as our body ages, we are invited again and again to rediscover its hidden blessings. For me, it has become a deep practice, an edge, to hold this fragile vessel's impermanence within a confidence in its momentary wakefulness. Yesterday, as I set off for a run on a chilly March morning in Boston, my knees stiff with the beginnings of arthritis, a prayer sprang into my mind…

> When I run, may I run in the wisdom wind.
> When I hike, may I hike in awareness.
> When I dance, may I dance in the temple.
> When I hold asana, may I surrender to humility.

Notes

1. Yang dgon pa rgyal mtshan dpal, Rdo rje lus kyi sbas bshad, in *The Collected Works* (Gsung 'bum) of Yang-dgon-pa Rgyal-mtshan-dpal: Reproduced from the Manuscript Set Preserved at Pha-jo-ldings Monastery (Thimphu, Bhutan: Kunsang Topgey, 1976), 424, 3–4. Sentence translated by Willa B. Miller.

2. Dge 'dun chos 'phel, *Dhammapada* (Berkeley: Dharma Publishing, 1985), 2. Sentence translated by Willa B. Miller.

Shadowing the Ephemeral
Embodied Emptiness Through Form

TOMIE HAHN

Paradoxical Loopings

For years I have been shadowing the ephemeral—enactive knowledge, embodied knowledge gained through action. My fascination with enactive knowledge stems from my practice of Japanese traditional dance, experimental movement improvisation, Buddhist meditation, and an ethnographic study of the senses. My object of study originally stemmed from a literal question: how do dancers learn? Complications arose. The embodiment of knowledge presented a paradox, a perpetual loop of nested transience that defied me. Although the body stands as a very real, physical entity in the world, the flow of knowledge into and from the body remained unclear, indiscernible. Emptiness. The body changes as it learns and embodies sensory information, continuing the paradoxical loop. Changes arise, transforming the body, heart, and mind; often the knowledge and transmission process transforms. Similarly, the research of movement—that which occurs only now, then vanishes—offers insights that disappear into the ether. In this way, the body mirrors the enigmatic, the ever-changing conundrum of being.

The paradox of practicing and observing the ephemeral, in time, in movement, in the body, inspires this chapter. The focus on lessons of the body directs my attention to relationships between dance, ritual, and everyday movements. Please do not run screaming from the room! I am not launching into the age-old question: what is dance? Rather, I hope that through observing a wider range of movement practices, the ephemeral qualities of being in the body and *practicing (in) time* might open several windows into enactive knowledge.

Warning Label

This essay contains short passages that can be read in any order. The sections were purposely written to defy sequential order, to question the linearity of time, and to provide interactivity between readers and myself. Please choose your own path. The theoretical intermingles with stories to encourage a pondering of movement from different points of view. I believe that flipping pages forward and back prompts body-mind activity and decision-making. Be willful—jump ahead, flip back, or start in the middle and spiral out. Consider how your movement-decisions influence the reading. Intentions. Causes. How might your choices initiate subtle movements of the fingers and hand? Are the choices a physical consequence, a mental process, or a heartfelt, intuitive process—all or none of the above? Also, consider how your particular sequence of passages shifts your embodiment of knowledge, comprehension, and creativity. Form.

During Japanese trainings or practices,[1] answers or conclusions are generally not offered directly. The training, then, demands involvement. Time. Digestion and contemplation of experience with the entire body-mind is practice. Introspection of dualities—though also through, with, and without dualities—enables the inertia of such a paradoxical cycle.

"Form is emptiness, and the very emptiness is form."[2]

Boundaries

While *nihon buyo* (Japanese traditional dance) is not strictly a Buddhist practice, the roots of nearly every Japanese traditional artistic practice are in some way indebted to the overwhelming influence of Buddhism during its formative eras. Japanese philosophers themselves directly draw a deep correspondence between the traditional arts and Buddhism.[3] Offering one example, the Buddhist philosophy of cultivating the body-mind through practice emphasizes direct experience over intellectualization. The significance of direct experience through practice deeply influenced Japanese culture, especially in the traditional arts where repeated practices of ritual and artistic forms enabled embodied learning. Below I juxtapose two stories to further link dance and Buddhism.

As background: I began studying Japanese traditional dance in Tokyo at the age of four. At the Tachibana school, dancers refer to our headmaster Tachibana Yoshie as "Iemoto" (headmaster). In the following passage, from my ethnography *Sensational Knowledge: Embodying Culture through Japanese Dance,* Iemoto folds the esoteric concept of *kekkai* into a lesson:

> During a visit to New York City in 2005 Iemoto explained to several beginner students why a fan is placed at arm's length on the floor when bowing to a teacher. She said something to the effect, "It is a kind of metaphor. The fan creates a line between the student and teacher, and draws attention to that space. The line symbolizes the spiritual boundary (*kekkai*) located between the two individuals, honored as a kind of devotional space. When you are bowing you are demarcating and acknowledging the distinction between your teacher and yourself, but your bow respectfully honors both of you." In the following days a fellow dancer and I corresponded via email about this lesson and she pointed out the importance of Iemoto's use of the word "*kekkai*," a word with spiritual overtones that carries the meaning boundary or barrier.[4]

In a personal conversation with Abbott Monshin Paul Naamon, spiritual head of Jiunzan Tendai-ji in upstate New York, I learned that Buddhist temples recognize spiritual boundaries referred to as *kekkai*. These thresholds stand as a literal boundary around or inside a temple (*hondo*), demarcating public versus private, or exterior versus interior space. Cultural concepts of *omote* and *ura* (*omote*, meaning public, exterior, or front and *ura*, meaning private, hidden or behind), as well as *uchi-soto* (inside and outside social groups), exist on a wide continuum in Japanese life, from everyday boundaries of etiquette and composure, to more esoteric boundaries. The following description of a liminal threshold inside the temple serves as an example of crossing thresholds.

Prior to entering the temple interior (*hondo*), *sangha* members remove their shoes and put on their *kesa* (robe). Between the outer hallway and the *hondo* there is a tall beam that delineates the inner *hondo* sanctity. Because the beam's height literally blocks fluid entrance, anyone entering the temple needs to move with awareness to step over it, as standing or stepping on the beam is taboo. In Tendai temples, one enters with the left foot and exits with the right. A conscious effort to step over the threshold (with the appropriate foot) signals an observance of one's entrance into or out of sacred space. As one can imagine, ritual movements within a temple become habituated and embodied through repetition much like dance movements.

Kata[5]

Training of the body is key for *ki* (energy) to flourish and develop. Specifically, a disciplined routine of specific movement and sound patterns must be practiced in order for the body to move freely with the spirit of *ki* energy. Yuasa wrote:

> When there is repeated training in the practice of performing techniques, the body-mind is disciplined, then the state of conscious movement changes into one which the hands, legs, and body unconsciously move of themselves. This is the state of "no mind."[6]

The performing techniques Yuasa refers to are *kata*. *Nihon buyo* dances are comprised of *kata*, formalized body movements that greatly aid the memorization and embodiment of pieces. *Kata*, or "precise exercise forms,"[7] are a distinctly Japanese formal device found in nearly every artistic practice, such as tea ceremony, archery, theater, *enka* (popular song),[8] and martial arts. Because most of the traditional artistic practices in Japan are taught through active engagement, *kata* are vital as the foundation for training. In *nihon buyo*, *kata* function as the fundamental building blocks for the foundation of dance expression. Rather than learning the discrete forms individually first, as is the case in ballet training, *kata* are learned gradually and contextually within dance pieces, but also from observing *kata* during other students' lessons. In a sense, this is similar to children's acquisition of language vocabulary; new words are heard and incorporated as they are needed.

Kata operate as artistic motifs that are standard and repeatable. They are also flexible. Structurally similar, *kata* may appear in a variety of pieces, yet for each dance and even within each phrase, a *kata* is performed with the nuance, or flavor, of that particular context. For example, a seated bow is a *kata* performed in many dances. However, the specific character the dancer portrays in a dance will modify the basic bow, depending upon the character's gender, social status, age, mood, or the social context of the bow (who s/he is bowing to). Formal bows in a classic dance will differ from a bow in a dance based upon a folk dance. It is important to keep in mind that there are *kata* for each movement unit. *Kata* are named and so have a pragmatic purpose in lessons, as teachers can call out a *kata* during a lesson.[9]

Patterning Continuity

Repeating and standardizing form—as in *kata*[10]—creates fascinating connections that span a continuum of time frames. *Kata* provide patterns to live within and through.

Tomie Hahn (left) taking a lesson with Iemoto Tachibana Yoshie. The pose, from the dance "Seigaiha," depicts a woman on the beach holding up a shell. Tachibana dance studio, Tokyo, Japan, October 1993. Photograph by Walter Hanh.

What do I mean by this? In many Asian cultures, movement patterns are often incorporated into the practice of a tradition, from rituals, martial and aesthetic arts, to spiritual activities. They represent "somatic attitudes"[11] that are believed to engage the mind through forming the body. To Westerners, the enactment of fixed patterns might seem rigid, yet, with some interpretation, the differences in body-mind philosophies of practice might shed some light. Meditation in the West, so associated with relieving an individual's stressful day, contrasts from the Buddhist aim—to meditate for the benefit of others. One evening, in a talk to the *sangha*, Abbot Monshin Naamon said "relaxation during meditation is a wonderful side benefit, but the true purpose of meditation is for the benefit of all sentient beings."[12]

Assuming a posture and enacting set movements connects living beings who have also assumed these postures over time. Centuries. Kasulis beautifully conveys the sense of enacted lineage in a passage discussing *kata* in tea ceremony:

> We should consider how the *kata* are learned. In general, the spiritual and artistic praxes are learned in discipleship to a master. That is, the student learns to a great extent through imitation.… So, when the student is turning the bowl, the master is turning the bowl, and the master's master is turning the bowl. This sense of tradition in the movement makes the behavior no longer simply the student's own. It opens the individual's integrated mind-body complex into an integration transcending the self.[13]

When I move, I enact my varied lineages. I am me and also not me, simultaneously reflecting that I am my mother, father, dance teachers, calligraphy teachers, Buddhist teachers, and others who contributed to my embodied sensibilities. Arriving at the cushion, I assume the posture. Arriving on the dance floor, I assume and move through postures. Admittedly, some days I resist, and other days I am eager. But postures curiously avail me of a process, a pattern to slip into, no matter where "I" am at the moment. Reaching outward from my space, I enact time in the sameness that others have enacted before, and will in the future. Differences matter little beyond the very moment.

Moving Within the World

As dancer-movers we know the core of life revolves around moving. According to neuroscientist Rodolfo Llinas, movement plays a key role in our being in the world. "In my view, from its very evolutionary inception mindness is the internalization of movement." Thirty pages later, in italics, he offers "*that which we call thinking is the evolutionary internalization of movement.*"[14] But how is the complexity of moving cells, muscles, and the body *in time* related to its ever-changing context, with infinite sensory possibilities at any given moment? Llinas explains:

> It is not difficult to understand that the externalization of any internal image can only be carried out through movement: drawing, speaking, gesturing with one's arms. What I must stress here is that the brain's understanding of anything, whether factual or abstract, arises from our manipulations of the external world, by our moving within the world and thus from our sensory-derived experience of it.[15]

Llinas's proposition that movement displays intention, *as* observable thought, reveals vital linkages of body-mind to that which is outside the body's realm. Boundaries. The key here is that forward-looking "intention" (not necessarily in the Buddhist sense[16]) imparts a prospective will to move that is expressed outwardly. Here, the observable enactment of movement reveals *something* has changed.

Moving Rituals

A few years ago Tendai Abbot Monshin Naamon noted my inclination for understanding *through* movement and sound. He suggested I consider learning a *mudra, mantra,* and visualization ritual to deepen my sitting meditation practice.[17] Japanese Tendai Buddhism incorporates esoteric rituals into the practice. Naamon wrote:

> Ritual practice involves body, speech and mind, thus opening additional channels for spiritual development.... Ritual also includes use of mudra (hand-gestures) and mantra (phrases, generally in Sanskrit) that contain the essence of a particular Buddha, Bodhisattva, or dharma practice. By performing these gestures and reciting the phrases, one is imbuing one's being with those qualities and acts as a conduit for them so they may be experienced by other sentient beings. Again, the underlying intention is that the practice is performed for the benefit of others.[18]

He explained that the body reveals insight through the *mudra* hand gestures, speech via *mantra,* and mind in visualizing the essence of the realm.

The ritual folded into my life. As Monshin predicted, I experienced a subtle experiential shift approximately six months after the transmission. While I cannot put into words the shift in my experience, I find it important to convey my struggle with the learning process itself. "I" kept getting in the way—the obstacle, the duality, as me, as emptiness, as form. The frustrations of trying to embody and ritualize the form fascinated me. At first, it took great effort to practice *mudra*, *mantra*, and visualization simultaneously—it felt as if every cell in my body demanded a keen focus to coordinate. I struggled with memory. Over time, the ritual gradually flowed more smoothly, as sound, movement, and consciousness became embodied, became fluid. Perhaps the nearly imperceptible experience of fluidity itself offers a momentary glimpse into a realm through body, speech, and mind. The ritual is the first practice art that I have learned not intended to be performed before "an audience"—instead, one performs *for* others, as in "for the benefit of others."

Flowing Form[19]

The concept of a (*nihon buyo*) dancer's form, or posture, is expressed in the word *katachi*. This word does not simply translate into "posture," it represents a structural system for cultivating the body, and, as Komparu Kunio points out, there is a connection between *kata* and *katachi*:

> Two Japanese words, *kata* and *katachi*, are closely related. *Kata* corresponds to pattern, model, or mold; it refers to set movements in the martial arts and to dance patterns in Noh.[20] The word *katachi* means shape, form, or condition, as perceived by the senses. We can generally translate *kata* as pattern and *katachi* as shape or form, but the terms may be very close in meaning. According to etymological dictionaries the work *kata* derives from *kami* (god) and *ta* (paddy or hand). Thus *ka-ta* involves god, agriculture, and the hand of man, and indeed the basic movement patterns of Noh are related to agricultural activities and sacred rituals.... The *chi* of *katachi* apparently is an indication of mystical powers and often appears written with the character for soul or spirit.[21]

Katachi is the form that the body assumes while dancing—the structural source for the flow of energy and movement. For dance, the notion of flow is apparent in a physical sense as well as an inner, contemplative energy. *Nihon buyo* movements derive from a strong core centered in the abdomen, or *hara*, where the body's energy and spiritual center resides. The body moves with a firmly grounded stance derived from a lowered center of gravity rooted in the *hara*. The basic stance reinforces this foundation—feet are firmly planted on the ground; the tailbone is tucked under so that the hips appear level with the floor; and the knees are always bent. Movements emanate from the *hara* region and radiate outward through the torso and limbs. The connection of the feet to the smooth wooden floor plays a vital role in dancer's carriage, balance, and movement vocabulary. More importantly, the connection of the body's *ki* energy to the earth is via tactile contact with soles of the feet. This is an energetic transmission flow between the dancer and ground.

Ink Trails

As a child I studied calligraphy with Kan Shunshin, a Buddhist minister and *kendo* (fencing) master. From time to time he would clutch my hand in his and gently guide my arm to form shapes in space that would ink shapes on paper. His deliberate movements informed my body of complex brush techniques—he propelled my brush conveying the momentum needed for lively strokes; the rolling of the brush between our fingers left a chiseled corner; the downward pressure of the brush bristles at the beginning of a stroke, or a lifting up to create a hooked shape. Grinding ink was also transmitted in motion. The methodical circular grinding of ink in water while perceiving the thickness of the ink through the ink stick could be meditative. Repeated each week, these kinds of lessons connected me to the brush, wet ink, paper, *kanji* characters, and Kan *sensei*. I remember watching him teach *kendo* and seeing aerial strokes.

Closings, or Far Beyond Beginnings

Perhaps you are reading this section prior to others. Perfect.

Movement, particularly movement improvisation or everyday movement, can reveal intention. It puts a mirror to volition and the intertwined nature of practice, habit, embodiment, choice, and desire. Because movement improvisation is not separable from the body, the ego easily steps in and stirs impenetrable commotion.

We become what we practice. Paying attention to how our (movement) repetitions shape our form, seems sensible. Atten*dance* bares presence.

Notes

1. See Carl Bielefeldt, "Practice," in *Critical Terms for the Study of Buddhism*, ed. Donald Lopez (Chicago: University of Chicago Press, 2005), 229–244.

2. Prajnaparamita Sutra, in *Buddhist Wisdom Books: The Diamond Sutra and the Heart Sutra*, trans. Edward Conze (London: George Allen and Unwin Ltd., 1958), 81.

3. See Yasuo Yuasa, *The Body: Toward an Eastern Mind-Body Theory* (Albany: State University of New York, 1987), Chapter 5.

4. Tomie Hahn, *Sensational Knowledge: Embodying Culture through Japanese Dance* (Middletown: Wesleyan University Press, 2007), 41.

5. Excerpt from Hahn, 61–62.

6. Yasuo Yuasa, *The Body, Self-Cultivation, and Ki-Energy* (Albany: State University of New York, 1993), 31.

7. John Singleton, "Situated Learning in Japan: Our Educational Analysis," in *Learning in Likely Places: Varieties of Apprenticeship in Japan,* ed. John Singleton (Cambridge: Cambridge University Press, 1998).

8. Christine Yano, *Tears of Longing: Nostalgia and the Nation in Japanese Popular Song* (Cambridge: Harvard University Asia Center, 2002).

9. For a clear description of the specifics of *nihon buyo*, see Chiyo Hanayagi, *Jitsu nihon buyo no kiso* [The practical skills of basic *nihon buyo* movement] (Tokyo: Shoseki, 1981).

10. Fixed postures or movements used in many Japanese traditional practices.

11. See Thomas P. Kasulis, "The Body--Japanese Style," in *Self as Body in Asian Theory and Practice*, ed. Thomas P. Kasulis, Roger T. Ames, and Wimal Dissanayake (Albany: State University of New York Press, 1993), 316.

12. Abbot Monshin Paul Naamon, Sangha talk on Buddhist practice, Tendai Buddhist Institute, East Chatham, New York, January 7, 2015.

13. Kasulis, 317.

14. Rodolfo Llinás, *I of the Vortex* (Cambridge: MIT Press, 2001), 5, 30.

15. Llinas, 58.

16. "Intention" has several meanings in Buddhism, depending on the context, culture, sutra, language, as well as the translation. Three examples would be *karma* (and *karmaphala, Sanskrit*), *samma sankappa* (Pali, "right intention," the second of the Eightfold Path) and *cetanā* (Sanskrit, Pali) perhaps comes closest to motivation.

17. For background information, see E. Dale Saunders, *Mudra: A Study of Symbolic Gestures in Japanese Buddhist Sculpture* (Princeton: Princeton University Press, 1985).

18. Tendai Buddhist Institute, "Tendai Practices." Accessed May 31, 2015. http://www.tendai.org/practices/.

19. Excerpt from Hahn, 62–63.

20. Noh is a highly stylized Japanese traditional theatrical form traced back as early as the 14th century. Many of the texts are drawn from Buddhist sutra and the influence of Buddhism on the aesthetics of simplicity, form, and artistry of masks.

21. Kunio Komparu, *The Noh Theater: Principles and Perspectives* (New York: Weatherhill/Tankosha, 1983), 221.

Cast

Exploring Ground, Path, and Fruition in Early Embryology

Kim Sargent-Wishart

Introduction

Bonnie Bainbridge Cohen, the founder of Body-Mind Centering® (BMC), describes the body as being like sand and the mind like the wind, noting that "it's difficult to study the wind, but if you watch the way sand patterns form and disappear and re-emerge, then you can follow the pattern of the wind, or, in this case, the mind."[1] Mind, in BMC, is not just the brain, but a process of consciousness that manifests and expresses through movement and presence. The process of discovering the movement of mind through kinesthetic awareness underpins somatic approaches such as BMC, reminding us that mind and movement are not separate processes.

Somatic awareness is similar to the meditative awareness found in the Buddhist meditation tradition, in which, according to Reginald Ray, "even thoughts are related to as somatic—as bursts of energy experienced in the body."[2] Over my many years as a practitioner of BMC, dance, and Tibetan Buddhism, I have taken a view of the body as dynamic display of consciousness. This perspective is at the heart of my dance-based research into early human embryological development—the beginnings of the body's creative appearance.

By exploring embryology through movement research and dance/film making, I consider embodied narratives of how the developing embryo expresses consciousness and the dynamics of universal, creative forces. This essay specifically concerns an early stage in which the embryo appears as a three-layered gestalt (comprised of the three germ layers of endoderm, ectoderm, and mesoderm), which I find to be strikingly resonant with Tibetan Buddhist teachings on the threefold dynamics of ground, path, and fruition. My path of research led to the creation of a dance/film called *cast*, which explores the embodiment of endoderm as ground, ectoderm as path, and mesoderm as fruition. The choreography for *cast* was created in collaboration with the two dancers who perform in the film, through a studio research process.

Ground, Path, and Fruition in Embryology and Dharma Arts Practice

At nearly two weeks after conception, our cells organize from a spherical cluster into three interrelated but distinct germ layers. It is here in this early pattern of organization, marking the first specialization of our embryonic cells into distinct functional relationships, that I sense an expression of (an embodiment of) the dynamics of ground, path, and fruition, terms found frequently throughout Buddhist teachings whose specific meanings vary depending on the context in which they are used. For this essay, I use Tibetan Buddhist master Chögyam Trungpa's explication of this "threefold logic" as the dynamics of "the background of manifestation, the potential of manifestation, and finally manifestation altogether."[3] These three aspects of ground, path, and fruition are, of course, inseparable; the "manifestation" of form is none other than the "background" of emptiness, the immeasurable and undifferentiated potential out of which and as which all form arises. However, despite being ultimately inseparable, the distinct articulation of these three aspects highlights the process dynamics of appearances, which is very useful when investigating embryology and art-making—two disciplines concerned with how things come to presence. The threefold perspective helps us to remember, when we view something like a work of art or a human body, that we are viewing a process of appearance (of presencing) rather than a independent, fixed form.

Within the Shambhala Dharma art teachings, Trungpa Rinpoche described this threefold logic as "a way of presenting a complete world"[4]—an arts practice that is responsive to the ground of making as much as to the thing being made. Dharma art practices, like somatic approaches to dance and movement, attune the senses, beginning with a basic sense of existence, of ground, then developing "slowly through the threefold process of perception: the sense of being, the sense of doing, and the sense of linking together."[5]

Many artists would recognize the experience of being with the pure potential of the unknown (ground), noticing a flash of insight or moment of perception (path), and the manifestation of this into form (fruition). Some have expressed this directly, such as the poet Allen Ginsberg, who organized his Mind Writing Slogans into three categories: (1) Background as "Situation, or Primary Perception," (2) Path as "Method, or Recognition," and (3) Fruition as "Result, or Appreciation."[6] The painter Agnes Martin suggested a similar threefold dynamic in the work of self-expression, dependent on a developing awareness: "Behind and before self-expression is a developing awareness in the mind that expresses the work. This developing awareness I will also call 'the work.' It is a most important part of the work. There is the work in our minds, the work in our hands, and the work as a result."[7]

The ground-breaking experimental composer John Cage, deeply influenced by his studies of Zen Buddhism, used the characteristically playful terms of nothing, making, and something, encouraging artists "not to make a thing but rather to make nothing … by making something which then goes in and reminds us of nothing."[8] Cage, like Ginsberg, understood the artist's path of action to be one of beneficial activity, through which the fruition (the something) aims to lead the perceiver back to the ground (the nothing). From a Buddhist perspective, one function of arts practice and production is to foster awareness of the emptiness and interdependence of all things. As Ginsberg claimed, "The only thing that can save the world is the reclaiming of the awareness of the world. That's what poetry does."[9]

Creative arts practice, with its implied aim to make a something that warrants being paid attention to, presents one of the more visible examples of this threefold poetics in action. Although we commonly find metaphors from gestation and birth used to describe creative projects, what is less visible is the actual narrative of embryology as it describes the creative process of our embodied appearance. Bainbridge Cohen teaches an embodied approach to embryology that, like Dharma art practice, acknowledges the spaces, the basic ground, in which and as which the embryo appears. In BMC, the embryo *is* the realization of space.

To somatically explore our embryological selves requires imaginative access to our earliest history, through what Bainbridge Cohen describes as "re-membering in the original sense of this word—to be mindful of again. We recognize the truth of this memory through the consciousness of its current manifestation in our bodily awareness and emerging reality."[10] The BMC approach to embryology engages movement practice to sense fundamental dynamics (like the wind) in our present embodiment (like the sand) that relate to structures and spatial relationships that are no longer present.[11] Through this process we animate an embryological narrative, beginning with the fruition, the form, to inquire into the ground and path as the form's essence. The shape-shifting embryo, continually in flux, shows us at our most mercurial, when we were always becoming, and not yet attached to any identity,[12] with each stage of development presenting a full-body *gestalt* that is foundational to our current organization.

Introduction to the Three Germ Layers

The embryological stage that inspired *cast* occurs at nearly two weeks post conception, when our embryo transforms from a spherical cluster of pluripotent cells into a flat two-layered disc with a differentiated front and back. The dorsal (back) layer, called the ectoderm, comprises the cells that will give rise to the nervous system and our external surfaces such as the outer layer of skin, the lens and cornea of the eye and the outer ear. The ventral (front) layer, the endoderm, will give rise to the gastrointestinal tract, the inner linings of many glands and organs, the bladder and lungs. Thus the front/back relationship of the body is established first, through the relationship of endoderm and ectoderm, which creates the conditions for the appearance (in humans and other bilaterally symmetrical creatures) of a third, middle layer between them—the mesoderm. This results in a trilaminar disc, or gastrula.

The gastrula is continuous with a yolk sac in front (providing nourishment) and the amnion behind (providing a protective space). The developmental narrative of this stage is thus in the context of these adjoining front and back spaces, created by the same cells as the embryo proper. In the embryo's subsequent enfolding into a cylindrical organism, the front and back layers, along with the yolk and amniotic sacs, become our interior and exterior worlds, respectively.[13] Throughout my movement exploration of these developing layers and spaces, I have noted sensations of what Bainbridge Cohen describes as "the embodiment of space,"[14] rather than structure, suggesting a connection between Western embryological narratives and those presented by Tibetan embryology, in which the body forms primarily as energetic channels.[15]

Cast: Embodying Ground, Path, and Fruition Through Dance and Film-Making[16]

The first section of *cast* embodies the ectoderm, which Bainbridge Cohen associates with the "pathways of flow between the ground of being and the form of manifestation or expression"[17]; providing the potential for communication, creative activity, and perception. The cells of this layer give rise to those aspects of us that meet the exterior world and enable communication between interior and exterior experience, what Elizabeth Grosz calls the "becoming-brain." This is "a mode of connection, working through various circuits that indirectly join the inside to the outside in every living thing."[18] It is the aspect of us that is not only porous with and enmeshed in a milieu, but is continually shape-shifting in response to the meeting of internal and external experiences. Our capacity for beneficial activity lies in this compassionate connection with our environment, based in awareness of the dynamics of communication and relationship.

In rehearsal, the dancers explored following flows of sensation and motor impulse, tracing how external information enters in and circulates with cortical intelligence and imagination. They initiated physical contact through the back of the body and explored enveloping the surrounding kinesphere and each other in partnering, entering the negative spaces between things. I noted these images that arose in dancing:

> Curiosity, exploration, meeting places and people, shaking hands.
> Leading and being led.
> Threading through a crowd.
> The spaces between things, like the wind.
> Seeing.
> Listening.

The opening section of *cast* takes place on a busy pedestrian bridge over the Yarra River in downtown Melbourne. The urban setting naturally draws one's attention outward, to the environment, and to one's progress through the space, to *doing*; as we moved out of the studio onto the site, our kinespheres expanded as the dancers began to incorporate the seemingly unending movement of people plus wind, water, birds, boats, buskers, and voices echoing across the space.

A bridge is a literal path—often the only path—like a nerve, directing movement into a forward momentum. The flow of pedestrians became a central focus of this section, a crucial "cast of extras" on location, whose visible movement is the result of flows of desire, habit, intention, and possibility—all expressions of mind. The dancers begin a duet on a wide area of the bridge, just out of the flow of traffic, a space I came to relate to as a kind of eddy, a space that allowed them to open to how the exterior flows circulated with their interior experience. In editing, I found the eddy created a space akin to sitting meditation, in which one notices the ongoing flow of thoughts without hooking into the storyline that they contain. The changing camera angles reflect our ever-changing points of perception and highlight the continuity between the spaces we move through and the movements within us. As the body is shaped by circulatory flows, life events, thoughts, and emotions, so too "places are not a stable ground that are simply subject to flows of ideas, people, information and money; the experience of place is *produced* by such flows."[19]

The dancers part abruptly, each entering into opposite pedestrian flows across the bridge and along opposite sides of the river. They reunite in a grassy, shaded area on the south bank, in an embrace. This begins the next section, embodying the endoderm, with a slower, sustained tone, and more internal focus. Intimate camera angles show points of contact and sharing of weight.

Bainbridge Cohen associates the endoderm with the "ground of being,"[20] invoking Trungpa Rinpoche's "sense of being," noted earlier. It embodies qualities of meditative stillness and internal calm, a relaxed, aware presence that is settled yet ready to respond when the need arises. Embodying the endoderm, in my experience, engenders an openness to this basic ground of the situation. In BMC this is based on yielding—a fundamental presence underlying the foundational movements of push, reach, and pull.[21] The yield is the baseline attention to what is, meeting the situation without attachment or aversion. Grounded in what Bainbridge Cohen calls cellular consciousness, this is the mind of not coming or going, but being simply present.[22] As is taught by most schools of Buddhism, this often requires slowing down, noticing internal sensations, and taking a break from "doing."

Exploring the endoderm during rehearsal, the dancers initiated movement through the tone and presence of their organs, responding to the slower rhythms of digestion, and the wisdom of the enteric nervous system (the "gut brain").[23] They moved with deep internal sensation, finding the subtle intimacy of being in contact without having to achieve anything.

In rehearsal I wrote:

> Inside of a snake.
> Heat condensed but spacious, inner space, digestion, processing.
> Soft belly, gut instinct, no eyes no ears.
> No place to go.
> No before or after.
> Going in to go out, going out to go in, and not going anywhere, and already everywhere.

This section of the film sees the duet more secluded in the shadows and contained by trees, supporting the dancers' ability to slow down and focus more internally on subtle weight shifts. They seemed to move outside of time, as a pause in the rush, a decoupling from enterprise; the sound also stills to birds and distant voices. In a sense, nothing happens. The dancers then transition together into walking, gradually re-emerging into an increasing volume of riverfront urban activity. In viewing this section I am reminded of the experience of transitioning into sitting meditation practice and then re-emerging into daily life activity with freshened sense perceptions.

Before the third germ layer appears, the ectoderm and endoderm already embody an archetypical relationship between exterior and interior, surface and depth, male and female, being and doing. The organizational gestalt of the embryo at this stage of existence (as two layers) is, to me, suggestive of the united deity and consort relationship in Vajrayana Buddhism's *yabyum* iconography. Experientially, the front/interior of the body (the endoderm), embodies the deeply internal wisdom of the ground, the female aspect of the *yabyum* deity, while the back/exterior of the body (the ectoderm), embodies the more outwardly aware perceptual and creative activity of skillful means, the male aspect of the deity. The *yabyum* embodies the inseparability of wisdom and skillful means. Embryologically speaking, our flesh and bone presence only arises out of the relationship of these primary two layers. Fruition arises in the unity of ground and path.

The mesoderm begins at what will be the perineum, growing upward like the stalk of a plant, in the space between the two "parent" layers, along a central line called the primitive streak. As this layer emerges between front and back, it also inscribes the embryo's midline, initiating our subsequent enfolding into three-dimensionality (interior/exterior). I find it significant that Tibetan embryology also names this central midline space as primary to development. Machik Labdron, the 11th-century Tibetan saint and yogini, instructed that "the body develops first from the navel. The navel channel is the first support from which the body gradually develops."[24]

From this initial central growth the mesoderm spreads laterally and establishes what will become the more dense and substantial aspects of the body—the meat of our physical presence, our beating heart, our skeletal strength. Bainbridge Cohen relates the mesoderm to the "form or manifestation of expression."[25] Our embodied substance, like any fruition, results from the ongoing dance between the ground (of being) and the path (of beneficial activity and wisdom perception).

Moving from the musculoskeletal system is familiar territory for dancers. The revelation, for me, in moving from the mesoderm as the basis of the musculoskeletal, lay in the experience of it as a product of the relationship between the other two layers. The support I gained from these other two aspects—yielding into the ground and attuning to the flow of path—gave me an amazing sense of effortless strength, a wider range of expression, and playfulness. My notes:

> "Sure, I can hold up the world," said Atlas.
> The child equally supported by mother and father.
> Power, muscle, biceps flexing.
> Resonance with ground brings nourishment for physicality.
> Resonance with space for effortless expression.
> It's a team effort.
> And we are so much more that what our bodies can do (D. Hay), but they can do so much more than we think they can.[26]

The mesoderm section of *cast* occurs on a concrete terrace, traversing from one end to the other in a playful push and pull duet across the space. I was drawn to the space for its literally concrete presence and clear, hard, structural form. In our several on-site rehearsals the space was sparsely inhabited; perhaps one or two people passed through. On the morning of filming, however, not only had builders appeared with their scaffolding and power tools, fitting out a new restaurant and filling the scene with the sounds of industry and materiality, but, as we shot the first take, a large group of people emerged from the far side of the terrace, crossing in opposition to the dancers, creating a palpable, formal tension with the duet. This was the only section where I felt the dancers were truly, tangibly acknowledged by other people in the space, as a part of the space, and I realized that the evolution of the piece was marked by an evolution of the dancers' presence: by first connecting into pathways of flow in the space (the path), then yielding to internal presence (the ground), they could come into full physicality and strength, and thereby into fuller visibility (fruition). This section marked the development of the dancers claiming space. Though physically tiring, it was in some ways the simplest, and the most playful section of dancing, reminding me of the easy physicality of a child's ballgame, the kind of dancing that gets you "out of your head," or the simplicity of Cage's directive to "just make something."

The final section of *cast* explores the enfolding, interdependent relationship of the three layers, reflecting the complexity of our adult physiology and embodied experience, as well as the inseparable dynamics of ground, path, and fruition. Trungpa describes this

Fiona Cameron and Jason Marchant in a still from the dance/film *cast*, Melbourne, Australia, September 2013.

as the "king principle,"[27] the wholeness and completeness of a situation, recognizing the unity of these three aspects. The dance here occurs in and around a large metal sculpture of wavelike forms,[28] with curved surfaces that reflected the dancers' images in the sunlight. The hard steel of the sculpture, a seemingly permanent something, became a surface of fleeting reflection, of images temporarily cast by movement, light, and color. The character of this section, unlike the others, did not take shape until post-production. In the editing process, I chose to highlight ephemerality, flux; I chose snippets of movement relationship arising, then gone; a breath, a suspension, a reflection, a footstep, the ringing of a bell. In the final images I wanted the fruition of the piece to bring the viewer back to the ongoingness of path, and ultimately, to the open potential of ground.

Further Considerations

Entering into the dynamics of these three distinct aspects of embodied experience through dance presents an exciting opportunity to rethink the way we define and experience "body." When I kinesthetically wake to the experiential qualities of ground, path, and fruition, I sense a glimpse of the *trikaya*, the three bodies of the Buddha, as the essential nature of my ordinary embodiment. This is highly complex territory, which I will attempt to introduce briefly based on my limited understanding. According to Traleg Kyabgon,[29] the three bodies are the *Dharmakaya*—the formless body, related to the ground of being; the *Sambhogakaya*—related to path and the ability to communicate (both verbally and nonverbally)—a body of bliss that is not physically or spatially located; and the *Nirmanakaya*—the "physical aspect of an enlightened being," as well as the potential of our own bodies once purified through correct practice. Traleg Rinpoche instructs us that "both the *Sambhogakaya* and *Dharmakaya* aspects are already embodied within each sentient being, and fruition [*Nirmanakaya*] is a matter of coming to that realization."[30] The Great Perfection tradition also teaches that these three bodies are the "triune dynamics of the Universe itself ... present within the core of all living beings at their heart as the ultimate pure source-potential of their psycho-physical vitality,"[31] but again, having forgotten our essential nature, we need to come to that realization. In this sense the practitioner's path is one of returning to the embryological moment, as an opportunity to rethink the narrative of who and what we are.

The movement research behind creating *cast* gave me the opportunity to play with the felt experience of these ideas in a highly kinesthetic and perceptual way that, for me, only dancing can do. Most of the insights I have had on this journey have arisen from dancing with and as the material at hand. Likewise, the creative practice of making the film—choosing locations, editing, having a dialogue with the moving image—suggested new relationships and working theories. The creative practice itself—the path of bringing something to fruition—embodied the embryological narrative, as the narrative came alive in what I was making. My aspiration is that the film, the something, simply go in and "remind us of nothing"; that is, I hope it creates some spaciousness and playfulness, and reminds us of our dynamic, radiant nature.

NOTES

1. Bonnie Bainbridge Cohen, *Sensing, Feeling and Action: The Experiential Anatomy of Body-Mind Centering®*, 2nd ed. (Northampton: Contact Editions, 2008), 11. Body-Mind Centering® is a registered service mark, and BMC is a service mark, of Bonnie Bainbridge Cohen. The author is a certified practitioner of BMC.

2. Reginald Ray, *Touching Enlightenment: Finding Realization in the Body* (Boulder: Sounds True, 2008), 45.

3. Chögyam Trungpa, *True Perception: The Path of Dharma Art,* ed. Judith L. Lief (Boston: Shambhala Publications, 2008), 128.

4. Trungpa, *True Perception*, 127.

5. Trungpa, *True Perception*, 76.

6. Allen Ginsberg, "Mind Writing Slogans," in *What Book: Buddha Poems From Beat to Hiphop,* ed. Gary Gach (Berkeley: Parallax Press, 1998), 197–201.

7. Agnes Martin, *Agnes Martin: Writings*, ed. Dieter Schwarz (Berlin: Hatje Cantz Publishing, 2005), 67.

8. John Cage, *Silence: Lectures and Writings* (Middletown: Wesleyan University Press, 1961), 129.

9. Allen Ginsberg in Mark Olmsted, "Genius All the Time: The Beats, Spontaneous Presence, and the Primordial Ground," in *The Philosophy of the Beats*, ed. Sharin Elkholy (Lexington: University Press of Kentucky, 2012), 191.

10. Bonnie Bainbridge Cohen, "Embryology—the Process of Consciousness," in *School for Body-Mind Centering® Training Manual, Embodied Developmental Movement and Yoga Program* (El Sobrante: The School for Body-Mind Centering, 2010). The author served as a teaching assistant for the course from which these materials are drawn.

11. Bainbridge Cohen, *Sensing, Feeling and Action*, 167.

12. This study, though based in Tibetan Buddhist theory, relies on Western embryology via the experiential anatomy approach of Body-Mind Centering. Entering the territory of Tibetan embryology is a complex endeavor, and beyond the scope of this paper. Frances Garrett has written a comprehensive and fascinating book on the subject in which she considers Tibetan "narratives of human development as vital and creative venues for addressing fundamental questions about identity, responsibility, and personal creativity" (Frances Garrett, *Religion, Medicine and the Human Embryo in Tibet* [London: Routledge, 2008], 56). Garrett's use of the term "narrative" has been influential in my approach to embodied embryology.

13. See Bainbridge Cohen, *Sensing, Feeling and Action*, 163–74, for further explanation and

guided practices to explore these spaces. Bainbridge Cohen relates the embodiment of these two spaces to the development of our internal and external "sea of chi," based on her study and practice of Tai Chi.

14. Bainbridge Cohen, *Sensing, Feeling and Action*, 163.

15. Machik Labdrön and Sarah Harding, *Machik's Complete Explanation: Clarifying the Meaning of Chöd: A Complete Explanation of Casting Out the Body As Food*, trans. Sarah Harding (Ithaca: Snow Lion Publications, 2003), 185–204.

16. Readers can find a link to view *cast* at kimsargentwishart.com.

17. Bonnie Bainbridge Cohen, "Aspects of the Front Body, the Back Body, and the Middle Body," in *School for Body-Mind Centering® Training Manual, Embodied Developmental Movement and Yoga Program* (El Sobrante: The School for Body-Mind Centering, 2007).

18. Elizabeth Grosz, "Deleuze, Ruyer and Becoming-Brain: The Music of Life's Temporality," *PARRHESIA* 15 (2012), 3. Accessed May 6, 2015. http://www.parrhesiajournal.org/parrhesia15/parrhesia15_grosz.pdf.

19. Kim Dovey, *Fluid City: Transforming Melbourne's Urban Waterfront* (Sydney: University of New South Wales Press, 2005), 3. Emphasis mine.

20. Bainbridge Cohen, "Aspects."

21. Susan Aposhyan, *Natural Intelligence: Body-Mind Integration and Human Development* (Baltimore: Williams & Wilkins, 1999).

22. Bainbridge Cohen, Sensing, Feeling and Action, 15.

23. The enteric nervous system, sometimes referred to as the "second brain," or "gut brain," is a self-regulating system, containing more neurons than the spinal cord or peripheral nervous system. See Michael Gershon, *The Second Brain* (New York: HarperCollins, 1999), and Mark Taylor, "Accessing the Wisdom of Your Body: Balancing the Three Brains," *Currents: A Journal of the Body-Mind Centering Association* 15.1 (2012), 10–17.

24. Labdrön and Harding, *Machik's Complete Explanation*, 189.

25. Bainbridge Cohen, "Aspects."

26. The week I wrote this I had attended a Q&A session with choreographer Deborah Hay. She spoke of her desire to transcend a focus on what the body can *do* in dancing, that she identifies with more than that measurement of achievement. My experience here was that in dancing from the mesoderm as an expression of endoderm/ground and ectoderm/path, the range of what my physical body could do became much wider.

27. Trungpa, *True Perception*, 128.

28. Inge King, *Forward Surge* (1974), at the Melbourne Arts Centre.

29. Traleg Kyabgon, "The Three Kayas—the Bodies of the Buddha," teaching given at Karma Triyana Dharmachakra, Woodstock, NY, November 1989, ed. Sally Clay. Accessed May 6, 2015. http://www.kagyu.org/kagyulineage/buddhism/cul/cul02.php. A later version of this talk appears in Traleg Kyabgon, *The Essence of Buddhism* (Boston: Shambhala Publications, 2001), 119–133.

30. Traleg Kyabgon, "The Three Kayas."

31. David Germano, "Poetic Thought, the Intelligent Universe, and the Mystery of Self: The Tantric Synthesis of *RDzogs Chen* in Fourteenth Century Tibet," PhD diss., University of Wisconsin, 1992, 835–36.

Guided Practices

Earth Breathing
Practice Instructions

Reginald A. Ray

One of the purposes of somatic meditation is to enable us to examine what we could call the *ego body*—that is, the body as it's viewed by our ego, through the filter of our concepts, as a static entity. It's the body that we think we have, the body we that we believe we experience. When our meditation practice is body-oriented, however, we quickly realize that there's a big difference between that body and our actual naked, direct, nonconceptual experience of the body. If you ask people about their experience of their body, you usually get what they *think* about their body, and what they *think* their experience of the body is. It's very interesting—they say what they think. What you're getting is a map of their left-brain concepts about their body. Circumstances can have an impact on this; when someone becomes very ill, for instance, then you start to get something else. But normally, unless something happens to us to disrupt our concepts, the body that we think we have is really a facsimile version. It's not the real body of our actual experience. It's very limited, and it's based on culture—different cultures have different mental maps of the body that are taken to be the actual body.

What we're doing with this practice, and the other bodywork practices that I teach, is bypassing that map and taking a look to see what's really there. It's a slow process. In an optimally functioning human being, you might say, the information from the *actual* body is received by consciousness. There are neurological links between our left-brain and our Soma, mainly through the corpus callosum, but in the modern world, those links have largely atrophied. As they say in neurobiology, if you don't use it, you lose it, meaning that if you don't attend to your body, you soon lose the capacity to even feel your body.

Because many of us are starting from a very rudimentary level of somatic awareness, we have to rebuild. We have to do these somatic practices over and over in order to begin to awaken and develop and even grow new neurological pathways linking our ego consciousness, our ego mind, with our somatic awareness. We do that by bypassing the mental map and beginning to tune in directly to what's actually going on in the body. In the face of direct experience, beliefs about the size of the body, the extent of the body, the shape of the body, what the body includes and doesn't include, all of these are up for grabs.

The practice described here raises questions about the relationship of our body to

Reginald A. Ray (top center) leading guided bodywork practice at a winter Dathün retreat at Blazing Mountain Retreat Center in Crestone, Colorado, December 2009. Photograph by Corey Kohn.

the earth, and about the apparent experience of separateness that we have as a mental construct. These are called into question by what we see. We begin to explore what the actual somatic experience of the earth is, beyond our preconceived notions. By connecting with the macrocosmic body of the earth in this experiential, embodied way, we can begin to identify with and feel supported by the earth. This experiential earth becomes an incredible resource for the spiritual journey, grounding and stabilizing us deeply.

This practice is best done lying down, especially when you are first learning it, as deeper physical relaxation facilitates the practice. Try keeping your feet flat on the floor, about a foot apart, with your knees bent and upright; you can tie a yoga strap or belt just above the knees. This allows your legs, hips, and lower back to completely relax without falling open or to either side. The arms are by your sides, with your hands crossed over your lower belly; a small cushion can be placed under your head if that is more comfortable.

First, simply be in your body. Feel your body. Try to let your awareness be bounded by your skin. At this point, the awareness of the body is what's happening. I don't mean the mind's awareness of the body, but the body's awareness of itself. You are not looking from the outside; you are feeling and sensing your body from within. Tap into it. The body is aware of itself. The ego mind has no particular relevance right now. Just give in. Let go.

Begin to tune into the tension in your body, working with the body as a whole. Feel into the body, feeling the tension, and on the in-breath, exaggerate the feeling of tension and holding in your body. On the out-breath, release that energy down into the earth. The in-breath is the last breath of your life; the out-breath you die into the earth. Just let go, and let yourself dissolve into the earth. Just do that over and over, on the out-breath, letting go of everything.

After working with that for a little while, on the in-breath, breathe in, feel the tension, feel the holding, feel the density, and on the out-breath, release downward and let your awareness go down about a foot under you, into the earth. You're going to follow the tension down into the earth about a foot. On the next out-breath, go down two feet. You're extending your awareness down into the earth, on each out-breath dropping down another foot.

Next, go down about ten feet, but on the in-breath, leave your attention ten feet under you. Leave it there, and on the next out-breath, extend another ten feet, and then leave it there on the in-breath. Then drop another ten feet on the next out-breath, and repeat, so each time, you're going down ten feet further.

Then drop down to fifty feet; and then a hundred feet; and then two hundred, three hundred. Use your imagination. Five hundred. Then just open to a thousand feet under you; and then two thousand. This is something you can do. And then a mile. Then just let your awareness go down and down and down, falling in a steady manner. It's independent of the breath now. It's just opening downward and outward, without stopping. You're surrendering your awareness into the vast, empty, open space of the earth below. It's like falling snowflakes, continuous and steady, at about that speed, opening down and down and down and out. Fifty miles, a hundred miles, a thousand miles down.

Then, let it plummet like a stone through space, at an almost exhilarating speed. Just *let go*. If you run into obstacles, thoughts, memories, ideas, or preconceptions, just let them go; let your awareness open down continuously.

As your awareness continues to fall, and your attention is thousands of miles under you, notice how your body feels on the surface of that immensity. Open the back of your body to that immensity under you. Open your skin, the muscles, your bones, your organs, so that your whole body is one with that immense space under you. You're still opening. Your awareness is still plummeting, becoming deeper and deeper.

Notice the quality of the space under you. It's not cold. It's warm. It's almost soothing, comforting. There's a kind of tingling energy in the space itself. One feels almost blissful, protected, being held within the folds of the earth womb. Just let yourself give in. Let go of the thinking mind and let the body open and dissolve in the space of the earth. Feel it in your body. Feel the energy of the earth. It feels very healing, soothing, comforting, protecting, nurturing. It's the somatic experience of love. You are a tiny baby in the arms of the most loving of all mothers. Let it be that way. And any wounded or diseased part, any mental distress or physical pain, just open, and let it dissolve and be flooded by the all-embracing energy of the earth. Just give it up. Don't hang onto it. Any tension—just release it.

There's a strange intensity in our body when we do this. Our lower belly feels very alive. Our heart feels very full. Our throat almost wants to sing, and our body feels tremendous well-being. So, you continue opening down, and at the same time you're feeling everything in your body.

Keep connecting. Keep deepening your awareness of the earth and bringing more and more parts of yourself into the open field of nurturance and healing. Your ego wants to hang onto your problem, your needs, your hang-ups. What we're doing here is opening that whole array of maintenance strategies, letting them go, and allowing the earth to heal us. Feel the energy of the earth filling the body.

Can you see any end to the depth of the earth when you look down with your awareness and feel down into it? Or is it endless under you?

This is a wonderful thing to do before love-making, before going on the stage at the Met, before anything. It is wonderful way to go to sleep at night, connecting with the earth in this way. And if you feel distrust, lie on the earth; if you feel ill, lie on the earth. It is also a very useful preamble to seated meditation, anchoring you in the depth of your somatic awareness. If you'd like, you can sit up on your cushion and continue to work with the practice while seated. To close this practice session, simply drop all techniques and rest in your body, feeling the space of your body, and noticing the awake and present quality of your mind, *in your body.*

Accessing the Subtle Energy Body

BHIKKHUNI THANASANTI

It's helpful to open up the joints before meditation, because the joints tend to be places where energy gets jammed up. When our energy pools and jams, we don't have as much access to the subtle energy body—the subtle sensations that are connected to meridians, channels, and flows. This subtle energy body is a great asset in meditation because the more refined our consciousness, the more powerful our insight.

Begin standing with your feet about hip-width apart and your knees pointing over your feet. Reach down to cup your knees in your hands. Slowly rotate your knees in circles, first one direction and then the other. Then shift from rotating your knees to rotating your ankles, wrists, and shoulders. First start in one direction and then go in the other. With your shoulders, begin by bringing your shoulders towards your ears, then let them roll back, down, and forward. To reverse, bring them up to the ears, forward, down, and back.

Now put the back of your hands in the lower part of the back for some neck rolls. It's important to move slowly. Using your chin to lead the movement, take care to stay within a pain-free range of motion. Roll your neck twelve times in each direction. If you feel some pain or clicking in your neck, slow down until you are just creeping through the part that is painful or clicking. See if by doing that the pain releases.

Now rub the palms of your hands together sixty times. After you have rubbed them, hold them about a foot apart and feel the tingling sensations and sense of pull between your hands. This energy that we feel in our hands is a physical expression of qi, or life force energy. Life force is in everything. It's in our bodies, the carpet, the floor, the trees, rocks, waters, food, animals. When we have access to this energy and the ability to direct it, we open up possibilities that we don't have otherwise.

When we have a sense of this life force energy, we don't need to make so much personal effort. Will is balanced with breath, awareness, and life force. When we do these exercises, we want the muscles to remain as relaxed as possible and the joints as open as possible, as we allow our bodies to become like unobstructed hose pipes for this life force.

Now stretch the hands up above your head, toward the heavens, and imagine this life force to extend past the finger tips, a thousand miles into the heavens. As you draw your hands back towards your shoulders, you draw in the energy from the heavens.

Now extend your arms out to either side, parallel to the floor. Draw your hands in toward your body, and then extend again out to the sides. Fingers remain like open tubes,

223

extending a thousand miles, extending and drawing in. Keeping the elbows and muscles as soft as possible. Repeat this five times.

Bring your hands in from the sides and push straight down in front of your chest with your fingers pointed outwards and your palms facing the floor. As your arms extend, your fingers point towards the floor. As you push your hands toward the floor, imagine the qi energy extending through your fingertips a thousand miles into the earth. When you bring your arms up, imagine drawing qi from the earth. Repeat this five times.

We'll now do a gesture called "separating and connecting heaven and earth." As you breath in, allow one hand to reach down toward the earth with your fingers pointing out towards the side, while the other extends up to the heavens, reaching out with the life force and extending both upwards and downwards, a thousand miles up into the heavens and down into the earth. As you breathe out, bring your hands together to meet in the middle of your abdomen with the high hand on top and the low hand on the bottom, palms facing each other, mixing heaven and earth. Then, breathing in again, the low hand reaches up and the high hand extends towards the floor. Extend, mix, and extend on the other side.

We can feel our physical body and breath moving. We can also feel our subtle body, the sensations and pulsing of the meridians of our subtle body, as we move our life force. Sometimes we can sense tingling moving through a particular pattern through our body. This is how acupuncture was first discovered—meditators became aware of the way energy flows throughout the body.

Now bring the feet out so they are about shoulder-width apart. Point the knees over the feet. Unlock your knees and tuck your sitting bones under—if you had a big bushy tail you would tuck it between your legs. Let your weight sink into the floor as your spine elongates and your shoulders roll back. Let the breath and the life force lift the arms up, so there's not so much a sense of your willful effort. It feels more like your arms are floating up, by themselves. Keep the fingers pointed to each other, palms facing your chest, arms rounded. Stop when the fingers are about at collarbone height. Let your elbows point down. You should be in a position somewhat like holding a very large beach ball. This is "standing like a tree." Though the posture is still, it's incredibly dynamic. We will hold this posture for a few minutes.

When you breathe in, extend the belly, and when you breathe out, extract the air and try to squeeze it all out.

Now, shifting the posture, raise your arms so you're looking up at the ceiling through a triangle made by the tips of your two thumbs touching and your two index fingers touching. Palms are facing upward towards the sky. Change the breathing to contract the pelvic floor and diaphragm when breathing in, and relax completely on the exhalation. This is reverse breathing, which gives the internal organs a massage.

Now bring the hands down to about waist level and out to each side in front of you, palms facing the floor, fingers extended straight outward. Continue to contract the pelvic floor and diaphragm while breathing in, and relax while breathing out.

Allow your fingers to drop by the sides of your legs. Continue reverse breathing.

Now take a few breaths with regular breathing.

We're going to close this exercise by drawing in energy that is around us into our lower energy center, three finger widths beneath our navel. Women, bring the right hand underneath the left. Men place the left hand underneath the right. The tips of the thumbs are touching each other. With your hands in this posture, extend your arms away from you, bringing your hands up to eye level. On an out breath, bring your hands down from eye level in to rest on the body just below the navel. Breathing in, lift your hands out towards the height of your heart. Breathe out and draw the hands down to the same energy center. Breathe in and bring your hands directly in front of the lower part of your abdomen, and draw the energy to your lower energy center on the next out breath. Now, take your hands and raise them directly above your head as you breathe in. Allow the palms of your hands to face the front part of your chest and draw the energy from the top of your head all the way to the lower energy center as you breathe out. We do this last movement three times.

Now begin to pat down the body with your fingertips, like raindrops falling on you. Begin with your head, tapping lightly. Then move to your face, heart, legs, up your inner legs, outer arms, inner arms.

When we activate the subtle energy body, it then becomes available to us in meditation. Our attention settles much more quickly when we are relaxed and our energy is flowing. We are able to focus and see things with a level of clarity that otherwise would take a lot longer to achieve.

Change your posture into a seated posture for meditation. Consider—if the body is comprised of many changing things, nothing permanent that you can put a net over and catch, constantly moving, changing, dynamic flow, then where am I? Who am I? If I am not my body and my body is not one thing, then who am I? Where am I? Use this as a reflection, more than as a cognitive question calling for a cognitive answer. Feeling the subtle energy body can help us reflect on "who am I?" When we ask a question, there's often a longing to know an answer. See if it's possible to resist a cognitive frame of this answer. See if it's possible to let awareness rest in something that isn't changing, fluctuating, moving, isn't made of parts.

The space that holds the awareness that knows isn't made of parts. When we are able to let attention rest in awareness, what happens? When we lean into awareness rather than the object of what awareness knows, what happens?

From this place that's still and grounded, bring forward some of the questions or doubts that you may be having in your life. Notice what happens when you bring a thought that has been disturbing into this space that's still, and vast, and peaceful. Can you watch the impact of a thought, and the movement that arises from a thought? Do the thought and the impact of the thought go anywhere? Track the impact of the thought, until the thought dissolves.

Try seeing if you are able to make adjustments to your posture or the rhythm of your breathing from the stillness. Notice how different this feels from making an effort because something is a "good idea." Allow refuge—this still, vast, spacious awareness—to be the basis of movement, rather than an interruption of movement.

Whenever you end the seated meditation, see if you can allow any sense impressions that enter to be received by this field of awareness, this space that holds things. The invitation is to make all your movements while staying connected to refuge—the still, vast, spacious awareness. May this be the place from which movement originates, is known, received, and to which it recedes.

Authentic Movement
Moving and Witnessing

Joan Wittig

Authentic Movement is a profoundly simple form in which movers close their eyes and wait for an impulse to move, and then follow the impulse where it leads. This work is sometimes described as moving meditation. As in meditation, movers bring their attention to what is happening in the moment with a non-judging awareness. Movement occurs in the presence of a witness whose task it is to watch the movers and accept them and their movement without judgment or interpretation. As in meditation, the work of the witness may appear easy, but is only accomplished through experience. As such, people who wish to facilitate Authentic Movement groups are strongly advised to undergo the extensive training and practice that is required in order to learn how to witness with the necessary skill and care. Authentic Movement groups and facilitator trainings can be found in many cities across the country.

The Witness

The witness begins by preparing the space for the movers, clearing it of any objects that could present a danger to people moving with their eyes closed. The task of the witness is to watch the movers and to accept movers and their movement without judgment or interpretation. Before the movers begin, the witness will give directions as needed, reminding the movers of the guidelines. The witness explains to the movers the process of waiting for an impulse and then following it into the movement. The witness decides how long the movement will be. In the beginning, movement is relatively short, perhaps ten minutes or so. As the movers become more experienced, the movement time can be longer. It is the witness who keeps time, indicating to the movers that it is time to begin, and that it is time to end. The witness can use her voice to signal transitions, or can use a bell, a chime, or a singing bowl, something that will signal the movers without startling them.

During the movement, the witness sits and silently gives her full attention to the movers. While she watches, she opens herself to her own experience: her thoughts, feelings, memories, and physical sensations. She allows herself to be touched, metaphorically, by what she sees. The witness carries the larger responsibility for consciousness, especially early in the work. She brings a particular kind of attention to the experiences of the movers. As Janet Adler explains, the witness is not so much looking at the movers, as listening to them, seeing them. The witness creates a container, a safe space in which the movers can do their work. The witness does not interact with the movers. If a mover touches her while moving, she does not move away, nor does she respond. She allows the mover to make all the choices. If a mover moves out of her line of sight, she does not move to see the mover, but rather trusts that the mover's unconscious desire is to not be seen at that moment. The witness enters the movement space only if a mover is in danger, for example if someone is moving with speed or force and has forgotten to open her eyes.

The Mover

The mover begins by entering the movement space and choosing a place to begin. She settles into a spot and closes her eyes so as not to be distracted by what she sees around her. Closed eyes make it easier for the mover to access the unconscious and to listen for impulses. The impulse to move may be an image, a memory, a dream, or a physical sensation. For example, the mover may have an image of long grass waving in the wind, and begin to sway gently. Or perhaps the mover remembers sitting at the edge of the sea, and being gently rocked as the waves roll onto the shore, and begins to rock back and forth. Or maybe the mover feels restless and anxious, and begins to pace. The idea is to create a space within, and then wait for something to come into that empty space. The mover must learn to wait until something changes. That change is the impulse, the reason to move. Once the impulse emerges, the mover follows it where it leads. Should the mover have an impulse to run around the room, or start kicking or jabbing, she must open her eyes a little bit to make sure she doesn't hurt herself or anyone else. Otherwise it is suggested that the mover keep her eyes closed as she listens to her impulses.

Some General Considerations

Authentic Movement is practiced in silence, without music. There really is no way for a witness to choose music that will support each mover's work, because it is impossible to know what that work will be. The motivation for movement is completely inner-directed, coming from inside each mover. Music may interrupt or disrupt or somehow interfere with the inner impulses that are emerging. However, movers are welcome to make their own sounds as they are so moved. Banging on walls, stomping on floors, clapping, snapping, tapping, are all welcome. Also, singing, humming, shouting, screaming, weeping, wailing, laughing, are all welcome. Movers are invited to follow their impulses to make sounds in the same way that they are invited to follow their impulses to move.

Authentic Movement is most often practiced in groups. As such, movers may gently encounter other movers in the space. When this happens, each mover's task is to listen to her inner impulse, and recognize whether she wants to stay and move with this other, or whether she wants to step back and continue alone. She must try not to make her decision based on what she thinks the other wants from her; rather she must try to stay true to herself.

There are situations when movers feel restricted in their choices, as they worry about the impact of their choices on other movers. For example, a mover may have an impulse to shout or scream, and doesn't follow this impulse because it may disturb the other movers. Or maybe a mover has a deep feeling and wants to lie on the floor and weep, but she doesn't because she is afraid other movers will feel obligated to come and comfort her. Or perhaps a mover encounters another and wants to join her, but doesn't because she is worried the other doesn't really want to move with her, but will feel obligated. The impulse not to follow an impulse is also an impulse, and one we can choose to follow. When an impulse isn't followed, the mover's work is to observe her choices, to see what and how she chooses. In the beginning, movers may judge themselves rather than simply observing. Over time movers learn to observe without judgment, to be curious. Ultimately this will allow greater freedom. Meditators new to Authentic Movement may draw upon the wisdom of their sitting practice for guidance in following what arises with gentle curiosity.

Speaking Together

When the movers have finished, the movers and the witness speak together. The witness provides directions for speaking, guiding the movers into sharing their experiences. She also reminds the movers that when she speaks, she is speaking of her own experience, and not making any assumptions about or interpretations of the movers' experiences. Movers and witnesses are encouraged to speak in the present tense, for example saying, "I raise my arms and drop to my knees," or "I see you raise your arms and drop to your knees." Speaking in the present tense invites movers and witnesses to re-enter the experience in an embodied way, rather than just remembering.

The witness invites the movers to speak, sharing anything about their movement that they feel it is important to share. This may be everything; or it may be just one or two moments. After this explanation, the movers speak first, one at a time. The witness listens in silence until the first mover is finished speaking. Then the witness shares her experience with the mover. She, too, shares only what she feels is important to say. The witness is careful to make "I" statements, and to be clear that she is speaking of her own perceptions and feelings, and not the mover's.

It is useful for both to begin by speaking of the movement itself, and then of sensations and images, and finally of emotions. This allows for an integration of the experience of moving, sensing, and feeling. There is no discussion after the speaking. The mover offers her experience, the witness offers hers, and then the next mover speaks and the process continues.

The relationship between mover and witness is deep and complex. We long to be seen and we wish to be invisible. Over time, as movers find they are not judged, but rather are seen and known, they are able to allow themselves to be vulnerable. Authentic Movement allows movers to engage in movement as an in-depth exploration of self.

Basic Contemplative
Dance Practice Form

BARBARA DILLEY

I. Opening Circle

Gather in a circle and begin with a bow. Introduce bowing as a gateway to being together and acknowledging the space. Invite people to introduce themselves, saying their first and last names and why they have come. Give a brief overview of the practice. Invite everyone to find a sitting place around the edge of the room (where there are meditation cushions, pillows, or yoga blocks for people). Ask everyone to keep their place for the duration of the practice.

II. Sitting Practice

Ring the meditation bell two times. Give simple instructions: the upright, relaxed posture, the sensation of breath moving, and letting thoughts come and go. Invite micromovements into the posture, those smallest of movements because of the breath and heartbeat and the settling of bones under gravity. Use words that are real for you.

After about twenty or twenty-five minutes, ring the bell one time and announce "Personal Awareness Practice."

III. Personal Awareness Practice

In Personal Awareness Practice, invite practitioners to explore their way of bringing meditation awareness into movement in this very moment. Begin to stretch on the cushion and, at your own tempo, move out into the room. Listen for the voice of body mind, and use everything you already know. It's time for self-care, research, and courting the unexpected. Wait for images and sensations to surprise you, to move you. Follow them. Develop them. And rest often. Encourage "kinesthetic delight."

In a three-hour session, Personal Awareness Practice lasts about forty minutes. Then invite practitioners to slowly find their way back to their cushions. When everyone is more or less settled, ring the bell one time and announce "Sitting Meditation Practice." After three or four minutes of Sitting, ring the bell again and announce "Open Space."

IV. Open Space

In Open Space, we enter individually and bring with us everything that is stirred up. It's an invitation to host this moment as a guest, right here, right now. Each one enters Open Space with a standing bow. Demonstrate, and when you are ready to exit, also bow. We are practicing, not performing. The commitment to stand and bow and enter takes time. It's a big moment when one chooses to stand. Fear arrives in its many guises. Open Space holds each one of us as we are. It is rigorous because awareness moves between inner and outer noticing and we are tracking the nowness of it all. Invite practitioners to come and go from their cushions as often as they like.

Sometimes the space is empty for a while. When we enter we may be alone, with everyone watching. Sometimes everyone decides to come in! Who knows what will happen? There are two rules: take responsibility for yourself, and don't cause harm. Sitting around the edge of the room, we become Well-Wishers and On-Lookers. We enjoy the presence of others and the room and the light. We witness without judgment or comparisons. If we have a notebook and pen, we might write about wonder and sorrow. We rest.

Watch the time so there can be discussion. Ring the bell and invite practitioners to return slowly to their places around the edge of the room. When everyone has returned, ring the bell again and announce "Sitting Meditation Practice." Sit for a couple of minutes or so, ring the bell two times, and conclude with a bow.

V. Closing Circle and Conversation/Discussion

Gather in a circle for comments and discussion. Sometimes there is a lot to say and sometimes not much. Invite people to speak from two places: "what I experienced" and "what I saw." Clarify the time for the next practice session and end with one final bow.

Permissive Movement

Brian Kimmel

This form can take as short as you want and as long as you want. When doing Permissive Movement in groups, designate one person as the facilitator who tracks time and gently guides the form. The following are suggested formats and the main objectives of Permissive Movement that you, as the facilitator, can read aloud to movers in the space. If done solo, the format is up to you. You can still read the following material as you go along for inspiration.

The main objective of Permissive Movement is to be more conscious of your body and mind, specifically impulses guiding you toward actions of body, speech, and mind. An impulse can come from a feeling anywhere in your body, an intuition, or a response to something external like a touch or a sound. Use all your senses to guide you. This includes the sense of yourself in space, images that come up in your mind, memories, and even thoughts.

The secondary objective and effect of Permissive Movement, of becoming conscious of your body and mind, is learning the skill of following impulses toward action while discerning whether you do those actions based on what feels right and real to you. These are moments of congruency of body, speech, and mind. When one is congruent in their actions of body, speech, and mind, one is no longer separated, but whole, being as one body and mind. Ideas of what we *should* do or think fade away as an authentic and natural state of being and moving is fostered.

The premise of Permissive Movement is "Do No Harm." No harm here extends to self, others, and the space around you and beyond. Permissive Movement is a time to experiment responsibly and responsively with your body and mind.

Sample Formats

Group Format (20 minutes, time negotiable)

The following is an example of a warm up you could do and what you can read aloud:

Group Warm Up (6 minutes)—I am going to lead you in a gentle warm up. Warm ups as a group help prepare you for more free-form improvisation. Sometimes having something familiar and simple to do may be less daunting than just jumping into the unknown. This can be the case even in the middle of a Permissive Movement session.

Find a standing posture or a posture that works for you. Become aware of your breathing. Maybe place one hand on your belly to feel the rising and falling of the belly with each breath. Breathing in. Breathing out. [Repeat as necessary.] Release your hand. Now on the inhalation, lift your shoulders toward your ears. Hold them there. Exhale, release. [Repeat two more times.] Now, begin rolling your shoulders with the inhalation and exhalation. Inhale, moving the shoulder towards your ears, back, and exhale, continue by moving the shoulders down and forward. [Repeat two more times.] Now, reverse the direction.

Personal Awareness Practice[1] *(7 minutes)*—Now, continue this movement as long or as short as you would like, or if you feel ready, begin to move your body as you would like to move. Open to the awareness of your body from the inside out. Focus your attention on your body in space. What is called to move? What is calling your attention? Listen to your body. The only restriction is "Do No Harm." Not to harm yourself, anyone else, or the space. Move as you move. Be still as you are still. This is a time for you. [Give yourself some space to listen to your body as you refrain from speaking. Repeat any part of the prompt as necessary.]

Open Space (7 minutes)—Now, become more aware of others around you. Become aware of your body in relation to others. Maybe you are aware of someone moving in a certain way that appeals to you. Maybe you would like to try that movement or posture or gesture on. Allow yourself to be inspired, to pick up influence of others and to leave it when you are finished. [Give some silence and space here. Repeat any part of prompts when necessary.] Now, perhaps you are called toward interacting with others. Now is the time to explore. You have the freedom to say no to others, to engage, disengage, and re-engage again with them. You have the freedom to move and to be just as you are. [Give some silence and space here. Repeat any part of prompts when necessary.] In a few moments we will end. What is left that you have not done that you would like to try? Now is the time. This is it. [Give some silence and space here. Repeat any part of prompts when necessary.] Now, finding an end. End.

Solo Format (20 minutes, time negotiable)

Anything goes as long as it does not harm yourself or the space in solo practice. You may read the guidelines for group format if that might inspire you. It is important in solo practice to remember to be gentle and kind to yourself. Practice more slowly if that helps you to be more mindful, more present and awake in your body. Solo practice can be very challenging for those who are accustomed to receiving direction externally. That's okay. Use the time in solo practice to be more mindful, more in touch with how you feel, where impulse comes from in your body and mind. You can also explore, more deeply, images and memories that have particular potency for you. Give yourself physical space to move freely. Start out with sitting and/or walking meditation, breathe, and set a timer for ten minutes or any length of time that feels not too much or too little for you to really get a sense of yourself, to really come home. Move, or be still, in any way you like.

Considerations on Sound

You may like to begin and end Permissive Movement periods, just as you may with sitting meditation, with the sound of a bell. During the session or practice period, use recorded or live background sounds, soundscapes as I call them, like singing birds, water-falls, ocean waves, or traffic noise. Try not to use music other than soundscapes as this can be too leading for movement. Music often guides us in certain ways and evokes memories, emotions, images, and other associations. While proficiency can be developed in minimizing or harnessing the influence of music while moving, it's best to begin practicing Permissive Movement with only soundscapes. This way, the impulse to move will more likely come from within, and greater learning about and expressing of our own personal experience may be available to us.

NOTE

1. Barbara Dilley's Contemplative Dance Practice (CDP) was a main influence in the creation of group Permissive Movement. While I use some of her terms to refer to the phases of Permissive Movement (Personal Awareness Practice and Open Space), these terms apply to somewhat different practices between CDP and Permissive Movement.

Tune in, Stand Around
Four Postmodern Dance Improvisation Scores

Karen Nelson

1. Come to Standing

Slow down all doing and simply stand. Let your doing be just the standing, natural and easeful. Watch what happens as you stand.

Sense your alignment. Let your feet stand naturally forward with some space between them. Have soft knees. Invite attention to roam through your body, letting your skeleton support you. Relax completely while maintaining the stand.

Inner reflexive movements keep your body erect. It is a very small dance that causes itself. Steve Paxton, founder of Contact Improvisation and whose life work has inspired this exercise, named this dance of standing "the small dance."[1]

Let your breathing be easy. Feel the movement of the diaphragm up and down as you breathe. Sense the mass of your pelvis, ribs and shoulders, and head as they counter balance on the spine. Relax tensing muscles again and again. Let the organs be supported by the bowl of the pelvis. Let the earth have you and let your skeleton receive the unconditional support the earth gives back.

Stay for a while in this meditation, five, ten minutes or more. Sense the earth below the soles of your feet and the space above your head. The sensations can get more subtle and vivid. The mind can grow to sense the whole body at the same time. You can notice the mass of your body swaying, constantly falling and catching itself. Feel the space your body takes up.

It took your baby body about a year to learn how to stand. Since then it's been an unconscious reflex. In standing we can hear the reflexes.

When you are ready to take a break from standing, begin to consciously move. Take your time. Find the antidote movements. Take a walk; sense how weight shifts through your bones. See how this reflex experience underlies your every movement.

2. The Third Thing: Partner Head Dance

Stand facing a partner. Someone of similar height is easiest at first. Close your eyes and sense into your stand.

After a period of sensing your small dance, open your eyes and see your partner. Wait until you are both ready, open eyes will be the signal. Using your hands if it helps, bring your foreheads together at a point near the top of each forehead. Allow this contact to have a bit of pressure, a comfortable bit of leaning into it. Return your hands and arms to hanging at your sides. Drop in again to your small dance meditation. Sense the contact with your partner's head.

Through the point of touch on your heads extend your awareness into noticing your partner's small dance. Can you sense their skeleton and the little or big waves of movement?

Sense each other and let your small dances entrain. Listen for an invitation by something that is mutual between you—a third thing. Let that third thing invite movement that adjusts to the balance—the skulls may begin to roll a little or a lot, perhaps a sliding might occur. You may find that moving your feet is a way to stay in contact. Always keep at least the same amount of contact pressure that you felt at the beginning. How does this dance evolve?

As you become ever more entrained with each other's small dance, let the exploration expand to more unknown possibilities. The score is to keep the touch to the heads. It's amazing how much surface area there is between two skulls—infinite, like two spheres. Notice how the movements affect your whole body. Keep tuning your awareness to what is happening in your balance, your small dance, your partner, and the third thing between you.

After a while notice when the dance seems to finish. Find a place to pause or sense an ending together. Gradually part from your partner's head. Take some time to move on your own, and eventually come to standing by yourself. See how you relate to your small dance now.

3. Interplanetary Dances

Sit back to back with a partner. Lean comfortably towards the other. Play with that. Sit on your pelvic sitting bones and let your back connect with your partner's. Your support environment has now expanded to include the earth below you and another planet: your partner. Sense both the warmth and support of your partner's body, and contact with the earth below you. Feel your own and your partner's breathing. If movement begins to come, see what it's like to follow it.

The feeling may be similar to the rolling Head Dance, except it starts at your back. The movement may invite you to lay back and stretch over your partner or to take the weight of your partner. Listen to your comfort. Take care of your self. You are the only one who knows if some part of you is uncomfortable. You can move anytime to help yourself feel safe. That is part of communicating your situation. Experiment with rolling together. Remember you are on the earth and are already dancing. Your first partner is yourself in awareness.

4. Tuning an Instant Duet (Trio, Quartet, Etc.) Using "Pause" and "End"

These are some Tuning Scores influenced by inventions of Tuning Scores founder Lisa Nelson, and made to compose dances in space.[2] The score offers an opportunity for communicating a direct desire and to experience consequences in relationship with others. Learning to track one's compositional desire is a practice of honest self-listening and experimentation, not unlike meditation in action.

To begin this Instant Duet score, the group of warmed-up players gathers at the edge of the dance composing space. One person enters to begin a solo. The other players watch within themselves and within the space, for a desirable place to create an instant duet. Each individual will bring their own style of watching, for example visually, kinesthetically, emotionally, through story making, or through a variety of lenses.

When a watcher notices the moment that her compositional desire yearns for, she calls "pause." Pause creates a stillness in all players. Take opportunities to watch your inner life within this collaborative group process. During the stillness created by pause notice the sensations and emotions in your experience. Perhaps the sudden change to stillness feels to be a surprise, a delight, an interruption, an insult? Allow curiosity to fill your whole body and experience.

The player who made the call enters the dance as the second in the duet. No need to rush, yet the dancer goes directly to join the first soloist in stillness at the place they imagined the instant duet beginning.

This second dancer who enters can move directly into contact with the soloist or can situate their body in space away from the partner. During the ensuing stillness everyone senses, "How does the space change with the second person entering?"

Notice the range of sensation and emotions including anticipation, boredom, predictability, frustration, appreciation, understanding, complicity, rebellion, or unknown?

The two dancers feel for the simultaneous moment to begin moving in their instant duet. They "self-start" themselves from the stillness of pause. Everyone is noticing from their own vantage point, and wondering, "How does the relationship evolve in the duet and within me?" Watchers are active players. Everyone is in the dance, holding agency for their own participation, even on the edge of the space.

Once the duet begins, all players begin looking for the inevitable end of this duet. Notice the sense of impermanence and fleetingness of what seems solid and real. Everyone has a unique measure for meaning. The dancers on the inside are looking inside themselves for sensations, perhaps of completion. Players on the edge are being present, perhaps with their sense of fulfillment. This looking for an end may be experienced as boredom, desire to change things, or satisfaction. Perhaps it is a desire to get in there and dance? Players taste the full array of experiences as they pass through the body and awareness. Frustration can be a real motivator.

One of the players calls "end," which clears the space allowing a new dance to begin. When end is called, take the time to feel the completion of the image. Someone in the group has exposed their private meaning. This is a moment of tuning and the whole group can resonate by comparing, within themselves, their own measure.

A tuning score can evolve from this basic ritual of communication. It's important to note that the rhythm of calls and actions is made by the nature of the group on that particular day and time. It's generally easier to start simple and to notice how the layers of complexity emerge.

After having experienced a number of successful duets with endings, a group might expand beyond duet to trio, quartet, etc. Using the same pattern as the instant duet, a third person may enter to make a trio after calling pause. Following the protocol (or eventually letting it go) where the watcher who calls pause is the person who enters, the dance can expand and tune itself to the desires of the players. Sometimes two people will have the same impulse at the same moment to enter or to make a call. This is a natural progression of complexity and a miracle to celebrate.

As the tuning progresses, dancers on the inside can also make calls. They can call pause to still the dancing for whatever reason they may have. Making up your own calls or developing your own ways of unfolding a score is a natural evolution of tuning.

A call could be made simply to hear the musical sense of the dancing or to satisfy someone's need for order in chaos or to relish a visually stunning moment. Dancers can also ignore any call at any time. Implementing a call is an act of collaboration. By participating we get to learn something about what the caller was hoping to experience. Ignoring a call is a collaborative choice that sends a strong message of individual preference.

Afterword

Once, at a Buddhist retreat, I explained Tuning to a fellow practitioner. She turned to me and said, "So, Tuning is the opposite of meditation!" I think she meant that a meditator is "supposed to" rise above desire. For me Tuning and meditation are about getting intimate with the process of desire as it experientially unfolds.

NOTES

1. Please visit contactquarterly.com for information about Steve Paxton and Contact Improvisation.

2. Please visit contactquarterly.com for information about Lisa Nelson and Tuning Scores.

Zenful Dance
Leading Breath Movement Meditation
Leah Joy Malberg

Zenful Dance is a breath movement meditation practice based on the principles of *Anapanasati*, or awareness of breath flow. The seven parts of Zenful Dance are each aligned with one of the Seven Factors of Enlightenment, as taught by the Buddha. The practice can be done in as few as thirty minutes and as long as two hours, with longer formats allowing each part to be practiced several times in succession before moving to the next.

The class begins with everyone seated barefoot or with socks on a yoga mat or *zafu* and *zabuton* (meditation cushions) facing the instructor. Comfortable, loose clothing is recommended, preferably without prints or distracting colors. I usually have Tibetan singing bowl music playing low on my iPod and speakers throughout the class because of its warm, relaxing, and melodic quality. The lights are usually low or off, especially during the daytime, to create a calm environment. Begin the class by sharing the definition of *Anapanasati* and suggest that each individual breath is the "music" for the 7 Parts of Zenful Dance. You could also do a brief Q and A to take the temperature of the room and help the students feel comfortable moving into Part 1. Below, I present how I lead the practice; interweaving instructional comments I might say in class with information to assist you, the reader. Feel free to adjust the language to fit your style, as you like.

Section 1: Alone

Part 1. Breath Watching

Lying down flat on your back on a mat or *zabuton* (remove the *zafu*) with the eyes relaxed or closed, rest your hands on your stomach. Bring your attention to your breath for a few minutes. Watch the breath come in and go out, feel the chest rise and fall, feel the sensation of breath on the nostrils, all this without attempting to control the breath in any way. Should thoughts come up because of sensations in the body or because of distractions (i.e., sounds or smells or visual distractions) outside the body, acknowledge the thoughts and let them go, and bring your attention back to the breath. Be mindful. After a few minutes, shift the attention to more of an external focus—to sights or sounds happening in the room, to my voice. Then bring the attention back to an internal focus, and repeat the Breath Watching practice.

The first Factor of Enlightenment is *sati*, or mindfulness. This first part of Zenful dance serves to ground practitioners in mindfulness as a foundation for the rest of the practice.

Part 2. *Zazen* (Seated Meditation)

Seated on a mat or a chair with legs in a comfortable position to sustain for at least five minutes, sit upright with the eyes relaxed, gazing downward towards the floor a couple feet in front of where you are seated. Practice Breath Watching while seated in stillness. Conduct your practice with integrity and discipline, sitting as still as possible and watching thoughts as they come up without judgment and letting them go. Notice the ebb and flow of thoughts and sensations, how everything that arises has the nature to pass away.

The second Factor of Enlightenment is *dhamma vicaya*, or analysis into the nature of phenomena. In this seated posture we observe the passing nature of phenomena through our own experience.

Part 3. Stand

Put the mats away and come to stand in a spot somewhere on the floor facing in any direction. With feet shoulder-width apart, relax the knees in standing with the shoulders lined up over the hips. Allow your arms to hang by your sides or clasp your hands together in front of you and rest them on your lower stomach. Allow the eyes to relax, gazing downward toward the floor a couple feet in front of where you are standing. Practice Breath Watching while standing in stillness for at least five minutes.

The third factor is *viriya*, or persistence. Persist in stillness even if the body wants to sway.

Part 4. *Kinhin* (Walking Meditation)

From a standing position, take a moment to tap into the Breath Watching practice. Feel the chest rise and fall and the belly gently expand and contract. Notice and watch the breath for a few cycles without any attempt to control the speed, depth, or quality. Choosing one foot, allow the inhalation of the breath to move the foot forward as you take the first step. There is no special technique to take the step; no dictation of "heel then toe," or "toe then heel," or "flat foot." Just step. Allow the pace of your own, uncontrolled, natural inhalation to move the foot forward. Notice that depending on the breath, the step may be short or long in stride, fast or slow. Continuing to follow the pace of the natural breath, allow the exhalation to move the other foot forward to take the second step. Repeat with one foot then the other foot walking forward, allowing the natural, uncontrolled breath to lead and be the music for the movement. Inhale, one step, exhale, next step, and so on.

This is the first movement meditation part in the sequence. Allow yourself to feel *piti*, rapture and joy, the fourth Factor of Enlightenment, in moving your body to your breath. Practice for approximately five minutes; keeping the eyes relaxed and the gaze towards the floor a few feet in front of where you are walking. Direction is not important, but be mindful of your surroundings so as not to walk into your neighbors. Notice any unevenness in the pace of your steps that is an extension of your breath. Accept the movement as is. Bring your feet together back to standing as you shift your attention from Breath Watching back to the sights and sounds of the room for a short break. Repeat the *Kinhin* sequence.

Part 5. Dance

There are four movements that make up the Dance sequence in Zenful Dance. Because the majority of the 7 Parts of Zenful Dance repeat at least once, only the two-hour class allows for enough time to practice all four movements. In my sixty-minute and ninety-minute classes, we choose only one or two of the four movements to focus on. Each movement is done for about five minutes. The four movements are:

1. In and Out—This is an action of contracting and releasing. Stand with your feet planted slightly wider than shoulder-width apart. Allow the arms, head, torso, and knees to contract as you curl forward into a standing ball. Then straighten the knees, expand the chest, arch the back, and lift the chin and eyes upward while releasing the arms up and behind the torso to reverse the movement. Allow the pace of the uncontrolled, natural exhalation to contract the body, and the natural inhalation to stretch the body outward. Depending on the pace and depth of the natural breath, the movements may be quick or slow, erratic and staccato at times, while graceful and longer at other times. Enjoy the unevenness of the dance. Dance is a metaphor for life. We are not machines. We are naturally uneven.

2. Across and Over—This movement brings the arm from across the body up and over to the outside of the body. The arms alternate moving. With the feet standing slightly wider than hip-distance apart, choose one arm to draw and extend across the body to the opposite side. Bring the straightened arm up across the face and over to the outside of the body, in an "over the rainbow" movement, sweeping the arm. The breath leads the movement. On the inhale draw the first arm across the body and up and as the arm sweeps in front of the face, the natural exhalation moves the arm to the outside. Change arms when the natural inhale leads into the next movement.

3. Down and Up—Stand with the feet slightly wider than hip-distance apart. Begin standing straight with the arms soft (bent) at the elbows. Exhale and bend the knees and lower the body while maintaining a straight back. Allow the natural inhale of the breath to straighten the knees and extend the arms out in the air on either side of the body. Draw one knee upward towards the chest while maintaining balance on the other leg. Upon exhaling, lower the lifted leg and foot down to the ground and bend the knees into a half squat. Soften the arms as the elbows bend into the sides of the body. Follow the next inhale and straighten both legs. Lift the other knee up towards the chest, balancing on the opposite leg and extending the arms out to the side for balance. When the breath is shallow, this movement appears more like a march in place; the movements are shorter and faster. When the breath deepens or is slower, this movement can resemble a very tame, gentle version of sumo wrestler foot stamping!

4. Side to Side—From a standing position with feet about hip-width distance apart and arms bent softly at the elbows, choose a foot to move out to the side (i.e.,

right foot moves a step to the right side). Shift all weight to the foot you have stepped on. Lift and cross the other foot behind the first foot to move a second step in the same direction. Shift all weight to the back foot. Lift the foot in front and again step out to the side of the body to move a third step in the same direction. Shift all weight onto the newly placed foot. Finally, lift the other foot without weight and place it together next to the foot you are standing on and return to the starting standing position. Every breath a step: inhale and step to the side, exhale and cross the other foot in back, inhale and step to the side, exhale and draw the feet together in standing position. Repeat in the other direction. This movement resembles a step in many dance styles referred to as the grapevine. Based on rhythm of the natural, uncontrolled breath, move mindfully and joyfully and surrender to the unevenness of the movement.

The fifth Factor of Enlightenment is *passaddhi*, or serenity. In each of these four Dance moves, feel the serenity in letting go of any urges to control the breath or movement. Allow the natural breath to move you. A sense of humor and light-heartedness is welcome!

Section 2: Partnership

Part 6. Dance with a Partner

Dancing with a partner requires concentration, or *samadhi*, the sixth Factor, on your own natural breath, while practicing the Dance in front of someone else. Both partners face each other without touching and choose one of the four Dance movements. Move to the pace of your own uncontrolled breath. There will be times when the natural breath of both partners is in sync, thereby allowing them to move together in harmony. In many instances, the breath rhythm will be different between partners and thus their movements. Allow and accept the differences and unevenness in the partnership. It is in the Dance as it is in life. Practice for approximately five minutes. Repeat the sequence if time allows.

Section 3: Group

Part 7: Dance in a Group

This final part is the ultimate practice in letting go and finding a state of equanimity, or *upekkha*—the seventh and final Factor. For approximately 5 minutes, practitioners form a circle facing the center and dance one of the four Dance movements, without touching each other, to the rhythm of their own individual, natural breath. Release expectations and allow on the breath to lead the movement. Invite all seven of the *Anapanasati* Factors of Enlightenment to come together in this final sequence: *sati* (mindfulness), *dhamma vicaya* (analysis), *viriya* (persistence), *piti* (rapture), *passaddhi* (serenity), *samadhi* (concentration), and *upekkha* (letting go). Repeat as time allows.

Once the group has proceeded through these seven parts of Zenful Dance, you can conclude the session by bringing the feet together and our hands in *gassho*, or prayer. Feeling our own awareness, vulnerability, humility, and humanity in our stillness, in silence we acknowledge and bow to all that we are within and all that we are without.

Ground, Path and Fruition

Kim Sargent-Wishart

This exploration is based in the methodological approach of Body-Mind Centering (BMC), which works somatically, engaging body and mind in investigating specific anatomical and physiological structures, states, and patterns. The material I am presenting is a synthesis of embodied embryology as taught by BMC's founder, Bonnie Bainbridge Cohen, with my studies and practice of Shambhala and Vajrayana Buddhism, and dance/movement improvisation.

This guided practice offers an embodied approach to somatic and philosophical inquiry; a place to physically "digest" and move with philosophical ideas and to reflect on what arises in your experience. I invite you to approach your own movement investigation, either solo or in a group, as a question, with curiosity and openness to what the experience may reveal to you. You can do this exploration anywhere that you feel safe and comfortable to move, though you may find it easier to begin the practice indoors, in a quiet, uncluttered room, to minimize distractions and create a container for your explorations. Working together with a small group of movers can support the deepening of the practice. When shared by a few people in the room, the "mind" of the work can be shared and reinforced, and this also gives you the chance to discuss your experiences and questions.

A strategy that I find very helpful to support this research process is timed stream-of-consciousness writing. If you wish to try this, be sure to have paper and pen within reach, so that you can pause after each section of exploration to write. Write for a set amount of time, maybe two to three minutes, without stopping to edit or think too hard. I suggest that you not try to specifically record what happened, but rather allow yourself to stay in the movement experience and let whatever words and images arise flow onto the page. If you are working in a group, you might read your writings aloud to each other, either before moving on to the next section, or at the end of the practice session. I find that this open writing strategy often reveals deeper and richer levels of experience than if I try to consciously describe or document what happened. As a further layer, you might choose to move in response to your own writing, or perhaps while someone else is reading aloud. Although not required, I recommend reading my chapter earlier in this volume prior to engaging with this practice.

Ectoderm as Path

Moving as you wish through the room, following your curiosity, bring your attention to the space around you, to your immediate environment. Gently opening your sensory perceptions, notice the pathways that make this perception possible—the nerve endings at the surface of your skin and the nerve tracks bringing information in to your consciousness. Allow this sensation to lead you into exploration. Notice how the sensory system brings the exterior world in to your interior experience. How do you receive sights, smells, sounds, and tastes? Notice the pathways from these sensory organs into your brain, or wherever you feel that they go. How does what you perceive become part of you?

These same pathways allow your internal impulses to express outward into space. Play with the give and take exchange between yourself and your environment. This might be quite subtle, a flash of perception or a thought, or the movement of imagination, or it might propel you into larger movement.

Sensitize the back of your body, as if you have feelers extending out into space from your back surfaces. Allow the space (including any other people who might be in the space) to circulate through you as you circulate through the space. The ectoderm, as the back of the body, is continuous with the amniotic sac, an active, protective space behind the body. Can you sense support from that space behind you?

When the embryo enfolds, the amniotic sac surrounds us, creating our immediate environment. What is the resonance between this external space, our perceptive surfaces, and pathways of flow in the nerves? How do you create your own space? How does the space become you?

As you move, notice how you feel in relation to close and far space, to the earth, to your sense of self, to others. What are you drawn to noticing? What do you feel like doing? What is the mind of the ectoderm?

Endoderm as Ground

Begin to shift your attention more internally, to your stomach, digestive organs, interior surfaces, deep in the front of your body. Close your eyes if you wish, or lie down to begin, to feel more contact with and support from the earth. Allow yourself to actively meet any surfaces you are in contact with, yield with the floor, or the earth, or anther person—actively meeting with full presence, but without having to do anything.

Notice any places in your body and mind that might be holding on to an agenda, any subtle grasping or resistance. Without trying to change this, invite a sense of equanimity and rest.

Allow your mind and body to rest in the ground of being. Allow every cell of your body to breathe and be simply present in all directions, with the support of gravity. As you yield to the earth, feel the earth's supportive yield into you.

The endoderm begins as what will be the front layer of the embryo, and is continuous with the yolk sac, a space of nourishment, in front. Allow your body to come into relationship with this space in front—can you sense support from that space?

As the endoderm folds inwards this yolk sac becomes our inner digestive organs, our deep nourishment. Invite the wisdom of the "gut brain," the enteric nervous system of the abdominal organs, to lead you in stillness and movement. Allow yourself time to settle into being rather than doing.

Notice the mind of the endoderm and the images and qualities that arise.

Ectoderm and Endoderm in Relationship

When you feel you have a clear sense of each layer, you can begin to play with the relationship between them. Begin by alternating your attention between them—the external awareness and pathways of flow of the ectoderm, and the internal state of presence and restfulness in the endoderm.

As you get more familiar with the mind of each, begin to sense how they influence and support each other. What feels most familiar to you? How can you work with these layers separately and in relationship to give yourself more support, more ease, or more vigor?

Invite the two layers to come into relationship, and bring your attention to the space where they meet, and the space in between, in the middle of your body. This is where the third layer, the mesoderm, arises.

Mesoderm as Fruition

The mesoderm begins at what will be the perineum, in the pelvic floor, and grows up as a central line in the space between the ectoderm and endoderm. It grows up a few inches and then, as it continues to grow upwards, the bottom retreats back down, orienting us to our verticality towards the sky with a rootedness into the ground, like the strong stalk of a plant.

Explore the appearance of this strong vertical stalk, extending to the earth and heavens. What qualities do you notice as this middle layer begins to arise?

From this central line (the primitive streak), the mesoderm then spreads laterally, bringing us into our side body and giving rise to bones, muscles and connective tissue.

Begin to feel your bones and muscles, your physical strength, pushing against the floor, pulling yourself through space, kneading, warming up, becoming more physically engaged in the space.

As your movement becomes more muscular and physical, notice your heart beating and blood pumping, throughout your body. Invite the intelligence of your heart to lead the movement of your muscles, bones and joints, to follow your passion and love in your dancing, perhaps playing with weight shifts, falls, and suspensions.

What can this physical body do? What do you want to create? What do you love to do? What is the potential of being embodied here and now?

Combining the Three Layers

Play with initiating movement in each of these three layers, exploring how they relate to each other in your movement and perception.

Ask questions of, and through, your movement. For example, how do the spatial pathways of the ectoderm support strength and vitality in the muscles (mesoderm, fruition)? How does yielding to organ presence (endoderm, ground) support clearer action and perception (ectoderm, path)? The possibilities for exploration are yours to discover.

To finish the session, be sure to allow yourself some time for open improvisation, moving without any instruction. If you are working in a group you may wish to witness each other moving, and to share your experience through writing, drawing, and/or discussion.

Once you are more familiar with the dynamics of these three aspects, you might explore them while engaged in other activities, such as taking a walk, singing, brainstorming, taking photographs, having conversations, or sitting in meditation. How does this exploration change your sense of what your body is and who you are as an embodied human being?

Geopoetics
A Buddhist-Inspired Site-Specific Performance Practice

Anna Tzakou

Geopoetics training is a contemplative practice of performance making in and with the landscape. "Geo-" comes from the Greek prefix *γεω-* which means "coming from earth." "Poetics" derives from the word *ποιητική*, which means the method of composing an artistic product. This chapter portrays a practical strategy to access a site and elaborate its embodiment toward the production of a performance event. The practice addresses theater and dance practitioners without being exclusive; therefore, it does not presuppose a specific training style. Based on a contemplative art-making tradition, the training evaluates the process as a product. It invites the practitioners to work from responding rather than acting, allowing the material to arise and direct them into a performance structure. It is an approach that presupposes trust and confidence in one's own process and cultivates a nonjudgmental curiosity about the world's phenomena.

Landscapes are divided into urban and nonurban. They are segments of space that may not have been contextualized by the human experience. Literally and metaphorically, landscapes enclose a view; a sense of perspective which one aims to resonate with and expose into sight/site through Geopoetics practice. The below suggested exercises refer to rural environments. If one is not familiar with working in nonperformance spaces, it is recommended to start with a natural landscape for several reasons: It is open, accessible, and beneficial when interrelating with it. It proposes a clear materiality to elaborate, and it functions as a transparent feedback mechanism. Although these features are applied to all sites, in the rural ones these attributes are amplified and thus more easily listened to. This chapter is organized according to Anna Halprin's three-structure discipline of working with nature: "contact, explore and respond."[1] Integrating Buddhist and performance practices, Geopoetics is divided into a double-fold process: attunement and actualization. The first phase investigates movement, voice, and objects on site as a specific "being-ness." The second phase organizes the on-site experience into a performance structure. These processes could be applied to solo or ensemble work. The following étude exemplifies a group practice of attunement.

Select a Site—Make the Transition

The first task of attuning is to find a place where we feel drawn to work. It could be a familiar place that instinctively came to our mind as a first thought, or it could be a site discovered by wandering through a specific area. The working site must be a place where you feel safe, comfortable, and interested to spend some time.[2] Having chosen a location, learn more about it: How is it used and why? Does it have any historical and cultural context? What are the oral traditions or histories that encompass it? How do the local people and authorities consider it? The answers to these questions can ignite other performative material (texts, songs, objects, stories) that may later supplement and enrich the somatic process. This is a preparatory phase; once the information is gathered, keep it in the back of your head and return to it when structuring the material.

The practice begins with the transition to the chosen site. It is important to allow part of the transportation, if possible, to take place by foot. Walking initiates the mindfulness somatic practice of the landscape. Group walking practice is based on the walking contemplation found in the *Satipatthana Sutta*, but follows a more open and flexible structure. Practitioners may walk in a line an equal distance apart or with less order. In either case, the group walks with a sense of togetherness, in silence. Notice the moments where the feet meet the ground; maintain the gaze on the horizontal level without having a fixed point; pay attention to thoughts, associations, ideas, and images that arise while passing through the landscape. The walking practice effects the transition from the social self to the working process and the experience of the site. It opens the body and mind in the space, making it available to enter the landscape through active listening. Like an emptying or cleansing process, it introduces the body to a direct experience of the space and creates the "white canvas" through which the body-landscape interrelationship will take place.

Contact

Once the group arrives on site, allow some time to digest the walk and take some notes. Recording the experience after each exercise is essential. It is a way to train the mind to become a nonjudgmental observer. It also functions as an account of events to which you could return later in the performance-making process. The practice continues with sensory and spatial awareness exercises. These practices open up the bodily experience in the landscape and provide an intermediate zone for you to notice when and how the outer landscape meets the inner. Blindfolded walking and slow rolling are two exercises of the sensory awareness practice. Working with no vision can be overwhelming; therefore, if you feel that you need support, do the exercise in pairs where one acts as the "eyes" for the other. This does not mean you play a restrictive role for your partner; it is mostly to create a sense of support and safety. Walk barefoot and blindfolded from one point to another within a time frame of twenty minutes. The aim is to absorb the environment through a different sensory gate and notice what arises with the incoming information. Follow a pace that feels natural to you.

The rolling exercise entails rolling on the ground in slow motion with movement initiated by the eyes. Lie down on your front, place your hands on the ground aligned with your shoulders, palms facing down. Your head looks to one side; your gaze moves toward the sky and lifts your head from the ground; your eyes keep looking further behind you. Push with your hands and start to rotate your upper body, turning your torso and legs and eventually rolling onto your back. In the same manner, keep moving toward the other side. Find a slow and organic flow with an equal tempo during all the phases of the roll. The aim is to have a sense that it is the eyes' exploration of the space that makes the rolling happen. Notice where you hold back and release more of your muscles into the ground. The blindfolded walk and the rolling practices, as simple as they sound, provide a somatic frame to listen and contemplate the story patterns, memories, associations, and personal histories evoked by the moving body in the landscape.

Another way of investigating place is by positioning the body/ies on site and exploring the ways their placement creates meaning. The practice is one of spatial awareness and investigates the following questions: Why are some images on site more engaging than others? What do they activate in the place, in the bodies, and in the watchers? The following exercise is called the "still shots" and is inspired by and structured based on Barbara Dilley's "Red Square" practice. Select a specific direction of the landscape and set a frame as a stage. Define an audience side and a performance side. You can play with how near or far you want these sides to be. Your movement vocabulary is sitting, standing, lying, and stillness (allowing all of their variations to take place). The instructions are: Enter the frame; select a posture; sense and inhabit the image you formulate; offer it to the watchers; dissolve it; and leave.

The task could start as solos, duets, and so on. You could also supplement the process with objects, or as Dilley names them, "allies."[3] This also functions as an opportunity to explore the objects found at the site. In taking a posture, it is important to consider the relations the body creates with the natural elements and how they respond back into the image. Enter the frame either by envisioning a position of your body or by deciding at the very last minute through listening to the present moment. This is not about presenting a predetermined story already in the mind. It is about creating from scratch and working with impulse and intuition. You can also play with the tempo of the transitions between the images (in and out of the frames). The watchers could be calling out titles, as attempts to articulate possible meanings of the image. The aim here is to investigate the narrative lines of the space, when and how the bodies on site tell a story.

Explore

So far, we have been individually practicing our somatic connection with the land. Each one has been investigating his/her own experience on site within the confines of the group. We have been working alone together. The next step is to explore the impulses and the relational dynamics with the landscape not only on a personal level but also on a collective one. For such an objective, I use the improvisational practice of "Open Space" from Dilley's Contemplative Dance Practice (CDP). It is an open-structure movement improvisation that explores the somatic experience in the space as a development of *samatha* meditation.[4] I have been using Open Space in the landscape to practice relating directly to the environment and to act on site as responding. According to Dilley, the discipline synchronizes body and mind with the present moment and aims to explore the activity that is requested from our experience of the space. The practice includes a movement vocabulary of lying/crawling, sitting, standing, walking (or running), and their kinetic qualities of stillness, repetition, and tempo (fast or slow). Dilley also structures a twofold discipline of connectivity: being influenced and copying. You can apply this instruction as part of your practice in relating with the other or the site. In this way, the practice becomes a perpetual negotiation between sensing and acting, being and responding, being separated and belonging.

To practice Open Space outdoors, first define the site of the practice, set its borderlines. You could also name an audience side, although it is not necessary. Set a time restraint and a time keeper. Start from where you are; notice your body-mind presence within the atmosphere of the landscape and acknowledge it. Give permission to yourself to be enchanted by the outdoor environment's materiality (e.g., a tree, a rock, a cloud in the sky). Allow yourself to follow an instruction, either initiating from your body as movement or from the environment as a task-activity. There are many strategies to organize such an interaction. A direct way to coordinate it is by formulating the interplay as a task activity (e.g., carrying stones) or as a structured play (e.g., moving whenever you hear a bird sound). Again, the movement is not to be predetermined, but originates organically by your somatic presence on site. Have no expectations! You only need to be open to the stimulus received from the environment (and/or other participants) and attentive to your impulses that arise in response.

Each moment, be aware of the instruction you choose to practice, even if you eventually break it or drop it. It is very easy to space out or follow your habitual mind patterns, which could distract you from openly relating to space and others. If you notice this happening, start fresh and return to the practice. If you recognize your associations and impulses running freely, drop the practice and pursue your flow. The practice functions as an initiator and an anchor; hence, it is not something that you have to stick to. Notice whether you are initiating from an authentic impulse or perhaps from a sense of pressure to be active. This could be manifested as a busyness in your practice or a psychological action-reaction driven situation with your co-practitioners. Notice your work patterns: How long could you be in the space until something arises? Do you initiate from ideas in your mind or impulses in your body? As the practice unfolds, is anything else revealed (a feeling, an image, a memory, or a dream)? There is no correct answer. The key here is awareness.

Respond/Actualizing

After concluding the practice, discuss the experience as a group. Describe as precisely as you can the particular moments (even those that were vague and abstract) and try to decode the reasons you think they are worth revisiting. Use verbs in your descriptions. It could constitute the first material to create a score. This phase of the work functions as a distilment process, and its goal is to understand what worked, how, and why. As you practice more and more in the specific site, you may be inspired to infuse the process with voice material and texts. You may discover subtler levels of interrelation. This is the phase of actualization, when the landscape begins to talk back to you and the division between you and it begins to fade. It is as if you start listening to a melody that has always been there. Now you perceive the landscape experientially. Themes and intentions could arise. This is a good time to return to the site research you did in the beginning of your process. Do you make any connections? Do you foresee any seed of a story line or a question that relates you with the place? This is your starting point for formulating your site-specific performance. Good luck!

Notes

1. Libby Worth and Helen Poynor, *Anna Halprin* (London: Routledge, 2004), 89.

2. Whether you are a facilitator or practitioner of the work, it is important that you take some health and safety precautions—bringing the appropriate gear and being realistic about the group's capacity.

3. Barbara Dilley, "Allies." Accessed June 4, 2015. http://barbaradilley.com/excerpts.

4. See my earlier chapter in the Performance section of this book.

Dharma Jam
How to Lead a Buddhist Dance Ritual

HARRISON BLUM

Dharma Jam is a two-hour Buddhist dance liturgy. It has been impactful for dancers trying on Buddhism, Buddhists coming to dance, and those not identifying as either. Please use this template as is helpful, whether as a model for replication or a foundation for revision. One important disclaimer: you don't need to be an impressive dancer to facilitate a Dharma Jam. Your role is more about confidence and presence than aesthetic and ability. You are there to be a host and a guide, and to hold space for the experience. Present the structure clearly and sincerely. Be the facilitator, and also a participant.

Arrival: Creating Sacred Space

The tone of the Dharma Jam should be signaled before one enters the room. A sign placed outside the entrance to the Jam can welcome people to enter quietly and mindfully. The Jam space itself should consist of a large, open room with meditation cushions (if possible) and chairs circling the perimeter. Feel free to decorate or beautify the room as you like. You might arrange a simple altar or centerpiece in the middle of the floor. Dimming overhead lights or using rope lights can create ambiance. A pleasant space can add to dancers' experiences, but really all that's needed are props to sit comfortably and space to move freely.

Once Jam time arrives, play an extended track of ambient music (collaborating with live musicians can also work well, although I'll describe using recorded music here). This music continues the invitation of the welcome sign, supporting a period of personal arrival into one's body and the room. As people arrive, let them know they can move or be still as they like, and that the Jam will begin shortly.

By fifteen minutes in, formally begin the Dharma Jam by inviting participants to walk through the space with different qualities—slowly, quickly, toward open space, leading with different body parts, reaching and stretching as they go, etc. This brief "milling" period serves both to open participants' range of motion in their bodies and within the room itself. As appropriate, comments throughout the Jam can be tailored to people of different physical abilities.

After a few minutes, ask the group to form a standing circle—close enough to reach out and take hands, though not yet doing so. This refuge circle sets the tone and intention for the Jam. It is a time to honor our human potential (Buddha), paths of truth (Dharma), and practice community (Sangha). Speak to each of those briefly in your own words. This is also a good opportunity to speak to and normalize the range of emotions people may feel at the Jam, and the importance of creating a safe space together. You might welcome people to hold hands (as they're comfortable) during the Sangha phase of refuge.

Move on by inviting participants to drop their hands and take a seat on a cushion or chair around the edges of the room. During this transition from standing to sitting it's timely to now turn the music down or off. Once people are settled, offer an overview of what's to come. Having a rough idea of the Jam phases can help put participants' curiosity at ease and aid presence in the moment. Simply outline the main phases of the Jam—Tune In, Get Down, and Join Up. Tune In begins with a seated meditation, moves into standing, and then gentle movement. Get Down invites a fuller range of movement style and tempo, supported by increasing intensity of music. Get Down shifts the focus from the individual to the collective creation. The Jam closes with a dancing dedication and seated reflection circle.

Buddha: Tune In

Begin the seated meditation by offering a few words on the Jam's theme. This could be a line or two from a text you're drawing from, or an image or metaphor—something short, accessible, and tied to the sparse facilitation comments you'll be offering throughout the rest of the Jam. This is less a mini–Dharma talk and more a Dharma seed. Brief meditation instructions can then be shared as the last spoken words before you ring a bell, signaling the beginning of the meditation.

Ring the bell after ten to fifteen minutes to signal the end of the seated meditation, and invite participants to stand in stillness somewhere in the room, continuing their meditative attention. Once all are standing, call their attention to the felt sense of the standing body. Speak to the mutual presence of stillness and movement in the body. They are standing, one of the four traditional meditation postures taught by the Buddha (in addition to walking, sitting, and lying down). Standing is a posture based on consistency of form, on the still body. Standing is also referred to by Contact Improvisation dance founder Steve Paxton as "the small dance," the dance of breath and balance, the dance of small movements within relative stillness. Call attention to these seeds of movement and dance present within the standing body.

Guide participants to notice the body's impulses for movement, beginning to allow slow movement while still keeping both feet planted on the floor. Ask that after some moments of moving, they return to stillness in some new position when their moving gesture feels complete. Draw attention to the details of starting and stopping a movement, and the feeling of each new shape of relative stillness. Continue in this way for some minutes, giving participants time to alternate between slow movement and stillness. Next invite them to allow more momentum to the movement, coming back to stillness only when it feels wanted or needed, when there is no impulse for movement. Give permission for this expanded movement to bring people's feet off the floor and to move them through the space. This is a good point to turn the music back on, with the next 20 minutes or so building gradually from a slow to medium tempo. I like to keep music selections instrumental during this phase, with the exception of explicitly spiritual or prayerful lyrics.

For the remainder of Tune In, it can be good to offer occasional facilitation comments, encouraging practitioners to allow whatever the body needs. Stillness, slow movement, stretching, lying down, walking, and moving in place are each welcome. There is no right or better way to move. As the seated meditation attended to fostering beginner's mind, this phase is a dedicated time for cultivating beginner's body—a felt presence received anew in each moment. In focusing on and supporting the beginner's body, Tune In provides the crucial foundation for lifting up how the moving body feels over how it looks.

Dharma: Get Down

The next phase of the Jam gives permission for fuller movement while letting go of expectation. Let participants know that the music pace will start to build, and that they can just stay with movement that feels natural and honest, with their dance partners of breath and balance, movement and momentum. There's no need to match the speed or style of the music. Encourage participants to blur the boundary between movement and dance, perhaps thinking of dance as being playful with movement. Slowness and stillness are always available. We follow our joy, or whatever comes up, wherever it leads us.

As bodily activity increases, facilitation comments can be sprinkled throughout this phase to welcome expanded movement and maintained attention to the breath. While the pace and range of motion may increase for most people, the focus is still mainly inward. Remind them to lean away from controlling and toward receiving, to dissolve into rather than build up their dance. Your facilitation is a welcome into ritual dance space, where movers become the universe dancing with itself. As participants navigate their own authentic paths from stillness into movement and dance, so too should you.

The music for Get Down continues from the mid-tempo of Tune In and progresses gradually toward faster, more dance-able tracks. The duration of this and the next section, as with the previous one, should each be about 20 minutes.

Sangha: Join Up

Join Up increases connection by broadening attention from the individual to the group journey. Welcome awareness to shift from the personal to the collective dance, trusting the sincere practice each person has been doing during the Jam. State that this expanded attention is an orientation, not a requirement for movement. Participants don't need to copy anyone else. They don't need to dance with anyone. They don't even need to make eye contact, although all of these *may* happen. Invite practitioners to simply notice the qualities of movement around them, seeing if some of these qualities might be present in their own dance.

With increasing connection comes the second aspect of this phase—increasing safety. Knowing that increasing relation can bring up issues of comfort and safety for people, ask participants to pair their widened attention with a heightened sensitivity to the needs of others. Cue them to body language as an indicator of how interactive another practitioner wants to be. Together, you continue the shared work of making the Dharma Jam a safe space.

This phase can be fun and playful. By this point in the Jam, most people's comfort levels will have increased. Your clear permission to be only as relational as each person wants will free people up to exchange without obligation. Some will pair up for extended dances. Others will orbit each other more briefly, one person's spin momentarily aligning with a neighbor's curving arm or turning head.

Join Up blends the meditation hall with the dance club. You've spent the last eighty minutes or so establishing a strong mindfulness foundation for the Jam. During this phase the tone shifts from contemplation to celebration. Choose music that reflects this shift. The pace can remain mid to fast tempo, taking care to stagger your selections so as not to wear people out. At this point it can be great to dip into more popular tracks—oldies, Motown, hip-hop, etc. Whereas lyrics could have posed a distraction during Tune In or Get Down, they can now be a positive addition to the celebration, something to sing along to even. As this phase nears its end, it can be good to give dancers a heads up when the last track is beginning.

Closing: Dedicating and Reflecting on the Practice

The dedication tracks are a time for practitioners to come back to their center while sending the benefit of their practice outward. The music shifts from fast to slow tempo. Speak once again to their partners, their allies, of breath and balance. Call them into attunement with the world's suffering. They might think of all sentient beings, or a certain community in crisis, or of just one person. That person might be one's self. The dance, or stillness, is now an embodied solidarity with this suffering, as the practice is dedicated to the well being of others, to all our relations.

I give one to two tracks for this moving dedication. When the music ends, there will be a power in the silence. Give that silence time to be heard. After some moments, invite people to gather in a seated circle. This is a time to share spoken words about the practice, if anyone is inclined. Depending on the context, this can be followed by saying names around the circle and making brief community announcements.

Moving in Grace
How to Guide the Practice

Hilary Lake

The structure of Moving in Grace is based on moving through an imaginary day, starting and ending with sleep, and cultivating meditative consciousness and self-expression throughout. I will describe the stages of this ritual as I have experienced them in practice, and offer specific concepts or images, such as a seed growing, that align with each stage. The structure as a whole is based on the Six Buddha Families of the Kalachakra Mandala, with each Family having a corresponding spiritual quality, element, color, and more. I invite you to develop your own imagery and bring in whatever holistic model works for you. What is essential is that it resonates with your own life experience and helps you to deepen and expand into yourself as well as emerge into relationship with others. The more you can actually do the practice while guiding, the more you'll be able to experience your own transformation, which in turn creates the space in which everyone else can undergo theirs.

The musical choice will likely affect the energy of the space and influence the practitioners more than any other element, and needs to be chosen with an ear for artistry and care for the preferences and edges of the group that you are guiding. The feel of the music should reflect and evoke the different stages of the day and parts of the Mandala. While live musical accompaniment may be ideal, recorded music or silence can also work. As the guide I use my verbal direction and voice, sometimes toning and singing musical phrases that arise spontaneously, to hold the space and bring in the different energies that correspond to the stages of the day.

My intention as the guide is to help connect my own and the participants' inner spiritual and emotional experiences with the daily activities of self-care, work, service, and being in relationship. Ideally there is a greater awareness cultivated, on many levels, of the extraordinary present in the ordinary. Continue to stay open to what images, concepts, memories, and feelings arise for you while reading this chapter. These are the elements that will guide you into your own unique way of Moving in Grace and will help you to hold an authentic container for your own as well as others' awakening.

Setting the Space

The practice begins when you enter the space. Ask yourself how you are feeling and holding yourself. What are you noticing in the space? What needs your attention internally and externally? You're now creating a space that the participants will enter into that will help them to feel welcome, safe, held, clear, and encouraged to turn inward. You could have an altar with whatever elements, guides, or symbols are meaningful to you, and invite the participants to add to it as well. The lighting is the most important element of the physical environment. I prefer to begin with the lighting fairly dim, and sometimes will turn the lights up as we move throughout the day if it feels generative and supportive to the practice.

Welcoming In

As the participants arrive, greet them with peaceful music and a sign to welcome them into the space with mindfulness. There's no need, necessarily, to personally address each person, and you should be free as the guide to center and ground yourself as you warm up. Your own process of becoming fully present as the guide is essential to a successful practice. You might also set a clear intention either for yourself or for the experience as a whole. Include whatever personal prayers you like at this time. The mental framework and awareness that you, as the guide, bring to the practice is key to holding a safe, transformational space in which grace can truly show up through you.

Beginning the Practice

Once the participants have mostly arrived or you feel that it is the right time to start, invite them to sit in a circle with you. Meeting together in a circle is essential to create a welcoming, safe container in which everyone sees each other and at least hears one another's names. Stay present with them and with yourself as you arrive together, looking around the circle. Give a short explanation of Moving in Grace to offer a context for what you are about to share. This will provide participants with a map of the journey and a sense of what to expect. Let them know that aside from beginning and ending in stillness, the duration of the practice is a time for open, improvisational movement and dance. Welcome them to move throughout the time and space however their bodies are called to.

Invite them to really go inside and trust themselves. Reassure them that it's ok if at times they can't hear your guiding comments or don't understand what is going on. Following their own inner guidance is what is most important in this practice. If that means that they lie down and sleep or are shaking wildly for the entire practice, then that's the right thing for them to do.

The next step is to invite everyone to spread out and find their own space or piece of ground in which to plant themselves. They can either sit or lie down depending on what's most comfortable. Remind them that there will be a visualization of deep sleep during which they are welcome to shift posture and lie down.

Next comes a meditation. Invite the participants to be curious about their inner experience. The intention is to bring the participants into a greater awareness of their bodies and their physical relationship to their environment without using their eyesight. Guide them to be present to their breath, to follow the in and out breath. "Notice how it affects the whole body. Explore how breath relates to sensation." Then have them choose a place in their bodies where they can feel their breath the strongest and to call this place home. "This home will be returned to throughout the practice to come back to ourselves, our centers, and to feel safe and renewed before going back out again." Amidst whatever thoughts, feelings, and sensations arise for practitioners, guide them to continue returning to this home. "If something calls your attention repeatedly, stay with that thought, feeling, or sensation, giving it the attention that it craves. This place, this thought, is a seed. It is full of potential and possibilities for expression. Send your breath to this place and hold it with your focused awareness. Imagine that this place and part of you is a seed that you are planting into the ground below you."

Buddha ~ Sleeping ~ Planting ~ Deepening

"Then, like this seed in the darkness, imagine that you are deep in sleep in your bed. You are in the darkness, in the silent stillness. You are united in this darkness with all of life. You are waiting, renewing, and preparing for your growth as the seed and for the day to come. Feel the stillness. Receive the darkness and your response to its depths from within you. Can you feel the potential that moves through your body, through your breath? Notice your breath. Without trying, can it settle, or even still, for some moments? Are you able to renew and rest in this place? Allow whatever arises to be here, all thoughts, feelings, sensations, and let them go, allowing them to pass through, returning to what is left."

This is the Buddha Family that relates to the body. It corresponds with one's ability to have a mirror-like, reflective capacity to take in all the information from one's inner landscape. It also relates to the element of earth, which is grounding and stable, and the color yellow.[1]

Vajra ~ Dreaming ~ Stirring ~ Receiving

"The next stage is dreaming, in which we are stirring in our seed, or our body-mind, while deep inside. It is very early in the morning, before the light, and there is an inkling of the day to come. It is a time for deep listening and holding spaciousness for what may arise. What dreams, visions, insights, and feelings are emerging that call for expression in your life? What is arising to give you a focus, direction, or intention for this day? Choose one, and hold it in your vast awareness."

This is the Vajra Family that relates to the mind and discriminating awareness. This awareness notices the labeling that takes place to create a sense of order. This is the element of space that is clear, precise, and corresponds to the color green.[2]

Padma ~ Awakening ~ Emerging ~ Opening

"The sun is now peaking up and sending early morning light into your bedroom, calling you to awaken and grow into the day. At this stage come back to your home, to your breath. How are you feeling your breath? How does it relate to this state of being, between sleeping and wakefulness, in the ethers of your dream world? How are you able to embody the sensations of this vision or dream, and nourish this seed into greater awakening? Can you feed your breath to where you feel this dream, like water that flows around a seed, nurturing it to open? How do you continue to feed this seed of a dream, encouraging its life to open as you get out of bed and move into your day? What rituals and practices do you use to prepare yourself? Can you notice the energy of each moment, taking care of your entire being?"

This is the Padma Family of speech and communication, through which one is able to recognize the individualizing awareness. True love and compassion is cultivated towards oneself so that one can be more present to all beings. All are accepted and welcomed just as all visions and dreams are invited to express themselves. This is the element of water, which is nourishing and flowing, and relates to the color white.[3]

Karma ~ Co-Creating ~ Engaging ~ Releasing & Creating

"As the sun rises into the morning, you step out of the safety of your dwelling, where you've been preparing for the day. Maybe you just step into the day's work, if it happens to take place where you live. How are you staying connected to your inner home, and to your breath? How do you fully engage with others and the wide world while continuing to expand the feeling and potential of this dream with each move and action? How do others' dreams affect your own? Can you reflect someone else's dream, supporting its expression while still staying connected to you own? How do you respond to conflict when it arises as you're expressing your dream? Can you play with the tension of confrontation, redirecting the energy? How can you use this energy to continue moving? Do you return back to your inner home to reconsider and try again?"

This is the Karma Family that emphasizes one's influence on self and others, the actions that one takes, and the results of one's activity. It is forceful, generating movement and change as the element of wind to blow away what is not useful and to create connections for purposeful collaboration. This family is playful in its direct action, and relates to the color black.[4]

Ratna ~ Returning Home ~ Integrating ~ Sharing

"The sun is now arcing across the sky and beginning to set as the day is rounding out. You are returning to where you came from this morning, or setting out into your evening activities. What is the feeling in your body and where is your dream after all of this work and activity? How can you gather all that you've experienced today so far and integrate it together? Bring each experience, each memory, as a worthy ingredient and toss them all into the pot as the stew of your day. Feel each element as separate and valuable and bring them in with the intention to cook up a state of greater balance and integrity within you. How can you create this meal as an offering to those you love, as a way to share yourself with intentionality and enjoyment? Allow the fire to integrate all the day's experiences and ingredients together. How do you set the table for them to join you at this meal? Who's invited to dinner tonight and who's not? How do you serve the meal and relish each bite together?"

This is the Ratna Family that recognizes all good qualities through an equalizing awareness in which all parts are accepted and held in equal regard to create a sense of the whole. The element of Ratna is fire and corresponds to the color red and the symbol of the jewel. This jewel is a wish-fulfilling jewel that gives with endless generosity to one-self and others.[5]

Vajrasattva ~ Resting ~ Reflecting ~ Dedicating

"The sun has set and the darkness calls us back inward to rest as we reflect on the day. We are digesting the meal of our integrated experience and allowing ourselves to just be. What do you notice is still left of your dream? Who and what helped bring you to this place within yourself? Who, if anyone, are you grateful for today? What else are you grateful for? What intentions do you want to plant back into the darkness of this day and back into your being so that they can grow up into the next day and beyond? What are these seeds? Send them back into your home in your body and down into the Earth below us to rest until it is their time to grow into your life."

This is the Vajrasattva family. It is a state of deep, blissful awareness and the element of consciousness, corresponding to the color blue.[6] It is a place where all is one and ideally there is a visceral feeling of the deep connection between each person in the room and beyond to our loved ones and others who are being evoked through the guidance.

Closing the Practice

Allow people to stay inside in the expansiveness of their experience for a few minutes as the energy dissipates. This space allows people to be present to their bodies and minds in this hopefully relaxed and open state, as well as to integrate their experience more deeply. After a few minutes, invite the participants to open their eyes and gather in a seated circle. Take your time coming back to the circle, staying in the energy of the practice. When everyone has arrived, sit together for a minute or so, just feeling and noticing each other. When it feels right, invite the group to share any brief reflections, feedback, or experiences in words, actions, or sounds. After everyone who wants to has shared, you might close with some group physical action to release any extra energy. Then, officially end the practice.

NOTES

1. Alexander Berzin, "Practicing Tantra Effectively." Accessed May 15, 2015. http://www.berzin archives.com/web/en/archives/advanced/tantra/level1_getting_started/practicing_tantra_effectively/transcript_3.html.
2. Berzin.
3. Berzin.
4. Berzin.
5. Berzin.
6. Berzin.

References

Adler, Janet. *Offering from the Conscious Body.* Rochester: Inner Traditions, 2002.

American Dance Therapy Association. "Fact Sheet." Baltimore: ADTA National Office, 1966.

American Dance Therapy Association. http://www.adta.org.

Analayo. *Satipatthana: The Direct Path to Realization.* Cambridge: Windhorse Publications, 2010.

Aposhyan, Susan. *Natural Intelligence: Body-Mind Integration and Human Development.* Baltimore: Williams & Wilkins, 1999.

Avstreih, Zoe. "Achieving Body Permanence: Authentic Movement and the Paradox of Healing." In *Authentic Movement: Moving the Body, Moving the Self, Being Moved,* edited by Patrizia Pallaro, 270–273. London: Jessica Kingsley, 2007.

Bainbridge Cohen, Bonnie. "Embryology—the Process of Consciousness." In *School for Body-Mind Centering® Training Manual, Embodied Developmental Movement and Yoga Program.* El Sobrante: The School for Body-Mind Centering, 2010.

Bainbridge Cohen, Bonnie. *Sensing, Feeling and Action: The Experiential Anatomy of Body-Mind Centering®,* 2nd ed. Northampton: Contact Editions, 2008.

Barba, Eugenio. *Le Corps en Jeu.* Paris: CNRS Edition, 1994.

Bell, Catherine. *Ritual Theory Ritual Practice.* Oxford: Oxford University Press, 1992.

Berzin, Alexander. "Practicing Tantra Effectively." http://www.berzinarchives.com/web/en/archives/advanced/tantra/level1_getting_started/practicing_tantra_effectively/transcript_3.html.

Bielefeldt, Carl. "Practice." In *Critical Terms for the Study of Buddhism,* edited by Donald Lopez, 229–244. Chicago: University of Chicago Press, 2005.

Blum, Harrison. "The Mindfulness Allies Project: Partnering Insight Meditation Centers with Marginalized Communities." MDiv thesis, Harvard Divinity School, 2012. Available for free download at http://www.movingdharma.org/writings-resources/.

Blum, Harrison. "Mindfulness Equity and Western Buddhism: Reaching People of Low Socioeconomic Status and People of Color." *International Journal of Dharma Studies* 2:10, 2014.

Blumenthal, Eileen. *Directors in Perspective: Joseph Chaikin.* Cambridge: Cambridge University Press, 1984.

Bodhi, Bhikkhu, trans. *In the Buddha's Words: An Anthology of Discourses from the Pāli Canon.* Somerville: Wisdom Publications, 2005.

Bodhi, Bhikkhu, trans. *The Middle Length Discourses of the Buddha: A New Translation of the Majjhima Nikaya.* Boston: Wisdom Publications, 1995.

Boucher, Sandy. *Opening the Lotus: A Woman's Guide to Buddhism.* Boston: Beacon Press, 1997.

Braun, Erik. *The Birth of Insight: Meditation, Modern Buddhism, and the Burmese Monk Ledi Sayadaw.* Chicago: University of Chicago Press, 2013.

Broadhurst, Susan. *Liminal Acts: A Critical Overview of Contemporary Performance and Theory.* London: Cassell, 1999.

Buckwalter, Melinda. *Composing while Dancing: An Improviser's Companion.* Madison: University of Wisconsin Press, 2010.

Cage, John. *Silence: Lectures and Writings.* Middletown: Wesleyan University Press, 1961.

Caldwell, Christine. *Getting in Touch: The Guide to New Body-Centered Therapies.* Wheaton: The Theosophical Publishing House, 1997.

Campbell, Joseph. *The Hero with a Thousand Faces.* Novato: New World Library, 2008.

Celichowska, Renata. *Erick Hawkins (1908–1994)*. Dance Heritage Coalition, 2012. Accessed March 21, 2015. http://www.danceheritage.org/treasures/hawkins_essay_celichowska.pdf.

Core of Culture. "Cham." Accessed May 31, 2015. http://www.coreofculture.org/cham.html.

Daishonin, Nichiren. *The Writings of Nichiren Daishonin*. Tokyo: Soka Gakkai, 1999.

Debord, Guy. *The Society of the Spectacle*. Translated by Black and Red. 1967. Accessed April 8, 2015. http://library.nothingness.org/articles/SI/en/display/16.

Dge 'dun chos 'phel. *Dhammapada*. Berkeley: Dharma Publishing, 1985.

Dilley, Barbara. *This Very Moment: Teaching Thinking Dancing*. Boulder: Naropa University Press, 2015.

Dilley, Barbara. "Allies." http://barbaradilley.com/excerpts.

Dorje, Wangchuk. *lhan cig skyes sbyor gyi zab khrid nges don rgya mtsho'i snying po phrin las 'od 'phro* [*The Profound Instructions on Connate Union: The Radiant Activity at the Heart of an Ocean of Definitive Meaning*]. Translated by Ari Goldfield. Accessed May 6, 2015. www.dharmadownload.net/pages/english/Texts/texts_0051.htm.

Dovey, Kim. *Fluid City: Transforming Melbourne's Urban Waterfront*. Sydney: University of New South Wales Press, 2005.

Eliot, T. S. *Four Quartets*. New York: Harcourt Brace, 1943.

Feldman, Christina. "Long Journey to a Bow." *Tricycle Magazine*, Fall 2008.

Fields, Rick, Peggy Taylor, Rex Weyler, and Rick Ingrasci. *Chop Wood Carry Water: A Guide to Finding Spiritual Fulfillment in Everyday Life*. Los Angeles: Jeremy P. Tarcher, 1984.

"Find a Dance/Movement Therapist." American Dance Therapy Association. Accessed July 10, 2013. http://www.adta.org/Find_a_DMT.

Fraleigh, Sondra H. *Dance and the Lived Body: A Descriptive Aesthetics*. Pittsburgh: University of Pittsburgh Press, 1987.

Friedman, Lenore. *Meetings with Remarkable Women: Buddhist Teachers in America*. Boston: Shambhala Publications, 2000.

Fronsdal, Gil. *The Issue at Hand: Essays on Buddhist Mindfulness Practice*. Redwood City: Insight Meditation Center, 2001.

Fronsdal, Gil, trans. *The Dhammapada: A New Translation of the Buddhist Classic with Annotations*. Boston: Shambhala Publications, 2005.

Garrett, Frances. *Religion, Medicine and the Human Embryo in Tibet*. London: Routledge, 2008.

Genoud, Charles. *Gesture of Awareness: A Radical Approach to Time, Space, and Movement*. Somerville: Wisdom Publications, 2006.

Germano, David. "Poetic Thought, the Intelligent Universe, and the Mystery of Self: The Tantric Synthesis of *RDzogs Chen* in Fourteenth Century Tibet." PhD diss., University of Wisconsin, 1992.

Gershon, Michael D. *The Second Brain*. New York: HarperCollins, 1999.

Gilpin, Richard. "The Use of Theravada Buddhist Practices and Perspectives in Mindfulness-Based Cognitive Therapy." *Contemporary Buddhism* 9.2 (2008): 227–251.

Ginsberg, Allen. "Mind Writing Slogans." In *What Book: Buddha Poems From Beat to Hiphop*, edited by Gary Gach, 197–201. Berkeley: Parallax Press, 1998.

Glaser, Aura. "Into the Demon's Mouth." *Tricycle Magazine*, Spring 2012.

Glowacki, David R. "Using Human Energy Fields to Sculpt Real Time Molecular Dynamics." In *Molecular Aesthetics*, edited by Peter Weibel and Ljiljana Fruk. Cambridge: MIT Press, 2013.

Grosz, Elizabeth. "Deleuze, Ruyer and Becoming-Brain: The Music of Life's Temporality." *PARRHESIA* 15 (2012): 1–13. Accessed May 6, 2015. http://www.parrhesiajournal.org/parrhesia15/parrhesia15_grosz.pdf.

Grotowski, Jerzy. *Toward a Poor Theater*. London: Methuen Drama, 1968.

Guenther, Herbert V., and Chögyam Trungpa. *The Dawn of Tantra*. Boston: Shambhala Publications, 1975.

Gyamtso, Khenpo Tsültrim. Unpublished poem (2005). In possession of Ari Goldfield.

Gyamtso, Khenpo Tsültrim. Unpublished poem (2009). In possession of Rose Taylor Goldfield.

Gyamtso, Khenpo Tsültrim. Unpublished poem (2009). In possession of Ari Goldfield.

Hahn, Tomie. *Sensational Knowledge: Embodying Culture through Japanese Dance*. Middletown: Wesleyan University Press, 2007.

Halprin, Anna. *Moving Toward Life: Five Decades of Transformational Dance*. Edited by Rachel Kaplan. Hannover: University Press of New England, 1995.

Hanayagi, Chiyo. *Jitsu nihon buyo no kiso* [The practical skills of basic *nihon buyo* movement]. Tokyo: Shoseki, 1981.

Hawkins, Erick. *The Body Is a Clear Place: And Other Statements on Dance*. Princeton: Princeton Book Company, 1992.

Hay, Deborah, and Susan Foster. *My Body, the Buddhist*. Middletown: Wesleyan University Press, 2000.

Hay, Deborah. *Lamb at the Altar: The Story of a Dance*. Durham: Duke University Press, 1996.

Hefferon, Kate M., and Stewart Ollis. "'Just Clicks': An Interpretive Phenomenological Analysis of Professional Dancers' Experience of Flow." Research in Dance Education 7.2 (2007): 141–159.

He-ru-ka, Tsang Nyon. *rnal 'byor gyi dbang phyug chen po mi la ras pa'i rnam mgur* [The Life and Songs of Milarepa, the Great Lord of the Yogis] (1488). Translated by Jim Scott. Accessed February 7, 2015. www.tibet.dk/pktc/tibdtexts.php.

Hevajra Tantra. Translated by Rose Taylor Goldfield. Accessed May 6, 2015. http://tbrc.org/link/?RID= O1PD92753|O1PD927531PD92757$W20866#library_work_Object-O1PD92753|O1PD927531PD 92757$W20866.

Huizinga, Johan. "The Nature and Significance of Play as Cultural Phenomenon." In *The Performance Studies Reader*, edited by Henry Bial. London: Routledge, 2007.

Ikeda, Daisaku. "The Practice for Transforming our State of Life." *Living Buddhism*, November 2014.

Ikeda, Daisaku. "Three Thousand Realms in a Single Moment of Life." *Living Buddhism*, August 2014.

Kasulis, Thomas P. "The Body—Japanese Style." In *Self as Body in Asian Theory and Practice*, edited by Thomas P. Kasulis, Roger T. Ames, and Wimal Dissanayake. Albany: State University of New York Press, 1993.

Kāyagatāsati Sutta, Majjhima Nikāya 119. Translated by Thanissaro Bhikkhu. Accessed May 6, 2015. http://www.accesstoinsight.org/tipitaka/mn/mn.119.than.html.

Kerr, Catherine. "Mindfulness Starts with the Body: A View from the Brain." Talk given at TEDx College Hill, May 12, 2012.

Kerr, Catherine E., Matthey D. Sacchet, Sara W. Lazar, Cristopher I. Moore, and Stephanie R. Jones. "Mindfulness Starts with the Body: Somatosensory Attention and Top-down Modulation of Cortical Alpha Rhythms in Mindfulness Meditation." *Frontiers in Human Neuroscience* 7.12 (2013).

Kerr, Catherine E., Jessica R. Shaw, Rachel H. Wasserman, Vanessa C. Chen, Alok Kanojia, Thomas Bayer, and John M. Kelley. "Tactile Acuity in Experienced Tai Chi Practitioners: Evidence for Use Dependent Plasticity as an Effect of Sensory-Attentional Training." *Experimental Brain Research* 188.2 (2008): 317–322. Accessed November 21, 2014. http://link.springer.com/article/ 10.1007%2Fs00221-008-1409-6.

Knapp, Alex. "Catherine Kerr on the Science of Meditation." *Forbes Magazine* 9/9/11. Accessed May 6, 2015. http://www.forbes.com/sites/alexknapp/2011/09/09/catherine-kerr-on-the-science-of-meditation/.

Komparu, Kunio. *The Noh Theater: Principles and Perspectives*. New York: Weatherhill/Tankosha, 1983.

Kornfield, Jack. *A Path With Heart: A Guide Through the Perils and Promises of Spiritual Life*. New York: Bantam Books, 1993.

Kripalu Center for Yoga and Dance. "Calendar of Programs." Accessed June 20, 2015. https://www. kripalu.org/program/theme/CADAN.

Kyabgon, Traleg. *The Essence of Buddhism*. Boston: Shambhala Publications, 2001.

Kyabgon, Traleg. "The Three Kayas—The Bodies of the Buddha." A teaching given at Karma Triyana Dharmachakra, Woodstock, NY, November 1989. Edited by Sally Clay. Accessed May 6, 2015. http://www.kagyu.org/kagyulineage/buddhism/cul/cul02.php.

Kyabgon, Traleg. "Karma Triyana Dharmachakra." Oral teaching given in Woodstock, New York, November 1989.

Labdrön, Machik, and Sarah Harding. *Machik's Complete Explanation: Clarifying the Meaning of Chöd: A Complete Explanation of Casting Out the Body As Food*. Translated by Sarah Harding. Ithaca: Snow Lion Publications, 2003.

Leach, Edmund R. In *Anthropology in Theory: Issues in Epistemology*. Edited by Henrietta L. Moore and Todd Sanders, 70–77. Malden: John Wiley & Sons, 2014.

Levine, Debra. "A True Story." *Hemispheric Institute*. http://hemi.nyu.edu/journal/4_1/artist_presen tation/jt_eng/truestory.html.

Levine, Noah. *Against the Stream.* New York: HarperOne, 2007.

Levy, Fran J. *Dance Movement Therapy: A Healing Art.* Virginia: American Alliance for Health, Physical Education, Recreation and Dance, 1992.

Llinás, Rodolfo. *I of the Vortex.* Cambridge: MIT Press, 2001.

Lodro Thaye, J. *Phyag rgya chen po'i rdo rje'i mgur* [Song of Mahamudra]. Translated by Ari Goldfield.

Lowenthal, Martin, and Tenzin Wangyal Rinpoche. *Dawning of Clear Light: A Western Approach to Tibetan Dark Retreat Meditation.* Charlottesville: Hampton Roads, 2003.

Mahasati Insight Meditation Association. "What Is Mahasati." Accessed May 6, 2015. http://mahasati.inspiredlens.com/mahasati/.

Maitreya. *theg pa chen po'i rgyud bla ma'i bstan bcos.* [The Treatise on Buddha Nature]. Translated by Ari Goldfield. Accessed May 6, 2015. http://www.dharmadownload.net/pages/english/Texts/texts_0015.htm.

Martin, Agnes. *Agnes Martin: Writings,* edited by Dieter Schwarz. Berlin: Hatje Cantz Publishing, 2005.

McMahan, David. *The Making of Buddhist Modernism.* Oxford: Oxford University Press, 2008.

Mehling, Wolf E., Judith Wrubel, Jennifer J. Daubenmier, Cynthia J. Price, Catherine E. Kerr, Theresa Silow, Viranjini Gopisetty, and Anita L. Stewart. "Body Awareness: A Phenomenological Inquiry into the Common Ground of Mind-body Therapies." *Philosophy, Ethics, and Humanities in Medicine* 6.6 (2011). doi: 10.1186/1747–5341–6–6.

Michaelson, Jay. *Evolving Dharma: Meditation, Buddhism, and the Next Generation of Enlightenment.* Berkeley: Evolver Editions, 2013.

Midal, Fabrice. *Chögyam Trungpa: His Life and Vision.* Boston: Shambhala Publications, 2001.

Mipham, Sakyong. *Turning the Mind into an Ally.* New York: Riverhead Books, 2003.

Montano, Linda Mary. "Another 21 Years of Living Art." Accessed May 31, 2015. http://www.lindamontano.com/another-21-years-of-living-art-1998–2019/.

Motokiyo, Zeami. *On the Art of the Nō Drama: The Major Treatises of Zeami.* Translated by Thomas Rimer and Yamazaki Masakazu. Princeton: Princeton University Press, 1984.

Murcott, Susan. *First Buddhist Women: Poems and Stories of Awakening.* Berkeley: Parallax Press, 1991.

Nachmanovitch, Stephen. *Free Play: Improvisation in Life and Art.* New York: Jeremy P. Tarcher/Putnam, 1990.

Naess-Lewin, Joan. *Dance Therapy Notebook.* Translated and arranged by Stephen Batchelor. Washington, D.C.: American Dance Therapy Association, 1998.

Nagarjuna. *Nagarjuna: Verses from the Center.* New York: Riverhead Books, 2001.

Nhat Hahn, Thich. *Transformation & Healing: Sutra on the Four Establishments of Mindfulness.* Berkeley: Parallax Press, 1990.

Nhat Hanh, Thich. *The Heart of Understanding.* Berkeley: Parallax Press, 1988.

Olmsted, Mark. "Genius All the Time: The Beats, Spontaneous Presence, and the Primordial Ground." In *The Philosophy of the Beats,* edited by Sharin Elkholy. Lexington: University Press of Kentucky, 2012.

Pallaro, Patricia, ed. *Authentic Movement: Essays by Mary Starks Whitehouse, Janet Adler and Joan Chodorow.* London: Jessica Kingsley Publishers, 1999.

Paxton, Steve. "Fall after Newton." In *Contact Quarterly Omnibus,* edited by Nancy Stark Smith and Lisa Nelson. Northhampton: Contact Editions, 1997.

Pearlman, Ellen. *Nothing and Everything—The Influence of Buddhism on the American Avant Garde: 1942–1962.* Berkeley: Evolver Editions, 2012.

Prajnaparamita Sutra. In *Buddhist Wisdom Books: The Diamond Sutra and the Heart Sutra.* Translated by Edward Conze. London: George Allen and Unwin, 1958.

Rahula, Walpola. *What the Buddha Taught.* Oxford: One World Publications, 1974.

Rainer, Yvonne. "A Quasi Survey of Some 'Minimalist' Tendencies in the Quantitatively Minimal Dance Activity Midst the Plethora, or an Analysis of Trio A." In *Twentieth Century Performance Reader,* edited by Michael Huxley and Noel Witts. London: Routledge, 1996.

Ray, Reginald. *Touching Enlightenment: Finding Realization in the Body.* Boulder: Sounds True, 2008.

Relph, E. *Place and Placelessness.* London: Pion Limited, 1976.

"Research." Institute for Stem Cell Biology and Regenerative Medicine, Stanford School of Medicine. Accessed August 13, 2013. http://stemcell.stanford.edu/research/.

Robinson, Richard H., Willard L. Johnson, and Thanissaro Bhikkhu. *Buddhist Religions: A Historical Introduction*. Belmont: Wadsworth/Thompson, 2005.

Rose, Mitch. "Gathering 'Dreams of Presence': A Project for the Cultural Landscape." *Environment and Planning D: Society and Space* 24, 2006.

Roth, Gabrielle. *Sweat Your Prayers: Movement as a Spiritual Practice*. New York: Tarcher/Putnam, 1997.

Rumi, Jallaludin. *The Matbnavi*. Translated by R.A. Nicholson. Cambridge: Cambridge University Press, 1934.

Salzberg, Sharon. "Suffering and Its Partial Cure." In *Adventures with the Buddha: A Buddhism Reader*, edited by Jeffery Paine, 343–366. New York: W.W. Norton, 2005.

"Sangha News." Insight Meditation Society, February 2013.

Sangharakshita. *The Buddha's Noble Eightfold Path*. Glasgow: Windhorse Publications, 1990. Accessed April 9, 2015. http://www.sangharakshita.org/_books/Noble_Eightfold_Path.pdf.

Sangharakshita. *The Religion of Art*. Glasgow: Windhorse, 1998.

Saunders, E. Dale. *Mudra: A Study of Symbolic Gestures in Japanese Buddhist Sculpture*. Princeton: Princeton University Press, 1985.

Schmitt, Natalie Crohn. "Stanislavski, Creativity, and the Unconscious." *New Theatre Quarterly* 2.8 (1986): 345–51.

Silberschatz, Marc. "Creative State / Flow State: Flow Theory in Stanislavsky's Practice." *New Theatre Quarterly* 29.1 (2013): 13–23.

Singleton, John. "Situated Learning in Japan: Our Educational Analysis." In *Learning in Likely Places: Varieties of Apprenticeship in Japan*, edited by John Singleton. Cambridge: Cambridge University Press, 1998.

Sivanda Yoga Center and Vishnu Devananda. *The Sivananda Companion to Yoga: A Complete Guide to the Physical Postures, Breathing Exercises, Diet, Relaxation, and Meditation Techniques of Yoga*. New York: Simon & Schuster, 1984.

Soka Gakkai. *The Soka Gakkai Dictionary of Buddhism*. Tokyo: Soka Gakkai, 2002.

Soka Gakkai International. "Nichiren Buddhism and the SGI." http://www.sgi-usa.org.

Stanislavski, Constantin. *An Actor Prepares*. Translated by Elizabeth Hapgood. New York: Routledge, 2003.

Story, Francis. *Dimensions of Buddhist Thought: Collected Essays*. Sri Lanka: Buddhist Publication Society, 1976.

Strand, Clark. *Waking the Buddha: How the Most Dynamic and Empowering Buddhist Movement in History is Changing our Concept of Religion*. Santa Monica: Middleway Press, 2014.

Suzuki, D.T. *Zen and Japanese Culture*. Princeton: Princeton University Press, 1959.

Suzuki, Shunryu. *Zen Mind, Beginner's Mind*. New York: Weatherhill, 1975.

Taylor, Margaret. *Dance as Religious Studies*. New York: Crossroads Publishing, 1993.

Taylor, Mark. "Accessing the Wisdom of Your Body: Balancing the Three Brains." *Currents: A Journal of the Body-Mind Centering Association* 15. 1 (2012): 10–17.

Tendai Buddhist Institute. "Tendai Practices." Accessed May 31, 2015. http://www.tendai.org/practices/.

Thanissaro Bhikkhu, trans. *Handful of Leaves—Volume Three: An Anthology from the Aṅguttara Nikāya*. Sati Center for Buddhist Studies & Metta Forest Monastery, 2003.

Tolentino, Julie. "A True Story About Two People." Accessed May 31, 2015. http://www.julietolentino.com/TOLENTINOPROJECTS/Performance/Entries/2005/1/1_A_TRUE_STORY_ABOUT_TWO_PEOPLE.html.

Trungpa, Chögyam. *Born in Tibet*. Boston: Shambhala Publications, 2000.

Trungpa, Chögyam. *Glimpses of Space: The Feminine Principle & EVAM*. Halifax: Vajradhatu, 1999.

Trungpa, Chögyam. *Meditation in Action*. Boston: Shambhala, 1991.

Trungpa, Chögyam. *The Myth of Freedom and the Way of Meditation*. Boston: Shambhala, 1976.

Trungpa, Chogya. *The Path of Individual Liberation*. Boston: Shambhala, 2015.

Trungpa, Chögyam. *Shambhala: The Sacred Path of the Warrior*. Boston: Shambhala, 2007.

Trungpa, Chögyam. *True Perception: The Path of Dharma Art*, edited by Judith L Lief. Boston: Shambhala, 2008.

Valaoritis, Nanos. "Meta-Etymology." In *Exiled in Our Skin*, edited by Rigopoulou Calliope. Athens: Topos Publications, 2010.

Varela, Francisco J., Evan T. Thompson, and Eleanor Rosch. *The Embodied Mind: Cognitive Science and Human Experience*. Cambridge: MIT Press, 1993.

Wegner, William H. "The Creative Circle: Stanislavski and Yoga." Educational Theatre Journal 28, no. 1 (1976): 85–89.

White, R. Andrew. "Stanislavsky and Ramacharaka: The Influence of Yoga and Turn-of-the-Century Occultism on the System." Theatre Survey, no. 1 (2006).

Wilhelm, Richard, trans. *The Secret of the Golden Flower* (eighth century) with commentary by C.G. Jung. New York: Harcourt, Brace, & World, 1931.

Willis, Jan. "An African-American Woman's Journey into Buddhism." In *Adventures with the Buddha: A Buddhism Reader,* edited by Jeffery Paine, 267–316. New York; W.W. Norton, 2005.

Willis, Paul, and Mats Trondman. "Manifesto for Ethnography." *Cultural Studies–Critical Methodologies,* vol. 2, no. 3, August, 2002.

Woodbury, Joan. Mary Wigman at 70," *Dance Observer* 23 (8) (October 1956): 117–118. In Bearnstow Journal. Accessed May 31, 2015. http://bearnstowjournal.org/wigman-woodbury-70.htm.

Worley, Lee. "Mudra Space Awareness." *Performance and Spirituality,* vol. 3, no. 1 (Spring 2012) http://www.utdl.edu/ojs/index.php/pas/article/view/51.

Worth, Libby, and Helen Poynor. *Anna Halprin.* London: Routledge, 2004.

Wu-Men, Kuan. *The Gateless Barrier: The Wu-Men Kuan.* Translated by Robert Aitken. San Francisco: North Point Press, 1993.

Yang dgon pa rgyal mtshan dpal, *Rdo rje lus kyi sbas bshad.* In *The Collected Works (Gsung 'bum) of Yang-dgon-pa Rgyal-mtshan-dpal: Reproduced from the Manuscript Set Preserved at Pha-jo-ldings Monastery.* Thimphu, Bhutan: Kunsang Topgey, 1976.

Yano, Christine. *Tears of Longing: Nostalgia and the Nation in Japanese Popular Song.* Cambridge: Harvard University Asia Center, 2002.

Yuasa, Yasuo. *The Body: Toward an Eastern Mind-Body Theory.* Albany: State University of New York, 1987.

Yuasa, Yasuo. *The Body, Self-Cultivation, and Ki-Energy.* Albany: State University of New York, 1993.

About the Contributors

Helen Fox **Appell** studied Vajrayana Buddhism for many years in India and as an ordained Zen priest co-established No Abode Hermitage. She is the co-founder of Nritya Mandala Mahavihara and as teacher, performer, and creative and organizational director she is devoted to maintaining the spiritual integrity of Charya dance in its new setting.

Harrison **Blum** is the Buddhist spiritual advisor and Mindfulness Programs coordinator at Northeastern University. He also works as a staff chaplain at Franciscan Hospital for Children, where he teaches mindfulness meditation to adolescent patients on an acute psychiatric unit, and is an authorized Community Dharma Leader in the Insight Meditation tradition.

Prema **Dasara** founded Tara Dhatu in 1986 to support her creation of a Buddhist ritual dance that has since been taught and performed in over 25 countries. She studied Tibetan Lama dancing at the Tibetan Institute of Performing Arts and sacred Balinese dance from the Queen of Peliatan in Bali. She is the author of *Dancing Tara* (self-published in 2010).

Barbara **Dilley** studied and performed with the Merce Cunningham Dance Company (1963–1968) and the Grand Union dance improvisation group (1970–1976). She has taught at Naropa University since its founding in 1974 and was president of the university from 1985 to 1993.

Sean **Feit** is a scholar-practitioner writing on Buddhist contemplative practice in postmodern arts and culture. Two decades of Buddhist meditation practice and study, including Theravada ordination in Burma and Insight Meditation teacher authorization from Jack Kornfield, weave with classical piano and experimental performance training as a foundation for embodied scholarship and social action.

Wynn **Fricke** is the director of the dance program at Macalester College and former dancer with Zenon Dance Company. She has served on the faculties of the University of Minnesota, St. Olaf College, and Winona State University, and she has been a choreographer-in-residence for the Minnesota Dance Theater. Fricke is co-founder of Common Ground Meditation Center.

Charles **Genoud** co-founded the Vimalakirti Center for Meditation in Geneva. He studied the practice of sensory awareness with Michael Tophoff and Charlotte Selver and has practiced Tibetan Buddhism since 1970, studying with Geshe Rabten and Dilgo Khyentse Rinpoche. He is the author of *Gesture of Awareness* (Wisdom Publications, 2006).

Fran **Gilboy** participates in community building through dance and mindfulness with her Canadian prairie dance troupe, FadaDance. She has trained at the Spirit Rock Meditation Center in Woodacre, California (including the Community Dharma Leader program), and has presented workshops in integrating mindfulness into the dance studio internationally.

Rose Taylor **Goldfield** is co-founder of the Wisdom Sun Buddhist community, whose roots are in the Tibetan Karma Kagyu lineage. She teaches body-based meditation and Buddhist dance and is the author of *Training the Wisdom Body: Buddhist Yogic Exercise* (Shambhala, 2013).

Tomie **Hahn** is an artist and ethnomusicologist. She is a performer of *shakuhachi* (Japanese bamboo flute), *nihon buyo* (Japanese traditional dance) and experimental performance. She is an associate professor in the arts department at Rensselaer Polytechnic Institute, where she is also the director of the Center for Deep Listening, and is the author of *Sensational Knowledge: Embodying Culture through Japanese Dance* (Wesleyan, 2007).

Lucia **Horan** was born into the family of the 5Rhythms® and certified to teach the 5Rhythms in 1998. She is recognized as an international teacher of the 5Rhythms practice and a faculty member of 5Rhythms Global.

Anahātā **Iradah** is a senior teacher in the Mentor Teacher's Guild of the International Network for the Dances of Universal Peace. She is a musician, teacher, composer, songwriter, meditation teacher, DVD author, and documentary film producer. She orchestrates spiritual pilgrimages to India, Nepal, and Brazil.

Brian **Kimmel** is pursuing an M.A. in somatic counseling psychology at Naropa University. He is a longtime, ordained student of Zen master Thich Nhat Hanh and has toured internationally in France, Indonesia, Vietnam, and the United States with his community. He teaches mindfulness meditation in secular and Buddhist settings, often incorporating contemplative dance/movement explorations.

Hilary **Lake** is a non-traditional artistic community minister. She holds an MDiv in Buddhist ministry from Harvard Divinity School and was a member of the Moving Dharma Dance Lab from 2008 to 2009. She lives, works, and plays as a co-owner and manager of Nine Mountain Retreats.

Lalitarāja has performed with several major ballet companies, including the Scottish Ballet. He is the director of Oracle Dance Co. and choreographs and performs both improvised and set work. He is a senior lecturer in dance at Roehampton Institute.

Cristina **Livingstone** began her exploration of the mind-body connection, which eventually led her to Dance/Movement Therapy, during her 26 years as a professional modern dancer. She holds an M.S. in Dance/Movement Therapy from the Pratt Institute and works as a dance/movement therapist in an acute inpatient psychiatric unit in a New York City hospital.

Leah Joy **Malberg** has been a practitioner of Soto-Zen Buddhism for 15 years and a teacher of dance and movement for over 20. She founded Zenful Dance Breath Movement Meditation in 2006 and has taught workshops to many dancers throughout California, New Jersey, and New York City.

Willa B. **Miller** is the founder and spiritual director of Natural Dharma Fellowship and Wonderwell Mountain Refuge. She is a visiting lecturer in Buddhist ministry at Harvard Divinity School. She is the author of *Everyday Dharma: Seven Weeks to Finding the Buddha in You* (Quest Books/Theosophical, 2009) and co-editor of *The Arts of Contemplative Care: Pioneering Voices in Buddhist Chaplaincy and Pastoral Work* (Wisdom, 2012).

Karen **Nelson** encountered Contact Improvisation and Tuning Scores in the late 1970s, in the early days studying with originators Steve Paxton and Lisa Nelson, respectively. She has practiced, performed, and taught internationally for over 35 years and has co-founded several dance projects, including DanceAbility International.

Reginald A. **Ray** draws on four decades of study and practice within the Tibetan Buddhist tradition to address the unique spiritual imperatives of modern people. He is the author of numerous books, including *Touching Enlightenment* (Sounds True, 2008), *Indestructible Truth* (Shambhala, 2002), and *Secret of the Vajra World* (Shambhala, 2002). He is the spiritual director of the Dharma Ocean Foundation.

Kim **Sargent-Wishart** is a Ph.D. candidate in performance studies at Victoria University in Melbourne, Australia, conducting practice-based research through dance and filmmaking. She investigates embodiment and creative dynamics, with a focus on embryogenesis, the beginnings of the body, as informed by Western science, Tibetan Buddhism, and Body-Mind Centering®.

Bhikkhuni **Thanasanti** has been a Buddhist nun for 25 years and has taught meditation and intensive retreats for 20 years with body awareness as a cornerstone of her teaching. She was first ordained in the Ajahn Chah lineage at Amaravati Buddhist Monastery. She is the founder of Shakti Vihara Hermitage and Awakening Truth.

Anna **Tzakou** is a theater deviser and performer pursuing a Ph.D. in the drama department at Exeter University. She is interested in practicing the body-landscape interrelationship through movement and theater disciplines and examining narratives of identity, home, and belongingness.

Adrianne E. **Vincent** is an integrative medical educator, clinical counselor, bodywork practitioner, meditation teacher, and Buddhist Ritual Minister. She is pursuing a master of theological studies at Harvard Divinity School and has researched sustainability options for clinicians at the Adult Palliative Care division of the Dana-Farber Cancer Institute.

Joan **Wittig** is the director of the graduate dance/movement therapy program at the Pratt Institute. She worked for New York City Health and Hospitals Corporation for 16 years, including seven years as director of the Creative Arts Therapy department at Woodhull Medical and Mental Health Center.

Lori **Wong** is the founding teacher of Insight Meditation Central Valley. She is an empowered Community Dharma Leader in the Insight Meditation tradition and a practitioner within the Chen and Yang tai chi and qigong lineages. She is a board member of the Sati Center for Buddhist Studies and was a founding board member of the Buddhist Insight Network.

Lee **Worley** founded the theater studies program at Naropa University and also serves as one of four Western teachers in the Nalandabodhi Buddhist organization. She is a professor of theater and contemplative education at Naropa University and is the author of *Coming from Nothing: The Sacred Art of Acting* (Turquoise Dragon Press, 2001).

Index